Cambridge Imperial and Post-Colonial Studies Series

General Editors: **Megan Vaughan**, Kings' College, Cambridge and **Richard Drayton**, Corpus Christi College, Cambridge

This informative series covers the broad span of modern imperial history while also exploring the recent developments in former colonial states where residues of empire can still be found. The books provide in-depth examinations of empires as competing and complementary power structures encouraging the reader to reconsider their understanding of international and world history during recent centuries.

Titles include:

Tony Ballantyne
Orientalism and race
Aryanism in the British Empire

Peter F. Bang and C. A. Bayly (*editors*)
TRIBUTARY EMPIRES IN GLOBAL HISTORY

James Beattie
EMPIRE AND ENVIRONMENTAL ANXIETY, 1800–1920
Health, Aesthetics and Conservation in South Asia and Australasia

Robert J. Blyth
The Empire of the Raj
Eastern Africa and the Middle East, 1858–1947

Roy Bridges (*editor*)
IMPERIALISM, DECOLONIZATION AND AFRICA
Studies Presented to John Hargreaves

Kit Candlin
THE LAST CARIBBEAN FRONTIER, 1795–1815

Hilary M. Carey (*editor*)
EMPIRES OF RELIGION

Nandini Chatterjee
THE MAKING OF INDIAN SECULARISM
Empire, Law and Christianity, 1830–1960

Esme Cleall
MISSIONARY DISCOURSE
Negotiating Difference in the British Empire, c.1840–95

T. J. Cribb (*editor*)
IMAGINED COMMONWEALTH
Cambridge Essays on Commonwealth and International Literature in English

Michael S. Dodson
Orientalism, Empire and National Culture
India, 1770–1880

Jost Dülffer and Marc Frey (*editors*)
ELITES AND DECOLONIZATION IN THE TWENTIETH CENTURY

Bronwen Everill
ABOLITION AND EMPIRE IN SIERRA LEONE AND LIBERIA

Ulrike Hillemann
ASIAN EMPIRE AND BRITISH KNOWLEDGE
China and the Networks of British Imperial Expansion

B.D. Hopkins
THE MAKING OF MODERN AFGHANISTAN

Ronald Hyam
Britain's Imperial Century, 1815–1914: A Study of Empire and Expansion
Third Edition

Cambridge Imperial and Post-Colonial Studies Series
Series Standing Order ISBN 978–0–333–91908–8 (Hardback) 978–0–333–91909–5 (Paperback)
(*outside North America only*)

You can receive future titles in this series as they are published by placing a standing order. Please contact your bookseller or, in case of difficulty, write to us at the address below with your name and address, the title of the series and the ISBN quoted above.

Customer Services Department, Macmillan Distribution Ltd, Houndmills, Basingstoke, Hampshire RG21 6XS, England

Law, Disorder and the Colonial State

Corruption in Burma c.1900

Jonathan Saha
Lecturer in Modern History, University of Bristol

First published 2013 by
PALGRAVE MACMILLAN

Palgrave Macmillan in the UK is an imprint of Macmillan Publishers Limited,
registered in England, company number 785998, of Houndmills, Basingstoke,
Hampshire RG21 6XS.

Palgrave Macmillan in the US is a division of St Martin's Press LLC,
175 Fifth Avenue, New York, NY 10010.

Palgrave Macmillan is the global academic imprint of the above companies
and has companies and representatives throughout the world.

Palgrave® and Macmillan® are registered trademarks in the United States,
the United Kingdom, Europe and other countries.

ISBN 978–0–230–35827–0

This book is printed on paper suitable for recycling and made from fully
managed and sustained forest sources. Logging, pulping and manufacturing
processes are expected to conform to the environmental regulations of the
country of origin.

A catalogue record for this book is available from the British Library.

A catalog record for this book is available from the Library of Congress.

10   9   8   7   6   5   4   3   2   1
22 21 20 19 18 17 16 15 14 13

Printed and bound in Great Britain by
CPI Antony Rowe, Chippenham and Eastbourne

For Rachel

Contents

Preface

Before I embarked on this project I was employed for a short spell as 'out-sourced' agency staff at the UK Home Office, operating the phone lines that provided advice and updates on people's work permit applications. It was in this capacity in which I first learned about bureaucracy from the inside, rather than from the receiving end. I still remember my naïve shock at how careless, chaotic, and callous the state could be in its routine procedures. On reflection, it was probably in that call centre in Sheffield where the seeds of this book were sowed.

Many people have contributed to this project over the last five years. My PhD supervisor Ian Brown first drew my interest to the history of colonial Burma as a Masters student at the School of Oriental and African Studies. Since then he has continued to be my primary source of support and guidance. Without his encouragement and criticisms, this project would never have been realised. Thanks also to the Arts and Humanities Research Council who funded the doctoral research upon which this book is largely drawn. And thanks to SOAS history department for hosting me as PhD student and training me, particularly Sunil Kumar. Thank you to Tharaphi Than, John Okell and Justin Watkins who valiantly taught me all the Burmese language I know; only I am to be blamed for my deficiencies in this area. I am also grateful to Ian Phimister, Benjamin Zachariah and Clare Anderson, who were all supportive of my early academic aspirations.

The comments and encouragement of my examiners Christopher Bayly and David Arnold have been invaluable in restructuring the thesis into this book. Thanks to Richard Drayton for his support for the book, and for backing its inclusion in this series. I am indebted to the following people, all of whom have generously given their time to read and/or discuss various parts and aspects of the book: Steven Pierce, Erich De Wald, Aditya Sarkar, Stephen Legg, Erica Wald, Anna Gust, Uditi Sen, Jessica Dionne, Taka Oshikiri, Angus Lockyer, Eleanor Saha, Reuben Loffman, Christopher Vaughan, Gary Rivett, Arash Sedighi, my anonymous reader and Taylor Sherman. Whilst in Yangon Su Lin Lewis, Lalita Hingkanonta, Noriyuki Osada, Ko Aung, and Vance all provided much needed company and conversation. The Myanmar Historical Commission were also a fantastic inspiration, thanks especially to U Thaw Kaung and U Hla Thein.

Apologies to my family for time that I have been absent or distracted while working on this project, and I am thankful for their continued understanding and support. Finally, Rachel Johnson, more than anyone else, has lived with the book as it has been developed and written. Her critiques and suggestions have been vital. She shares in the successes, if any, of the book. All errors, empirical or interpretative, are my own.

It is necessary to provide a short note on my use of place names, as the controversy over whether it is best to use Burma or Myanmar rumbles on.[1] Since I am writing about the colonial period almost exclusively, I mostly use Burma. This is consistent with the use of place names by authors who generally prefer Myanmar over Burma.[2] My use of other place names too follow the English spelling of the time, such as Calcutta, Rangoon, and Irrawaddy. On the few occasions in which I refer to current times I use Myanmar, Yangon, etc., but where the period referred to encompasses the period before 1989, when the name was officially changed, I use Burma. Naming is unavoidably a political act, but in this case, as far as possible, I wish to remain agnostic over which designation is preferable for this particular 'imagined community'.[3]

Much of Chapter 4 was originally published in *The Indian Economic and Social History Review*, Vol. 47, No.3. © The Indian Economic and Social History Association New Delhi. All rights reserved. Reproduced with the permission of the copyright holders and the publishers, Sage Publications India Pvt. Ltd, New Delhi.

Introduction

At the end of the nineteenth century, among the dense network of streams and tributary waterways of the Irrawaddy River's tidal delta, tens of thousands of migrants mostly from Upper Burma settled to cut back the vast mangrove forests and replace them with lucrative paddy fields producing rice to be sold on the world market. It was a rapidly expanding agricultural frontier the scale of which was entirely unprecedented in the history of Southeast Asia.[1] Villages swelled into towns more than five times their original population in under a decade.[2] Steamships linked the new settlements moving goods and people across the watery landscape.

Hot on the heels of these pioneer cultivators lumbered the British colonial bureaucracy. Revenue collectors, surveyors, police departments, hospitals, and all of the paraphernalia of the state migrated to the delta. The growing population did not only have to come to terms with the seasonal flooding and malarial environs of the newly cultivated paddy fields,[3] but they also had to negotiate the expanding branches of the colonial state on a daily basis. This was no small challenge in the febrile climate of the delta: village headmen solicited bribes, policemen fabricated evidence, clerks embezzled government funds, township officers coerced women into sex, excise officers covered-up drug smuggling, and so on. These were mundane and quotidian state practices.

The Burma Delta was, without question, a disorderly place at the turn of the twentieth century; abuses of power were common among subordinate state employees and the recorded crime levels were among the highest in British India.[4] But the characterisation of it as a 'lawless frontier' does not capture the nature of this disorder.[5] There was not an absence of the colonial state and its accoutrements of judicial

1

procedures, bureaucratic structures, and coercive institutions. The disorder in the delta was not the result of a *lack* of legal state power. Instead, it might be said that the disorder in the delta had a symbiotic relationship with legal state power.[6] The pervasive corruption and misconduct in the region were intrinsically linked to the formalised, officially sanctioned rules and resources of the colonial state: subordinate officials used their legal authority to commit illegal acts, and these acts were of considerable consequence. For many in the delta, this everyday misrule was their lived experience of the state. In short, law and disorder were inseparable, and both were crucial to how the colonial state was performed and experienced.

In this book, I trace this relationship between law and disorder in the making of the colonial state in the Burma Delta, by studying numerous episodes of what was deemed by high-ranking officialdom to be 'misconduct' or 'corruption'. I suggest that through these cases, we are able to reveal the state as it was enacted by subordinates and experienced by the local population in their daily life. The colonial state from this quotidian perspective was less the rational, bureaucratic entity which it has often been depicted as by historians, but instead was something rather more amorphous and ambiguous. As we shall see in the proceeding chapters, to many of those encountering the colonial state in everyday life, it was duplicitous, theatrical, despotic, highly personalised, and masculine.

Exploring the state through episodes of misconduct makes several underpinning historiographic conventions seem problematic, even unsustainable: the inherently antithetical relationship between law and disorder; the clear division between the state and society; and the peripheral role of subordinate officials in making the colonial state. Each of these three often unacknowledged assumptions are briefly critiqued and refigured in this section, which foreshadows the more detailed study that follows. Overall, I hope that this book will go some way to 'defamiliarising' the state in Burma, exorcising some unhelpful yet stubborn historical frameworks. To pre-empt my argument, I intend to breakdown the image of the colonial state as a monolithic and alien entity intruding into Burmese society to reveal its complexity and embeddedness. The messy realities of state power in the Burma Delta provide an opportunity to critically reflect on the limitations of the deeper theoretical models of the state that have implicitly structured much historical writing and through this find new ways of understanding colonialism and its legacies.

Law and disorder

On 25 September 1896, H. J. Aston, the Judicial Commissioner of Lower Burma, heard an appeal for a most irregular civil case. In the village of Mezale in the Irrawaddy Delta, a rice trader called Maung Shwe Pa had been negotiating the sale of 1300 baskets of rice when the prospective purchasers seized the boat carrying the rice and attempted to get away without paying. Maung Shwe Pa immediately contacted the local head-man, Maung San Gaung, to recover the rice. The thieves made it as far as the next village before being caught. It was at this point that the initial legal dispute arose. Not a criminal case between Maung Shwe Pa and the rice thieves, but a civil case brought by Headman Maung San Gaung against Maung Shwe Pa. The Headman claimed that Maung Shwe Pa had promised to pay him Rs. 500 as a reward for the return of his rice, but on its return he had refused to pay. As a result, Maung San Gaung was taking him to court for breach of contract. But by making this claim, the Headman was effectively demonstrating that he had charged a fee to induce him to execute a task that in actuality was his legal duty. To put it bluntly, Maung San Gaung took Maung Shwe Pa to court in order to extract what was tantamount to a bribe.

Maung Shwe Pa's testimony corroborated the evidence that the Headman had solicited a bribe. He claimed to have agreed to pay the Headman for the recovery of the rice but only Rs. 50, a sum that he maintained he had paid up front. Regardless of the differing amounts, the evidence of both the defendant and the complainant unequivocally demonstrated that a bribe had been agreed. What made this episode exceptional was that the Headman won the case in court. Ignoring or overlooking the evidence of bribery, Civil Judge Maung Tha No found in favour of Maung San Gaung. He ruled that Maung Shwe Pa was contractually obliged to pay the Headman for performing the service of recovering his stolen rice. This decision must have been particularly irksome to Maung Shwe Pa since after further enquiries it was revealed that there was a heavy suspicion that the rice thieves were in cahoots with the Headman in what was an elaborate ruse to extort a bribe from Maung Shwe Pa.[7]

As Aston acknowledged, cases in which government services were solicited through bribes were usually hard to investigate and punish, as the parties involved conspired to hide the illegality involved. In the present case, however, this was not a problem as both parties had admitted in court the existence of the bribe, and the court had even recognised it as a legally binding contract. The decision was eventually overturned at appeal, but nonetheless this was a case ridden with ambiguities. Policing powers were openly acknowledged as being available for hire. A bribe was initially upheld as a legal contract through the decision of a colonial court. And there were suspicious, informal relationships between a subordinate state official and a group of suspected criminals. The official legal order and everyday disorder were deeply entangled in this case of misconduct. For Aston, this raised considerable concerns about the local administration of justice, and a misconduct investigation was launched into the Civil Judge. Yet despite these high-level concerns, the Headman was not himself investigated for misconduct and ultimately none of the officials involved were dismissed from government service.[8]

In many respects, this was not a unique case. It was typical of the 240 surviving files detailing cases of subordinate-level misconduct investigated in the Irrawaddy Division between 1896 and 1909. Containing petitions, internal official correspondence, court records, witness statements, and sometimes written explanations from those accused, the files are rich archival sources. This documentation was produced through the quasi-judicial framework established in the nineteenth century to 'discipline and punish' errant state actors.[9] As historians of criminality in colonial South Asia have done extensively over the last 20 years, in Chapter 1, I deconstruct the colonial discourses and disciplinary procedures involved in misconduct cases.[10] My study of the files shows that, as in the misconduct case discussed above, often the suspected officials escaped severe reprimands even when the veracity of the accusations against them seemed clearly established through evidence. Overall, the cases suggest that high-ranking officials often erred towards leniency when punishing misconduct.

My contention that the higher echelons of the colonial state tolerated misconduct and corruption jars with conventional historiographic wisdom. Most historians of colonial Burma have argued that the state identified and defined forms of illegality, and then sought to control and suppress them.[11] But this overarching impression of a 'coercion-intensive' state has largely been based on episodes of heightened conflict and widespread violence, such as the colonial 'pacification' campaign following the annexation of Upper Burma in 1885 and the Hsaya San rebellion in 1930.[12] The quotidian history of state power in colonial contexts has attracted comparatively little attention, in Burma and beyond.[13] On this everyday level, it appears that the relationship between state power and illegality was more ambivalent, as we have seen in the complexities of the Maung San Gaung case.

Indeed, tolerance, in general, has been an overlooked facet of colonial governmentality. Most post-colonial historians have been too consumed by exploring the ways colonialism engendered new subjectivities though the state's interventions in society to consider the effects that deliberately limiting intervention might have had.[14] However, recent studies of prostitution and colonial cities in Asia have begun to fruitfully develop this line of inquiry. Ashwini Tambe and Philip Howell have shown that colonial legislation created spaces where prostitution was condoned and law enforcers turned a blind eye to the related forms of gendered violence, outright illegality, and general disorder that then arose within them. Similarly, Stephen Legg has argued more broadly that the deliberate neglect of certain city spaces in colonial Delhi was the necessary corollary to the state's excessive interventions in other urban areas.[15] Thus, illegality and disorder did not always undermine or weaken the legal order. Instead, tolerating disorder was vital to the viability of colonial law. Likewise, subordinate officials' daily abuses of power did not constitute an existential threat to the colonial order. As I show in Chapters 3 and 4, these often malfeasant acts actually reinforced colonial racial and gender hierarchies.

As the anthropologist John Comaroff has persuasively argued, colonial law should not be treated as a functional, monolithic entity with a clear, ahistorical purpose. It was not simply an imperial tool for stamping out disorder. Instead, he argued, it should be treated as a changing assemblage of often improvised practices and institutions which were constitutive of colonial societies and used to mediate the tensions within them.[16] This insight concisely captures the fluidity and indeterminacy of how the law appears in cases of misconduct. Subordinate officials could use their legal state power duplicitously for their own ends, and at the same time the upper levels of the colonial regime defined such acts as 'misconduct' and attempted to combat its prevalence through the law.[17] In this attempt, however, they were willing to tolerate much of the pervasive misconduct in the delta. But Comaroff's insight also captures the importance of these ambivalent uses of legal state power in constituting the colonial state. Maung San Gaung's disagreement with Maung Shwe Pa over his bribe, his suspicious relationship with the rice thieves, and his initially successful use of the court to extract the bribe were all moments in which the state was made in daily deltaic life. In this way, cases of misconduct and corruption not only reveal the symbiotic relationship between law and disorder, but they also reveal how the state was performed in everyday life.

State and society

One misconduct file from 1906 records a heated exchange that occurred between Maung On Gaing, a township officer, and Maung Po Tun, a resident excise officer, both of whom were employed in Zalun, a town in the north of the Irrawaddy Division. It was reported that while Maung On Gaing was visiting the district's rest house in November 1905, he overheard Maung Po Tun speaking loudly and pointedly to a local police inspector. Maung Po Tun, apparently well aware of Maung On Gaing's presence, provocatively stated that he was 'afraid of no one but his superior officers.' Maung On Gaing then retaliated by asking Maung Po Tun how many wives he had, to which the reply given was three. Maung On Gaing then said, 'No, you have four, you are a dog and worse than a dog.' Later that evening Maung Po Tun stood in front of Maung On Gaing's house publicly proclaiming that he was unafraid of him. It appeared on investigation that this public feud had arisen after a woman who had been 'seduced and abandoned' by Maung Po Tun appealed to Maung On Gaing for redress.[18]

This seemingly trivial set of events would almost certainly have gone unrecorded if Maung Po Tun had not been under the scrutiny of a misconduct investigation due to accusations of regular insobriety. Although it was believed that Maung Po Tun had not been drunk on this occasion and that the evidence for his general drunkenness was unsubstantiated, he was transferred away from Zalun in the 'interest of public service'.[19] At his new station, he fared even less well and by November 1906 had been suspended for heavy drinking and involvement in a brawl.[20] But replacing him proved difficult. The District Superintendent of Police complained that three of the four potential replacements were 'useless and evidently dishonest', 'untrustworthy', and 'weak and incompetent', and the remaining candidate was completely inexperienced.[21] Banal as it is in comparison to the numerous cases of forgery, framing, bribery, and physical violence contained within many of the misconduct files, the case of Maung Po Tun sheds light on some of the most mundane of the daily problems in the colonial bureaucracy. It offers a perspective rarely interrogated in historical writing.[22]

The state that emerges out of this case, and others like it, appears to have been dysfunctional, understaffed, and ridden by fraught personal conflicts. In contrast, the historiography on the colonial state in Burma has long laboured under the narrative that through colonialism an increasingly rational bureaucracy superseded a more fractious and personalised one.[23] In John Furnivall's classic history of the earliest period of colonial rule following the First Anglo-Burmese War (1824–6), *The Fashioning of Leviathan*, he reconstructed senior officials' administrative battles to establish a flexible regime sympathetic to local customs against the relentless economic logic of East India Company bureaucrats.[24] While recent scholars have challenged the accuracy of Furnivall's depiction of early colonial governance in Burma and drawn attention to the twin influences of nostalgia and paternalism in his work,[25] his characterisation of the state has remained an enduring feature of subsequent histories. His narrative of a gradual rationalisation of state structures breaking traditional forms of authority during colonialism is a central argument in Robert Taylor's influential history of modern Burma, *The State in Burma* (recently revised and updated under the new title, *The State in Myanmar*).[26] This standard, established narrative of the history of colonial Burma portrays the colonial state by the early twentieth century as a rational, impersonal, bureaucratic actor, separate from, and yet increasingly intrusive in, society.[27]

This dominant narrative has created a dichotomous, Manichean picture of the relationship between the state and society that can be mapped directly onto the binary of the coloniser and colonised.[28] There is little room in this framework to examine the complexities of how the state was experienced in everyday life. Nor is there much scope to study the role played by the mostly Indian and Burmese subordinate state officials; a group on which precious little historical work has been published,[29] and which in general texts have been dismissed as no more than 'cogs in the machine'.[30] Examples of how the state operated in everyday life, such as Maung Po Tun's case, disrupt this narrative. They blur the assumed boundary between the colonial state and colonised society by focusing on subordinate officials who in their daily life inevitably straddled this divide. Just as Ann Laura Stoler, Fredrick Cooper, and John Comaroff noted in the late 1990s, historians have wrongly assumed the colonial state to have been a monolithic object and have consequently failed to break it down and study it at its different levels.[31] This critique still remains relevant for much published research on colonialism.[32] Usually, it is taken as a given that the colonial state was an identifiable, discrete entity clearly separated from the broader colonised society. When examining the lower branches of the colonial state, such an assumption cannot be sustained.

However, new conceptualisations of the modern state have emerged over the last 30 years which offer useful theoretical models for studying the colonial state from an everyday perspective. Philip Abrams's essay on the state, in which he argues that scholars must take seriously the state's ideological and mythical qualities, is justifiably seen as the milestone for these new approaches. For Abrams, the state is not a tangible and distinct object in history but is instead something that has to be imagined into existence by society and something that is imagined in historically contingent ways.[33]

Following on from this crucial insight, Timothy Mitchell has attempted to conceptualise how it is that states come to be imagined in societies, a process he calls the 'state effect'. For Mitchell, the 'state effect' is the result of two intrinsically linked, mutually constituting processes. On the one hand, certain practices in society become identified and legitimated as being state practices through a societal imagining of the state. On the other hand, the idea of the state itself emerges in society as a cumulative result of everyday practices. In short, the state is the metaphysical effect of everyday practices structured by the collectively imagined norms of that state.[34] As a result, Mitchell argues that it is inherently impossible to point accurately to where the state finishes and society begins and misleading to assume an inherent separation between the state and society. Instead the state–society boundary is an illusionary one that has to be performed in everyday life. In other words, by being recognised as performing the state, state actors were effectively making the state real.

These antecedent works have inspired a raft of anthropological (and more recently historical) studies of the post-colonial states in South Asia exploring how the state was experienced as a quotidian entity, an object of study that has been given the academic shorthand the 'everyday state'.[35] Within this field, authors such as Akhil Gupta, Craig Jeffrey, William Gould, and Steven Pierce, the latter through his rich work on Northern Nigeria, have identified 'corruption' as a central discourse through which the boundary between the state and society has been imagined.[36] This insight is also applicable to colonial misconduct investigations in Burma. The file on Maung Po Tun's feud with Maung On Gaing, his drinking, and his brawls demonstrates high-ranking British officials' desire for an ideal state bureaucracy in which subordinates officials' state responsibilities were separate from their private lives. As I show in Chapters 1 and 4, attempts to delineate public duties from private interests within the subordinate ranks of officialdom were crucial to the contemporary definitions of misconduct. In performing misconduct investigations, the upper echelons of the regime were imagining an ideal colonial state which was rational and impersonal. It was an ideal that was not attained in everyday life, as the misconduct files make clear, but despite this the ideal has been reified in subsequent histories from Furnivall to Taylor.

The documentation on misconduct reveals the extent of British officialdom's concern about their subordinates' competence and honesty. Indeed, if colonial archives can be read to reveal the 'epistemic anxieties' of imperial rulers, as Ann Laura Stoler has recently argued,[37] then the misconduct files as a whole indicate overarching British anxieties about the 'everyday state' in the Burma Delta. However, these anxieties were mild. As I have already noted above, on the whole, the British attitude towards misconduct was marked by tolerance. The files on misconduct demonstrate an attempt to monitor and police subordinate level corruption and incompetence, but not a desire to eradicate it.[38] This was because, as I have already noted, misconduct did not undermine key aspects of how the colonial state was imagined by the British, but paradoxically reinforced them, particularly the state's racial hierarchy.

In Maung Po Tun's case, although a range of witnesses were questioned about his behaviour, the investigation's conclusions rested largely on the evidence provided by European officials.[39] This reflected the general structure of misconduct investigations. The authority to conduct misconduct investigations was restricted to deputy commissioners, who constituted the frontline of high-ranking British officialdom.[40] The deputy commissioners had the authority to decide whether they would act to investigate and punish subordinate misconduct or not. But, at the same time, they saw themselves as above the fray of '"native" quarrels'.[41] As a result of this contradiction, as I discuss at length in Chapter 3, they were in effect bureaucratic despots and both the accusers and accused in misconduct cases could only appeal to deputy commissioners' capricious authority. By tolerating some cases of misconduct and punishing others, but always attempting to remain aloof from the indigenous population, deputy commissioners established their authority over their subordinates in everyday life. This may explain why while Maung Po Tun boasted that although he was unafraid of Maung On Gaing, he remained 'afraid' of his superior officers.

Overall, the existence of subordinate level misconduct, far from undermining the ideal state, was used to justify the racial division of the colonial state, a differentiation that Partha Chatterjee has argued was a defining feature of the colonial state.[42] Maintaining the separation of the white upper echelons of the state from indigenous society, including those in subordinate state employment, was of greater importance than maintaining a separation between the subordinate branches of the state and the rest of society. Indeed, the former division was actually reinforced by the breakdown of the latter.

Misconduct was a discourse through which the British expressed their concerns about how the colonial state was being enacted in everyday life, but it was a discourse marked by ambivalence.[43] Indeed, the colonial ideal of a state organised hierarchically according to racial difference was maintained by British tolerance of subordinate misconduct which seemed to blur the boundary between the state and society. This tolerance of practices defined as 'misconduct' implies that beyond the ideal state existing in the minds of high-ranking British officials (and since reified in historical writing), there was a quite different set of state practices taking place at the level of everyday life.[44] I argue, following Mitchell, that these practices also produced a 'state effect'. Subordinate officials, when breaking the rules, were also making the state. Unsurprisingly, given their conceptualisation of the colonial state as a rational entity, historians of colonial Burma have viewed misconduct and corruption as merely epiphenomenal to state formation.[45] But acts defined as misconduct are not helpfully conceptualised as aberrations from norms of state practices because they were pervasive and performative state practices themselves.[46] Misconduct was both a discourse for imagining the state and a set of practices through which the state was constituted.

Subordinate officials

In the wet season of 1901, a European secretarial subordinate who had been employed in the Chief Secretary's office for many years was convicted of cheating. The official, one E. Vanspall, was of Dutch descent and had a well-known elderly father living on a Government of India pension in Calcutta. As a result, the case came as a shock to some in the close-knit European community in Burma, although the conviction received a begrudging endorsement in the British colonial media for its salutary value. Vanspall had pretended to be the Chief Secretary to the Government of Burma in order to induce cultivators embroiled in land disputes to pay him to resolve the disputes in their favour. The unusual aspect of his case was that he had no authority, legal or otherwise, to resolve such disputes; in fact, he had absolutely no influence on the allocation of land. He was employed only as the superintendent of an office of largely clerical powers. But irrespective of his minor bureaucratic role, Vanspall had used his limited state position to create in the minds of the duped cultivators a truly imaginary state. The secretariat office became the 'high court', he used procedural terms such as 'court fees' and 'stamps' as a guise through which he could extort illegal payments, and he gave himself an outrageous promotion to one of the top administrative positions in colonial Burma.[47]

The case is fascinating for a host of reasons, not least of which was Vanspall's apparent use of his race to carry out his deception, but I want to focus here on his performance of the state. Clearly when judged against Vanspall's formal bureaucratic role, he was misrepresenting the state. He was not the Chief Secretary, his office was not the high court, and he was not collecting legitimate fees from the cultivators who had travelled from the delta to Rangoon to help their cause. The state he performed was a fiction.[48] However, this is a rather limited way to understand Vanspall's acts as this was a deception which was successful, a fiction which was believed: and why not? The cultivators need not have been ignorant or stupid to have been conned by Vanspall. He used legitimate state buildings, resources, and procedures to perform his duplicitous state. The state as he performed it would have looked and sounded much like the 'real' state as it existed in legal statutes, government gazettes, and in the official mind. Moreover, following Abrams and Mitchell, for the limited time in which he was successful, Vanspall's state was, in effect, real: he was believed to have been acting legitimately on behalf of the state by his victims. His case forces us to carefully reconsider the nature of the colonial state in Burma and the role of state actors.

Firstly, Vanspall's case reveals the protean nature of the colonial state. I have already noted the benefit of conceptualising the state as an imagined entity, and one imagined through myriad everyday practices. But 'everyday state' approaches have tended to imply the singularity of the state: the existence of a sole, historically contingent imagining of the state and a discrete set of related quotidian state practices. For instance, Timothy Mitchell argued that state practices were arranged into routines and evoked the state through disciplinary power, following Foucault. The nature of the state, being structured and maintained by disciplined practices, was thus stable. Modifying this position, Vanspall's case suggests instead that the nature of the state was in the eye of the beholder. What appeared to have been an incredulous deception to high-ranking British officials seemed entirely plausible to cultivators from the Irrawaddy Delta. John Comaroff has eloquently criticised the overburdened, implicitly singular meaning of the designation 'colonial state' in much scholarship. He quipped, 'to speak of the Raj, at the height of its elaboration, in the same breath as the administrations of, say, Lesotho or Zanzibar is not unlike treating an elephant, an emu, and an egret as the same kind of creature because they are all animals.'[49]

I would add that even in the same place and time, the colonial state connoted different things to different people.[50] To overlook this is not unlike assuming that the experience of an elephant was essentially the same for all, regardless of whether one was riding on top of it or was trampled beneath it.

Here it is worth briefly returning to the work of the great patriarch of Burma studies, John Furnivall. As an anomalous official who was a Fabian socialist, sympathetic to Burmese nationalism, and held a genuine interest in the culture and society of Burma, it is unsurprising that his depictions of the colonial state portray it as an inflexible, destructive monolith. Such a rendering is entirely consistent with his personal experience of bureaucratic frustration, as well as his previously noted nostalgia and paternalism.[51] What is at stake here is not the accuracy of Furnivall's description of the state. Indeed, accuracy might be a foolish aim when attempting to depict a chimerical and fluid entity as a state. The problem has been the privileged place of this particular perspective on the state within historical writing as if it were the only valid view of the state. It seems highly unlikely that Furnivall's imagining and experience of the colonial state corresponded with those of the cultivators making deals with Vanspall, the witnesses to Maung Po Tun's aggressive and drunken behaviour, or Maung Shwe Pa when attempting to negotiate the local Headman and courts to recover his stolen rice.

Secondly, the case of Vanspall reveals the role of subordinate officials in shaping what, for want of a better term, we might describe as subaltern imaginings and experiences of the colonial state. High-ranking British officials were mostly invisible to the bulk of the delta population. They appeared briefly in the smaller towns during their tours. They may have passed through more remote villages on steamers on route, or in the case of a scandal. In fact, at times of tidal flooding, the more southerly areas of the delta would have been almost entirely inaccessible to them. Instead, the upper-echelons of officialdom mostly resided in the central district towns. The vast majority of the visible state activities were performed by the predominantly Burmese and Indian subordinate officials. It was these low-ranking officials, such as Headman Maung San Gaung, Maung Po Tun, and Vanspall, with whom those encountering the colonial state would have interacted with. Subordinate officials were the ones who performed the colonial state in everyday life and as we have already seen, and will see throughout what follows, their performances were often duplicitous.

Describing subordinate officials as 'performing the state' should not suggest to the reader that these were somehow superficial or shallow acts. To the contrary, I mean to argue that subordinates' performances were constitutive of the colonial state. As conceptualised by Judith Butler, performances are much deeper than intentional, ornamental acts. Instead, they are reiterative, citational acts that produce the effects that name them; in her work a gender, in mine a state.[52] This is a theoretical approach encapsulated in the term 'performativity', one also applied to states.[53] In his work exploring the nineteenth-century pre-colonial state in Bali, Clifford Geertz argued that the courtly ceremonies and pomp of an exemplary centre were not adornments or devices for maintaining the state, 'they were what the state was for'.[54] For Geertz, this was a 'theatre state' in which performance was its *raison d'être* and not a decorative extra. His ideas, when refracted through the conceptual lens of performativity, can be taken further. The performance of the state made the state. In the Burma Delta, this did not occur through the theatrical rituals of priests and princes at an exemplary centre, as in the Balinese *negara*, but in the quotidian performances of subordinate colonial officials.

Bringing these two conceptual premises together—the protean nature of the state and the performativity of the state—the utility of cases of misconduct for historians becomes clear. These investigations sought to uncover everyday state performances and the files document the deltaic population's often routine encounters with subordinate officials. They provide a window onto the state as a quotidian entity, revealing how it was performed by subordinates and, from that, enabling us to infer how it might have been imagined and reified. From this everyday perspective, looking through cases of misconduct, the colonial state in the Burma Delta appears to have been a complex entity. It was duplicitous, personal, and negotiable, as in the case of Headman Maung San Gaung. It was internally divided and dysfunctional, as in the case of Maung Po Tun. As we shall see in Chapter 2, which focuses on the career of a notorious police inspector, it could also be violent, despotic, and intrusive. However, by far the most overlooked aspect of the colonial state in the Burma Delta as it has been depicted by historians has been its gendering as masculine.

Maung Po Tun's public feud with Maung On Gaing, it will be remembered, was apparently about a woman 'seduced and abandoned' by Maung Po Tun. This narrative reflected two aspects of how the colonial state was gendered, both of which are explored in the final chapter. Firstly, this story was related to a common trope in British depictions of Burmese society. The British imagined Burmese men as 'henpecked husbands' under the thumbs of their female family members. According to this discourse, Burmese women were viewed as a threat to the bureaucratic division of the public and private spheres. To British eyes, the case of Maung Po Tun was yet another example of meddling women undermining the day-to-day affairs of the colonial state. Secondly, the absence of the woman's voice, name, or, in fact, any details on her at all in the archive reflected the gendering of subordinate official's everyday state performances, particularly those labelled misconduct and corruption. Despite British claims to the contrary women did not have access to the resources of state power through either formal or informal routes. This was especially apparent in misconduct in rape investigations, in which women's criminal cases were deliberately sabotaged. Subordinate officials' abuses of power served to simultaneously marginalise women and perform the state as male.

Living with leviathan

As post-colonial theorists have long noted, formal colonialism may be over but its effects still haunt both former imperial and recently liberated nations and continue to shape and structure contemporary debates.[55] This is apparent in historical interpretations of the colonial state in Burma. For Michael Aung-Thwin, the colonial state was a brief blip in the otherwise continuous development of a Burmese order, resurrected in the second half of the twentieth century.[56] In his new book, written with his son Maitrii, they go as far to claim that, 'The vaunted "legacy" of the British exists largely in the minds and books of historians.'[57] The books which they may implicitly be referring to are those of Thant Myint-U. His argument that modern Burma was forged during the fall of the Konbaung Dynasty to the British is almost diametrically opposed to theirs.[58] This disputed interpretation of history is reflected in their politics. Although Myint-U has long been an advocate for liberal democratic reform,[59] Michael Aung-Thwin has been openly sceptical about what he once called a Western-inspired 'democracy jihad'.[60]

This debate exposes the current limits of historical imagination when it comes to colonial Burma (limits which have been overcome in recent work on the cultural history of the period).[61] Colonialism was either a superficial, fleeting moment or a transformative turning point. In both narratives, the colonial state was simply an alien entity imposed on Burmese society. Neither approach treats the colonial state as emerging from within society, as the imagined effect of embedded, daily practices. In only slightly exaggerated terms, the colonial state is instead treated as an abstract object to be either blamed for Burma's post-colonial historical trajectory or exorcised from Myanmar's history. The colonial state has been fetishised as a 'bad thing', to put it in the words of anthropologist Michael Taussig,[62] but it has not been adequately studied. Its nature has been assumed and its legacies have been reductively simplified, and this has contributed to limiting how any future state in Burma might be imagined, confining commentators to binaries of reform/retrenchment, foreign intervention/isolation, and unity/division. Things were, and are, more complex.

Furnivall wrote of the 'fashioning of leviathan', the high-level correspondence through which the foundations of the colonial state in Burma were laid. But it was subordinate officials who performed this state, and they did ambivalently, as the numerous files on misconduct attest. This book is an attempt to examine the state beyond its existence in official correspondences, gazettes, and legal statutes to explore its quotidian manifestation and what it meant to live with leviathan. Chapter 1 deconstructs colonial definitions of 'misconduct' and 'corruption' and outlines the disciplinary procedures developed to police them. As I have already noted, tolerance was as important as punishment in the economy of discipline which emerged. Chapter 2 uses the career of Police Inspector Fakir Pakiri to demonstrate how subordinate officials, through acts of corruption, were able to performatively enact the colonial state. In this case, Pakiri's prodigious malfeasance relied on his ability to evoke and engage the broader colonial coercive network of courts and prisons. Chapter 3 explores the relationship between high-ranking British officials and their subordinates. It details how the authority to investigate officials for misconduct was used to reify the racial division of the state. And lastly, Chapter 4 discusses how the colonial state was gendered, both in official practices and in informal acts of misconduct and corruption.

From a distant aerial view, or on a map, the Irrawaddy River's path from upland Kachin State to the Bay of Bengal seems clear. But when one focuses in on the delta alone, the illusion is lost. The once unified river disperses into unstable systems of narrow creeks and channels. The water eddies and pools; it ebbs and flows. The previously precise demarcation between land and sea dissolves into a shifting terrain, sometimes one, sometimes the other. In a similar way, the apparently monolithic colonial state becomes infinitely more complex and fluid when studied as an everyday entity. Its power too could flow in unexpected directions and gather in unwanted areas. Its boundaries were also imprecise and permeable. It could offer opportunity for some, whereas it could be unpredictable and destructive for others.

1
Making Misconduct

"[B]ut I think I shall fine him. Yes, it is not improbable that I shall fine him."

"And do you imagine that that will do any good?"

"It will do my pocket good to the extent of a rupee or two, provided of course, I do not remit later."

"But him, I mean—do you suppose that it will do him the least good? I doubt it myself very much."

"It will furnish him with further data for his misdemeanour tariff; that is about all."

"I don't understand," she said.

"He will get from the fine a rough idea of how much it will cost him to repeat an experiment of this kind. Next time he will count up and calculate. If he is not quite sure that the fun is worth the fine, he will deny himself."

Cecil C. Lowis, *The Machinations of the Myo-Ok* (1903)

Constructing an economy of discipline

Defining 'corruption' is notoriously difficult. Various authors with different disciplinary backgrounds have pointed out that the term has often been used to denigrate post-colonial regimes, depicting corruption as something that belongs to non-Western 'others'.[1] The sentiments of a recent commentator on corruption in Burma reveal how casually such essentialising moral judgements are made: 'Burma is one of those countries where corruption is well known to the point of being conspicuous. ... To Western eyes the flagrancy still comes as a shock.'[2] The recent scandals of Enron in the United States as well as those concerning BAE

Systems, parliamentary expenses, and the phone-hacking journalists at News International in the United Kingdom have somewhat muddied the waters of such patronising sentiments, but they persist.

Unsurprisingly, such a moralistic notion of corruption has an imperial lineage.[3] Herbert Thirkell White, the Lieutenant Governor of Burma between 1905 and 1910, wrote in his published memoirs, extolling the virtues of colonial rule, that, 'To all men were given the protection of equal laws and the assurance of even handed justice. The grasping avarice of officials was restrained, and corrupt practices were discountenanced.'[4] In a similar vein, Charles Crosthwaite, the Chief Commissioner during the 'pacification' campaign in Upper Burma, used the apparent corruption of King Thebaw's reign as a justification for colonial invasion.[5] British officials denigrated the pre-colonial state as utterly and irredeemably corrupt. At the same time, the absence of corruption was dubiously heralded as a marker of the beneficence of the colonial regime.

This portrayal of corruption has lasted into post-colonial historical writing. Apologists for empire have argued that the British introduced the ideals of an incorruptible state, if not its realisation.[6] D. G. E. Hall identified the Burmese corrupt treatment of two British sea captains as a critical causal factor in the First Anglo-Burmese War.[7] Like Crosthwaite before him, for Hall British imperialism was made inevitable, even invited, by the corruption of the pre-colonial Burmese state. These arguments have insidiously managed to find their way into more nuanced and critical recent histories of colonial rule in Burma. Even Robert Taylor, perhaps in parapraxis, described corruption under the colonial regime as a return to 'practices of the past'.[8] The abatement of corruption has been made a marker of modernity, one allegedly brought about by colonialism.

British officials consigned corruption to the pre-colonial past, and historians of Burma have by and large followed suit. That corruption was widespread in the branches of the colonial state did not disrupt this rhetorical strategy. It was viewed as an unfortunate inherited trait of states in Asia, stubborn 'practices of the past'. Later in his memoirs, White opined: 'Both in Upper Burma and in Lower Burma we inherited the traditions of a feeble Oriental Government, and it was impossible that evil practices should not abound.'[9] Corruption was conceived of as a problem particular to governing an Oriental population. Thus, the British largely blamed their subordinate Indian and Burmese officials for corruption, and the suggestion that corruption could be a product of the colonial bureaucracy was not countenanced.[10]

But corruption was a product of colonial rule: British officials discursively created corruption. This process was similar to the development of colonial discourses on criminality. Both corruption and criminality were defined as illicit through colonial disciplinary techniques and institutions.[11] Historians of colonial Asia have long studied the various ways that criminality was constructed through colonial policing, prisons, and courts in conjunction with discourses on race, gender, and psychology, among others.[12] This creation of colonial criminality was paralleled by the colonial construction of corruption through similar, though more informal, quasi-judicial practices put in place during the late nineteenth century. Corruption too developed alongside discourses of racial difference, particularly the perennial concern over the mendacity of the Burmese and Indian populations.[13] Despite the regular instances of corruption committed by Europeans in Burma, Asians were routinely depicted as inherently prone to corruption. Corruption was primarily about disciplining 'native' subordinate officials, just as criminality was about disciplining 'native' populations.[14]

The term 'corruption' is, however, slightly anachronistic. In their official bureaucratic correspondence, the British did not use the term to describe the malpractices in the subordinate branches of the state. It was an adjective applied to the pre-colonial state and was regularly used in the British colonial press in Burma for polemical purposes, but it was not the official nomenclature. British officials instead preferred the broader, euphemistic term 'misconduct'. Unlike corruption, misconduct encompassed acts of incompetence, negligence, and insubordination within its remit, although most of the recorded cases involved the types of wilful malfeasant malpractices now synonymous with the term 'bureaucratic corruption'. In official imperial rhetoric, the pre-colonial state suffered from endemic Oriental corruption, whereas the colonial state was afflicted by subordinate misconduct.

Although misconduct was the target of bureaucratic discipline, it was not the intention of British officials to eradicate what were pervasive malpractices. In fact, the misconduct proceedings that were put in place were based implicitly on tolerance as much as punishment. They constituted an economy of discipline in which both acquiesce and repression were common currencies.[15] Acts of misconduct were differentiated from one another; a repertoire of punishments was developed and calibrated to the different categories of misconduct; the severity of punishment was calculated according to a range of contingent colonial imperatives: in short, during the late nineteenth century, British officials developed what the novelist and colonial judge, Cecil C. Lowis, referred to as a 'misdemeanour tariff'. Intrinsically, within this economy of discipline, spaces were produced in which some misconduct was tolerated, overlooked, or punished leniently.[16] In other words, inherent to the misdemeanour tariff was the possibility that the fun *could* be worth the fine.

This chapter reveals the dual processes through which colonial rule made misconduct. Firstly, how misconduct was created as a colonial illegality. In other words, the process by which certain malpractices were defined as misconduct through the quasi-judicial proceedings put in place during the nineteenth century. Secondly, how these proceedings created spaces in which misconduct was tolerated, particularly when committed by township officers and Europeans. The final section then places these colony-wide processes in the local dynamics of the rapidly changing Irrawaddy Delta society and economy.

The arithmetic of punishment

Despite the gradual evolution of formal procedures for investigating and punishing misconduct during the nineteenth century, policing corruption was a peripheral concern throughout colonial rule. There was no specialised unit for enforcing bureaucratic conduct. There was no India-wide legislative basis for dealing with misconduct that was not already punishable under the Indian penal code. It was not a topic that featured in the official correspondence between the members of the upper echelons of the Raj.[17] Instead, misconduct proceedings were developed through a series of local standing orders issued by the chief commissioners of Burma (after 1897, the lieutenant governors). The proceedings that were eventually put in place locally were thin and were not uniformly adhered to. Nonetheless, they loosely constituted modern disciplinary techniques specifically targeting misconduct.

Before 1879, disciplining a subordinate official was an informal procedure. Deputy commissioners could dismiss them without framing formal charges, without giving them the opportunity to defend themselves, and without giving them the right to appeal decisions. It was decided in 1879 that, except in cases in which a subordinate had been found guilty of a crime and dismissed as a result of being jailed, officials being disciplined for misconduct must have the charges put to them in writing and then given the opportunity of defending themselves through a written explanation.[18] These written explanations were not simply window-dressing to give legitimacy to deputy commissioners' decisions in cases of misconduct. They were an effective form of defence, and subordinate officials were occasionally able to exonerate themselves through their written explanations.[19]

From this rather rudimentary, bare bones framework, a more intricate set of procedures developed that were increasingly of a quasi-judicial nature. In 1893, subordinate officials were given the right to appeal against decisions in misconduct cases. But at the same time, the Chief Commissioner ordered that witnesses questioned during misconduct investigations should not be placed under oath and that advocates should not be used. The rationale behind this was to maintain a lower threshold for admissible evidence in misconduct proceedings than was necessary for the criminal courts.[20] Although the proceedings were increasingly legalistic in their framework, they were clearly delineated from actual legal proceedings.

By 1901, the documents that subordinate officials were allowed to access in order to frame their appeals were clarified for the first time. In addition to the charges, the defence, and the decision, subordinate officials were entitled to access the recorded statements of witnesses examined in the enquiry. This was tantamount to being able to cross-examine the evidence. However, again this was limited as they were denied access to any internal office notes, reports, or correspondence regarding the enquiry.[21] Formal proceedings for punishing misconduct cases while being subordinated to judicial proceedings took on many of the same features, such as the use of witness and the right to appeal decisions.

However, it would be misleading to extrapolate from these written orders to directly infer how misconduct investigations were actually conducted. In 1898, it was necessary for the Lieutenant Governor to reinforce the earlier orders that the charges, the defence, and the decision should be reduced to writing and given to the accused official. In 1907, deputy commissioners had to be reminded of the orders again by the Lieutenant Governor of Burma, even though they had first been formulated in 1879. British officials would occasionally punish and dismiss subordinate officials without going through the established procedure, especially with regard to granting appeals.[22] Evidently, deputy commissioners in Burma often misconducted misconduct proceedings.

A further difficulty deputy commissioners faced when punishing misconduct was that it was not always clear what precisely constituted misconduct. The Indian penal code covered most malpractices, for example, bribery, accepting illegal gratifications, and extortion.[23] If the evidence of these illicit acts was not strong enough for a criminal prosecution, as was often the case, deputy commissioners instead pursued suspected subordinate officials through misconduct proceedings. At the other end of the spectrum, misconduct also encompassed negligence and general incompetence. Being either incapable or inefficient in their duties would occasionally lead to subordinate officials being disciplined through misconduct proceedings.[24]

But not all forms of misconduct were covered by the penal code or by negligence; indeed, there was some internal debate over whether some acts constituted misconduct at all. Two such unclear areas were: whether subordinate officials should be allowed to engage in private trade, and whether they should be allowed to gather donations from those attending their family ceremonies.[25] Both of these questions proved divisive within the Indian Civil Service in Burma. At the heart of these bureaucratic debates was an attempt to delineate the public and private spheres. British officials worried that if subordinate officials were allowed to engage in private trade, then they might be tempted to use their public office to illicitly further their businesses.[26] British officials also worried that if subordinate officials were allowed to collect donations for private ceremonies, then they might be tempted to use these donations as a guise for extorting bribes.[27] On the other hand, it was feared that barring subordinate officials from private trade or accepting donations for ceremonies would be an unfair restriction on their private lives.[28] It was in situations such as these, in which the public and private spheres overlapped, that misconduct charges were often brought against subordinate officials.[29]

Although the correspondence surrounding these two issues was often heated, both were ultimately of little consequence. Despite deciding that subordinate officials should be prohibited from engaging in private trade, the only official from the Irrawaddy Division charged with breaking the rule between 1896 and 1909 was not punished but praised for exhibiting commercial enterprise against the allegedly innate inclinations of the Burmese.[30] Likewise, the only official found to have breached the regulations on accepting donations for hosting private ceremonies was punished lightly with a transfer to a new township and retraining.[31] Although, in principle, British officialdom wished to clearly separate the public and private spheres, in practice, they were ambivalent about policing and punishing instances when the two overlapped but there was no evidence of malfeasance. In these cases, they showed leniency. There was a sliding scale of punishment.

Within the formal proceedings for investigating acts encompassed by misconduct, deputy commissioners had a broad repertoire of potential punishments at their disposal. Dismissal was the most severe punishment that could be sanctioned against subordinate officials, without criminal proceedings being brought against them. The implications of dismissal as a punishment may seem obvious enough but deputy commissioners regularly had to be reminded about them. The complication emerged from their failure to distinguish the penalty of 'removal' from 'dismissal'. If a subordinate official was removed from his post, he could still take up government employment in other posts. However, if a subordinate official was dismissed, he could no longer gain employment in any government position. Although the difference was quite straightforward and had been established since 1886, deputy commissioners had to be reminded of it through local orders in 1895 and once again in 1907.[32] Removal was thus intended to be a step below dismissal in severity, and below removal there was a wide range of less severe penalties, including fines, suspension without pay, demotion, or transfer. This hierarchy of punishments was applied according to the perceived gravity of the misconduct.[33]

But deciding upon the appropriate punishment was not solely based on the seriousness of the misconduct. Deputy commissioners took into account a number of other informal factors when deciding the severity of punishment. Subordinate officials with good reputations, before allegations were made against them, were often spared the full force of colonial discipline. Maung Po Thet, a village headman from Henzada, was charged with embezzlement in 1900 but the Deputy Commissioner argued that due to Maung Po Thet's 24 years of experience in government service, he should be spared the 'indignity of a prosecution with possible imprisonment'.[34] Embezzlement was often punished through criminal proceedings resulting in substantial terms of imprisonment; Maung Po Thet was fortunate to be treated with such leniency. Similarly, Tha Hmaing, a head constable of police found guilty of forging his diaries in an attempt to frame a township officer for misconduct, considered a very grave malpractice, had his punishment reduced because of his previous service. His commanding officer wrote, 'The present case is no doubt a bad one, but taking into consideration the Head Constable's length of service and previous good conduct, I think that reduction to the rank of 2nd grade Sergeant ... and transfer to a district in another division will be a sufficiently severe punishment.'[35]

There were numerous additional factors under consideration when deputy commissioners calculated the severity of a punishment. As well as the perceived gravity of the infringement and the previous record of the subordinate official, they took into account how the misconduct affected the subordinate's suitability for their role. For instance, Maung Po Byu, a township officer from the Sagaing division, who had been found guilty of 'gross irregularities' and acting beyond the remit of his powers, was punished with a transfer to the Irrawaddy Division. The Deputy Commissioner justified the lenient punishment by arguing that Maung Po Byu was unfit to wield the 'independent charge of an inaccessible township' but would be fine in a township that had better networks of communication and was more accessible.[36] Following a similar logic, the township officer Saw U White had his magisterial powers removed due to his negligence in civil cases and perpetual insobriety. But he was still deemed capable of less onerous administrative duties.[37]

Deputy commissioners' calculations of the severity of punishments were also informed by the difficulties they faced recruiting subordinate officials. Maung On Gaing, a township officer from Bogale, was spared his punishment of being transferred for embezzlement due to a lack of qualified township officers available to replace him.[38] These pressures were also apparent in the nearby town of Pyapon. Maung Shwe Hnit, a head constable of the police, faced a fine for failing to sign a register, but the Deputy Commissioner interjected, reasoning that, 'It is difficult to get recruits—I am told in Pyapon—fining thus a Head Constable will not make the force more popular.'[39] British officials had to take into account the strength of the pool of potential state employees and replacements when disciplining their subordinate officials.

The arithmetic of punishment was thus contingent on deputy commissioners taking under consideration a variety of factors: the gravity of the infringement; the subordinate's previous record; the subordinate's ability to continue performing their duties; and the amount of available replacements. This was an informal economy of discipline in which tolerance and repression were allocated according to the imperatives of the situation. This distribution of tolerance and repression varied particularly across different occupations and was often dependent upon whether the subordinate official being disciplined was European or not.

Even a cursory look at the list of individuals dismissed from government service across colonial Burma reveals that certain occupations were dismissed more frequently than others.[40] Most subordinates were dismissed from the civil police force and clerical staff, accounting together for more than half of all the dismissed subordinates across colonial Burma between 1886 and 1909. For the Irrawaddy Division, this figure was closer to two-thirds. Following clerks and police officers in frequency of dismissals were forestry staff, vaccinators, village headmen (*thugyis*), and jail staff.[41] But the frequency of dismissals did not always reflect the frequency of misconduct charges made against certain groups of employees. The most notable example of this disparity was township officers (*myo-oks*) of whom only a small number were dismissed despite the large number of misconduct investigations against them. Deputy commissioners tolerated misconduct within some branches of subordinate officialdom but not others.

A less overt contingent factor in misconduct procedures was the race of the subordinate official. Often this was an implicit factor, one difficult to tease out of the sources. It was not an easily identifiable or quantifiable factor to assess, unlike the occupation of the subordinate. Nevertheless, in cases of misconduct committed by Europeans, the often-implicit importance of race became more pronounced. Deputy commissioners expressed empathy and sympathy towards Europeans implicated in acts of misconduct, whereas this was absent in similar cases involving Burmese or Indian subordinate officials. They were generally more lenient in cases of misconduct committed by Europeans. However, at the same time, notions of racial prestige had to be maintained, and British subordinate officials thought to be undermining this façade were not tolerated.

The economy of discipline allowed certain subordinate officials, such as Europeans and *myo-oks*, space for misconduct, and deputy commissioners tolerated many of their malpractices. While for others, particularly clerks, punishments were applied strictly.

Clerical staff

Behind the civil police, the clerical staff made up the largest proportion of subordinate employees dismissed from government service between 1886 and 1909, responsible for around a quarter of all dismissals.[42] This can be accounted for largely by the sheer size of the clerical staff employed in the state. The actual total number is impossible to accurately fathom for a host of reasons. Firstly, individuals in clerical positions could actually be in a variety of roles. The clerical staff category comprised a range of different jobs: clerks, translators, treasurers, peons, and others, and within these categories there were further differentiations. Some of those employed as low-level clerks and peons were employed only on a temporary basis, and apprentice clerks were taken on without payment. The 'clerical staff' thus constituted a fluctuating and blurred group. Estimates are made even more difficult because the administration itself made little attempt to monitor the overall number of those employed as clerical staff, as it did for its more manageably sized and higher-waged branches such as the police force or the magistracy. Moreover, the clerical staff was spread across the varying departments of the colonial administration and not treated as one body. Even Alleyne Ireland's two-volume *The Province of Burma*, the otherwise encyclopaedic study of the colonial bureaucracy at the commencement of the twentieth century, could only vaguely comment that, 'the Government of Burma employs a very large number of persons whose duties are of a purely clerical character'.[43] However, although the large number of subordinate officials employed in clerical work would logically mean that many of the individuals dismissed from government service would have been from clerical positions, there were specificities in how the economy of discipline was applied to clerical staff.

Clerical employees, particularly clerks and interpreters, have often been cast as the archetypal colonial subordinate official. Recent literature on African colonial employees especially has focused on clerks as intermediaries between the European rulers and the indigenous population. These studies have emphasised the difficulties and tensions of African clerks' position between the coloniser and colonised, as well as their ability to use their position for their own purposes, both selfish and altruistic.[44] These insights provide an incisive assessment of the place of subordinate employees but they are not features that were specific to the work of clerks; indigenous vaccinators, policemen, magistrates, and a host of other positions could all be accurately described as intermediaries between the coloniser and colonised in a similar way. The difference between the clerical staff and the other positions in the colonial bureaucracy in Burma was that they were more expendable. As such, the economy of discipline was often more severe for clerks and other clerical employees, who could be punished harshly for comparatively minor infringements.

The offences that resulted in the dismissal of clerical subordinates could be remarkably slight. For example, Sunal Singh, a peon, was dismissed for 'making a noise under the circuit house' and was then denied the opportunity to defend himself.[45] In a similarly brusque decision, two other peons were dismissed for 'not aiding' someone attempting to submit a petition.[46] Other examples include one head clerk of a court in the town of Twante who was dismissed after being twice convicted of singing obscene songs, and a sub-treasury accountant dismissed simply for 'suspicious behaviour'.[47] However, by far the most common reasons clerical staff were dismissed were for misappropriation, embezzlement, and criminal breaches of trust.[48]

Treasurers, accountants, and clerks had ample opportunities for embezzlement since government revenue would often pass through their hands. Low-level clerical staff often dealt with the payment of fines, the payment of stamps, and other everyday transactions of small sums of money. They were also often the subordinate officials charged with maintaining the government records and files, and thus in a position to 'cook the books'. European high-ranking officials certainly believed embezzlement by clerks to be a considerable concern. The long-serving judge in colonial Burma, Cecil C. Lowis, premised his second novel about colonial Burma, *The Machinations of the Myo-ok* published in 1903, on the embezzlement of government funds by a cunning head clerk triggering a farcical chain of events in which other officials attempted to avoid the blame.[49]

That deputy commissioners took embezzlement seriously can be demonstrated further by the heavy punishments inflicted on those officials caught. Maung Taw Lee received a five-month rigorous imprisonment for the misappropriation of the small amount of just over Rs. 17.[50] In 1891, a clerk was convicted and dismissed for a criminal breach of trust concerning only Rs. 3.[51] Unsurprisingly, the punishment was even more severe when large amounts of money were concerned. Maung Maung, a head clerk in Pegu Division, was initially sentenced to a 10-year transportation for three counts of criminal breach of trust for an amount totalling Rs. 1166, although the sentence was reduced to four years of rigorous imprisonment on appeal.[52] Their position as intermediaries for the colonial regime in everyday monetary interactions with the public meant that they were peculiarly well situated for such acts of deceit, and deputy commissioners exercised little tolerance in dealing with the cases that arose.

Other common causes for dismissal among clerks were forgery and the falsification of documents. As with embezzlement, clerks were often in an opportune situation to commit such crimes, as they handled official documentation as a central part of their daily duties. For example, a particularly dilatory township officer in 1909 was found to have unwittingly signed numerous false bills for travel expenses made out to his clerks for journeys that they had not taken.[53] In a large number of cases, as in the previous example, forgery and falsification were either a means for enabling embezzlement or a method of hiding the evidence of misappropriation: but forgery was itself sufficient grounds for dismissal. In 1903, the head clerk of the township office in Wakema was dismissed for 'falsifying entries in registers', the motives for which were not stated. In what was perhaps a harsher case, a head clerk from the district of Katha was dismissed for forging a document in order to replace one that he had previously lost.[54]

Another regular use of forgeries and false documents was in connection with examinations. In 1906, two clerks were dismissed from the Pyapon township for possessing forged examination certificates purporting to demonstrate their proficiency in language.[55] Other clerks were found to have fraudulently acquired examination papers before sitting the examinations. Passing examinations and receiving qualifications were increasingly becoming the preferred paths for advancement in the subordinate civil service towards obtaining a first class *myo-ok*ship, although promotion from within departments still remained the most common route.[56] These changes seem to have created a market for illegally acquired examination papers, a market in which clerks could play an important role, as they did in an examination scandal of 1901. Because of this particular scandal, four *myo-oks* were removed from their positions for having acquired the examination papers in advance of a departmental examination. The *myo-oks* had bought the papers from a government translator who had compiled them with the help of three minor clerks who had 'dishonestly acquainted themselves with the contents of the examination papers'. The investigation revealed that the trade in examination papers spread from Mandalay all the way down to Rangoon.[57] In this case, as with other cases of forgery, clerks had used their proximity to government papers and records for ulterior motives.

It might have been expected that the higher echelons of the colonial regime were particularly sensitive to cases of embezzlement and forgery, these being crimes of some gravity affecting their revenue streams. The strictness of the economy of discipline for clerical staff, however, becomes more apparent in deputy commissioners' attitudes in the numerous cases of insubordination, negligence, and absenteeism. Cases of misconduct of this sort could often arise from fairly innocuous situations. One junior peon in the office of the Deputy Commissioner of Bassein found himself disciplined for an altercation stemming from his accidental mislabelling of a file as 'Miscellaneous' rather than 'Advocate'. The Deputy Commissioner alleged that when the peon, Maung Po Pan, was asked to correct his error, he became obstreperous and used 'inappropriate language'.[58] Unsurprisingly, Maung Po Pan saw the matter in a different light. He argued that he had not used abusive language but had only sought further clarification on the labelling and that the Deputy Commissioner had misunderstood him. He went on to write in his explanation, 'If superior officers [are] intending to find fault with juniors in such cases, I think, the latter will be found with a dozen kinds of such faults within 12 hours of a working day.'[59] Despite his articulate and spirited defence, high-ranking officials dismissed Maung Po Pan's explanation, since he had not dealt with the unacceptable character of his 'manner and tone'.[60]

A number of similarly trivial cases occurred in the Office of the Commissioner of the Irrawaddy Division during 1904 and 1905. One clerk was disciplined for being absent from work to attend his grandfather's funeral, and a peon was fined for missing work in order to get a haircut, his defence being that he did not want to appear before the Commissioner in a 'rough fashion'.[61] A third peon was disciplined for chewing betel in the office, and the superintendent of the office admitted that there were a few 'black sheep' among his clerks and apprentices.[62] Petty offences were not readily tolerated.

Working in close proximity to British high-ranking officials was, on occasion, an unpleasant situation for the indigenous clerical staff. Clerks in other colonial contexts were regularly at the receiving end of racial prejudice, and, partly as a result of these experiences, clerical staff often swelled the ranks of anti-colonial movements.[63] Burma was no exception to this; most of the membership of the first widespread anti-colonial political movement, the Young Men's Buddhist Association, was made up of young government officials and clerks.[64] The case of an apprentice clerk, also working in the Commissioner of the Irrawaddy Division's office, Maung Maung, who was denigrated by the superintendent in front of the office staff as lazy and rude is an example of the everyday humiliation clerical staff could face.[65] The superintendent's insults echoed broader depictions by contemporary British scholar-officials who portrayed the Burmese as lazy and quick to temper when provoked.[66] Cases of insubordination, absenteeism, and neglect may have been more a reflection of the conditions of work and prejudices of high-ranking British officials than the attitude and competence of the clerical staff.

Racial prejudices aside, the backgrounds of the low-level clerical staff were a cause for concern for high-ranking British officials. The Deputy Commissioner of Bassein discovered on a tour of the district's townships a clerical subordinate employed in a court who had previously been convicted of seven crimes including causing hurt, bad livelihood, theft, and housebreaking. The Deputy Commissioner commented on the case that, 'It is not surprising that such men commit blackmail, delay [the] service of summons and generally do what they want.'[67] Subsequent investigations revealed 12 other low-level clerks and peons working in the Bassein District with previous criminal convictions, including some serious crimes such as theft and stabbing.[68] Evidently, recruitment procedures were flawed and background checks on prospective clerical employees were not always carried out, resulting in individuals who had previously been punished under colonial law receiving clerical jobs.

The clerical staff contributed so highly to the number of individuals dismissed from government service, not only because there were more of them, but because they were more expendable in the eyes of deputy commissioners. Holding a lower position in the bureaucratic hierarchy meant that for clerks the economy of discipline was more severe. Take, for example, the case of financial irregularities that occurred in the town of Thabaung in the Bassein District, the result of which was that the *myo-ok* had formal misconduct charges levelled against him. In his explanation, the *myo-ok*, Maung Myat Min, drew attention to his previous long and blameless record in government service and blamed the irregularities on his clerks, whom he claimed he had mistakenly trusted.[69] This excuse did not hold much water with the Deputy Commissioner who wrote in reply, 'His clerks whom he trusted were extremely incompetent. At least one of them was almost certainly dishonest with stamps, and all three would tell a lie at any time to suit their purpose.' But he went on to write, 'I believe that Maung Myat Min knew this and was too weak and too good natured to take action against them.'[70] Although the *myo-ok* was held ultimately responsible for the government's financial losses, it was the clerks who were punished the hardest; one was put under observation, one was removed, and the remaining clerk was dismissed.[71] Maung Myat Min was disciplined more lightly, with a demotion and a transfer.[72] The stakes were higher for clerks than for other government servants when charged with misconduct.

Myo-oks or miniature monarchs

One group of state employees that are conspicuous in their absence from the list of individuals dismissed from government service were *myo-oks*. Between 1886 and 1909, the number of *myo-oks* dismissed from government can be counted on one hand. It should not be assumed from this that *myo-oks* were less likely to be corrupt or incompetent than other officials. If anything, sources suggest that the opposite may have been the case. The general British population in Burma viewed *myo-ok*ships as one of the most corrupt subordinate posts. Within the British colonial media, excepting the civil police, no other group of state employees received the same intensity of almost constant berating in newspaper columns. This widespread suspicion was reflected in official attitudes. Among the misconduct files, alongside civil policemen, *myo-oks* appear as the most regular group under investigation or to have accusations made against them. Despite this, they were rarely dismissed. The reason that *myo-oks* so often avoided the ultimate departmental punishment of dismissal despite the suspicion surrounding them was because deputy commissioners tolerated much of their misconduct.

Myo-oks were responsible for the administration of the townships. They also had civil and criminal magisterial powers, powers that increased with the higher grades of the office. It was this aspect of *myo-oks'* duties and less their myriad administrative tasks that attracted the disapproval of the British colonial press. Many of the contributors to the *Times of Burma* newspaper were either barristers or otherwise familiar with court procedures. Having come into contact, and often conflict, with *myo-oks* on such a regular basis in court, it is unsurprising that their depictions were mostly disapproving. In some ways, their journalistic accounts of court cases seem analogous to contemporary gossip pages, satisfying a voyeuristic desire for scandal while inviting the reader to make moral judgements.

Another cause for this disproval of *myo-oks* was the prevalent sense of racial superiority, specifically the newspaper's concern about authority passing into the hands of the Burmese. An article from the *Times of Burma* from 1899 titled 'Justice in Burma', reviewing a number of cases of corrupt *myo-oks* that had previously been reported in the newspaper, captured this concern about the suitability of uneducated Burmese to carry out the magisterial powers invested in them:

> Although a Burman who knows English and a little law, may be trusted with ordinary cases to pass intelligent orders ... it does not follow that other Burmese gentlemen, who cannot speak English, knowing little and caring nothing about the law as it stands in the Manuals and Codes, are capable of gracing a seat in Her Majesty's dominions ... one has to have only a slight acquaintance with the subordinate judicial courts scattered throughout the province to find out the approximate number of utterly incompetent Myooks: and the grievance of the public is made all the greater by the lack of conscience and honest principles in those who are not straight.[73]

According to the author, even a fully trained Burmese township officer could only be trusted with 'ordinary cases'. As *myo-oks* were among the most prominent and powerful indigenous officials, it is unsurprising that the British colonial media, perennially concerned with power slipping from British hands in the administration, singled out *myo-oks* as incompetent and corrupt.

The dishonesty of the *myo-oks* was a recurring journalistic theme. In March 1902, the *Times of Burma* devoted three pages (the paper was only eight pages long excluding pages for advertisements) to an article taken from the *Moulmein Advertiser* simply titled '*Myo-oks*'. The long and polemical piece likened the authority of *myo-oks* in their townships to that of absolute sovereigns. The author called them 'Miniature Monarchs'.[74] In the article it was argued, as in earlier articles but in greater detail, that the corrupt practices of the *myo-oks* meant they were able to live in great comfort and that the position had become the aspiration of all Burmese schoolboys—a claim often made in the *Times of Burma*. According to the author, *myo-oks* lived lavish and affluent lifestyles, well beyond their officially sanctioned pay.

Such was the strength of the article that it immediately elicited a response from a *myo-ok* in defence. He wrote, 'That *Myooks* are all corrupt, I know from experience, is a false—absolutely false—statement ... In my varied experience of fourteen years, I have seen much public spirit; much real subordination of interest to duty; and a sensibility to honest fame and reputation among *Myooks*.'[75] A few of the articles on the subject that appeared in the *Times of Burma* also acknowledged the existence of few honest and competent *myo-oks*. But, it was commonly lamented, these few honest township officers were not encouraged or supported by the administration. A sub-theme in the paper was that blame did not lie entirely with the individual *myo-oks* but with the institutional framework in which they worked. Too little pay, poorly constructed courtrooms, and a lack of training were all cited as factors discouraging honesty among township officers.[76] But, although they were not perceived to have been entirely to blame, the British colonial press overwhelmingly depicted *myo-oks* as being corrupt and open to bribery.

This depiction of *myo-oks* as dishonest and intriguing was also present in literature written by colonial officials. Cecil C. Lowis' 1903 novel, mentioned above, evoked this idea in its very title, *The Machinations of the Myo-ok*. The plot revolved around the comic farce that ensued when a *myo-ok* discovered that the contents of the treasury had disappeared and attempted to fake a robbery, which went badly wrong.[77] The rotund, manipulative *myo-ok* of Cecil Lowis' writing foreshadowed, both in character and physicality, the more famous fictional Burmese magistrate U Po Kyin of George Orwell's novel *Burmese Days*, although

U Po Kyin's somewhat darker schemes ended in tragedy rather than farce.[78] Given the apparent general distrust of *myo-oks* and their ubiquitous characterisation as dishonest among the British community, it is all the more perplexing to comprehend why deputy commissioners rarely dismissed them.

In order to better understand how *myo-oks* avoided dismissal, the chequered career of Maung Gyi is illustrative.[79] The various misconduct cases against him occurring between 1903 and 1906 demonstrate two things. Firstly, that gathering concrete evidence against *myo-oks* was often a fraught and difficult process, and secondly, that in comparison to low-level clerical staff, there was a broader repertoire of punishments that could be preferred against a *myo-ok*, with high-ranking British officials displaying notable tolerance towards them.

Maung Gyi first appears in the misconduct files in March 1903 after making accusations of nepotism against another *myo-ok*, Maung Po Thi, in the town of Bogale in the newly created Pyapon District. The allegations that he made were found to be largely untrue by the District Commissioner of Pyapon, who suspected that Maung Gyi was attempting to besmirch the reputation of Maung Po Thi who, Maung Gyi believed, was giving evidence against him in an ongoing bribery case. Maung Gyi had sent his letter making his accusations to the Deputy Commissioner, the Commissioner of the Irrawaddy Division, and to the Burma secretariat, in an attempt to smear Maung Po Thi in the eyes of high-ranking British officials.[80] The British officials attached some urgency to dealing with Maung Gyi's false charges. The Deputy Commissioner of Pyapon dramatically advised that 'there can be no peace in the land as long as this gentleman [Maung Gyi] is allowed to go unpunished & whatever is done should be done as soon as possible'.[81] Despite this consternation, as well as the fact that Maung Gyi's explanation of his actions simply consisted of a reiteration of his allegations against Maung Po Thi, Maung Gyi weathered the storm and remained in his position as *myo-ok* and additional magistrate in Pyapon Township.[82]

Maung Gyi reappears in the misconduct files just a month later in connection with the bribery case alluded to above. The charges in this case were made against one Ba Cho. It was alleged that Ba Cho received a bribe of Rs. 400 from Po Sin to pay Maung Gyi in exchange for a decision of acquittal in a theft charge. The evidence that Maung Gyi had orchestrated the bribe and that Ba Cho was his tout was circumstantial but revealing nonetheless. The theft charge against Po Sin was described by the government advocate in the case against Ba Cho as a 'trumpery complaint' and was made without any evidential support. Despite the flimsiness of the complaint, Maung Gyi still issued a warrant for Po Sin's arrest. After Ba Cho had received the bribe from Po Sin, Maung Gyi held the trial, examined the witnesses, and, correctly according to law, dismissed the charges against Po Sin. The government advocate reasoned that 'Maung Gyi was not accepting a bribe as reward for a wrong decision: he was rather using this trumpery complaint for the purpose of extorting a bribe'.[83] The benefit of this strategy was that the legal decision made by Maung Gyi was a correct one. When the proceedings of the case were forwarded, his superior, the subdivisional magistrate, would not be able to detect any fault of law or have reason to suspect foul play. It was only Maung Gyi's issuing of an arrest warrant against Po Sin for a frivolous charge that implicated him with Ba Cho.

The problem that the government advocate confronted when attempting to frame a charge against Maung Gyi was that he was unable to directly link Maung Gyi to the Rs. 400 given to Ba Cho. It was self-evident that Ba Cho was enough of an acquaintance of Maung Gyi to be seen by Po Sin as a figure capable of conveying a bribe to him; otherwise, presumably Po Sin would not have paid Ba Cho the bribe. There was even some evidence that Ba Cho and Maung Gyi communicated in court via messages sent by the clerk Ba Tin, messages that coincided with the time that Po Sin was waiting to hear whether his bribe had been accepted. However, it was considered that this evidence would not have been strong enough to secure a criminal conviction. Part of the difficulty was that much of the government's evidence relied upon the testimony of Po Sin, who having given the bribe, was considered a collaborator and as a result was likely to have been discredited in court. The government advocate in the end conceded that he felt that the evidence was such that ultimately a conviction against Maung Gyi would have been unlikely. He lamented:

> These cases are always difficult to establish: the accused are generally men of ability with an intimate knowledge of all the facts connected or apparently connected with the case and money at their backs. There is in my opinion sufficient material to justify a prosecution, but I do not feel able to express any confident opinion upon the result of a prosecution if instituted, it is doubtful whether a conviction would be obtained.[84]

Deputy commissioners faced great difficulty proving cases against *myo-oks* such as Maung Gyi who possessed both the financial means and the authority unavailable to lower-ranked subordinate officials.

Maung Gyi had successfully avoided leaving any incriminating evidence through his use of legitimate court procedures and the employment of intermediaries, both Ba Cho and the court clerk Ba Tin. Maung Gyi once again lived to fight another day and other departmental enquiries.

1904 was a relatively quiet year for Maung Gyi. During that time, he attracted only one misconduct complaint, which was for the minor indiscretion of allowing photography at a durbar.[85] However, in early 1905, he was again embroiled in serious trouble. The Deputy Commissioner of Bassein, the station where Maung Gyi had been transferred as a departmental punishment for his connections with Ba Cho in the bribery case, reported in January that he had been informed that Maung Gyi had been involved in a fight at a festival and additionally that he had been prowling the streets at night soliciting women.[86] Following these all too public displays of private indiscretions, Maung Gyi was transferred once again, this time to Wakema. Once there, it was only a matter of a few months before he was again the object of yet another misconduct enquiry, even more serious than the previous ones. In this case, Maung Gyi was suspended and eventually removed from his position (but it must be noted, not dismissed from government service) for abusing his authority to protect a friend from prosecution in a case of sexual assault.[87]

The misconduct investigation that all but ended Maung Gyi's administrative career began with a petition from a *taikthugyi* (circle headman) called Aung Dwe. Aung Dwe alleged that Maung Gyi held a grudge against him, a grudge born when he had refused to 'procure women for him'. He went on to allege, more specifically, that on 5 March 1905, Maung Gyi's friend Po San had trespassed into the house of Me Sein and sexually assaulted her. Me Sein happened to be Aung Dwe's wife's cousin. When she brought a criminal complaint against Po San, Maung Gyi attempted to frighten her and any witnesses from giving evidence against Po San by using the colonial powers of surveillance available to him for use against individuals suspected of having 'bad livelihoods'.

After the police had investigated the case against Po San, it was sent to the Subdivisional Magistrate of Wakema. Incredibly, the Subdivisional Magistrate delegated the case to be tried by none other than Maung Gyi himself. Maung Gyi made the most of this suspiciously fortuitous turn of events by not only granting bail to Po San, but also providing it himself, allegedly joking in court, 'Do not run away I am your surety.'[88]

Maung Gyi did not stop there. According to Aung Dwe, while the case was pending, Maung Gyi had two witnesses for the complainant Me Sein arrested, along with Me Sein's husband and another of her male relatives. As one of the witnesses was Aung Dwe's servant, he went to provide bail for those arrested. But Maung Gyi refused to grant bail and had the four who had been arrested locked up in the police guard. That night, at around 11 o'clock, Maung Gyi, armed with a revolver, forced himself into Aung Dwe's house followed by four other men carrying sticks and knives. Maung Gyi accused Aung Dwe of supporting Me Sein's case and threatened him allegedly remarking, 'If my man is troubled you should be troubled too … You take care.'[89]

Due to Aung Dwe's allegations, Maung Gyi's actions were investigated both criminally and departmentally. In court, he was found guilty of house trespass and intimidation and was sentenced to a fine of Rs. 30, a seemingly light punishment considering the gravity of the charges against him and in comparison to the sentences passed against clerks convicted of embezzlement. Through misconduct proceedings, he was also removed from his position and was paid only a quarter of his salary for the time he had been suspended while under investigation. Although removal was a strong punishment, Maung Gyi had been spared the severest departmental penalty of dismissal from government service. The then Lieutenant Governor of Burma, Herbert Thirkell White, the highest authority in colonial Burma, believed that Maung Gyi 'though unfitted for the position of magistrate may not be incompetent to discharge the duties of a less responsible position'.[90]

Despite the fact that Maung Gyi possessed a blemished record in the subordinate service, to put it mildly, there was still a place for him within the administration. He had made false allegations against another *myo-ok*, been strongly suspected of extorting bribes, been fighting in the streets, soliciting women, accused of using his magisterial powers to help a friend, and been found guilty of house trespass and threatening a man with a revolver, all in the course of just three years. During these years, he had been twice punished with a transfer to a new township, had his powers reduced, and in the end he was removed from his position. Yet, even after all these punishments, Maung Gyi was still deemed eligible for employment as a subordinate official by the highest ranked British official in Burma.

It is worth considering why Maung Gyi was reduced, transferred, and removed, but not dismissed. The Lieutenant Governor of Burma did not provide an explanation to justify why he recommended Maung Gyi be removed not dismissed, beyond the somewhat vague statement quoted above. It may be that the level of Maung Gyi's training and particularly his standard of English and his knowledge of colonial law were qualities too rare and treasured in subordinate officials to be ignored.

Dismissing highly trained staff was not a decision to be taken lightly. Deputy commissioners increasingly relied on *myo-oks* to perform the bulk of the administrative tasks as well as to man the civil courts in the Irrawaddy Delta during the nineteenth century, as we will see below. Such administrative pressures certainly informed disciplinary decisions: a few years before Maung Gyi's case, a *myo-ok* from Bogale was spared transfer after being found guilty of embezzlement because the deputy commissioner could not find a first class *myo-ok* to replace him.[91] As Maung Gyi was a subordinate of precious skills at a time of acute overwork, it is probable that high-ranking British officials preferred to resort to a variety of lesser punishments rather than opt for dismissal.

Another less circumstantial and more structural explanation is that tolerating misconduct among township officers served to reify the racial division of the colonial bureaucracy. The denigration of these officials, the highest ranked of the indigenous subordinates, served to justify their continued supervision by British officials. The paradoxical manner that subordinate-level misconduct served to bolster the authority of British deputy commissioners is explored in detail in Chapter 3. For our purposes, here it suffices to note that unlike clerks, *myo-oks* were not expendable to high-ranking British officials. Despite considerable concern among the British population regarding the extent of *myo-oks'* authority, the misconduct of subordinate officials such as Maung Gyi was largely tolerated.

European subordinate officials

Partha Chatterjee argued in his book *The Nation and its Fragments* that the colonial state was distinct because 'the central premise of its power was the preservation of the alienness of the ruling group'.[92] This he dubbed the rule of colonial difference. Until the second decade of the twentieth century, recruitment into the colonial bureaucracy in Burma partly reflected the racial division of rule that Chatterjee emphasises; the Burmese rarely held positions higher than *myo-ok*, and deputy commissioners until 1908 were always British.[93] Nonetheless, throughout colonial rule in Burma, there were Europeans in the subordinate ranks of state employment, most commonly in the civil police and excise departments. As a result, some Europeans were lower than Burmese officials in the colonial hierarchy, even while Burmese officials were barred from entry into the higher echelons of the administration. It was possible, but unclear whether it actually occurred, that Burmese or Indians could be in positions of direct authority over British subordinate officials. This racial overlap should not be overstated. Europeans were not employed in the very lowest rungs of colonial bureaucracy. Nonetheless, there were Europeans in the subordinate branches of the administration and, just like Indian and Burmese subordinate officials, European officials were on occasion subjected to misconduct procedures. In these cases of misconduct concerning Europeans, the otherwise implicit notions of race that shaped the decisions of the higher echelons of the administration became more pronounced.

Race was crucial to the conceptualisation of corruption in the non-official British colonial press in Burma in ways that paralleled official understandings. Although the British newspapers in Burma generally looked upon *myo-oks* with suspicion as Burmese above their station, the presence of Europeans in the subordinate service was thought beneficial. The newspapers bemoaned particularly the promotion of Burmese officials ahead of British officials in the police force. The following comment from the *Times of Burma* was typical:

> The Local Government some little time ago ruled that Europeans in future should not be appointed Inspectors of Police as formerly; but that Burmese should be given these appointments until the civil police service throughout the province should be eventually composed in the proportion of 5 Burmese to three Europeans. A few years hence the Burmese will say that this is the proportion in which appointments to the higher grades of the public service should be made. By and bye, this policy will succeed in creating a Burmese babu, from whom Great Scott deliver us.[94]

The promotion of Burmese officials to the higher ranks of the colonial administration was perennially attacked in the columns of the *Times of Burma*. Part of the concern of the British community was the belief that the Burmese inherently had a greater propensity towards corruption than Europeans. As a result, the corruption of Burmese officials was always an unmitigated scandal and disgrace, but when faced with European subordinates committing acts of misconduct, occasionally gross acts of misconduct, the response was considerably more ambiguous.

In the case of the notorious police head constable Hadden in 1899, who during his two trials was accused of having committed acts of extortion and bribery as well as suppressing evidence in a rape case, the *Times of Burma* initially supported him against the criminal accusations.[95] When Hadden was acquitted in his first trial (a feat he managed by intimidating the witnesses, as we shall see in Chapter 2), one of the correspondents of the *Times of Burma* even went to congratulate him.[96] During his second trial in which he was convicted of bribery, the newspaper's coverage was considerably more muted. Following this embarrassment, the newspaper mounted a more subtle response to European corruption in the case of Vanspall, Superintendent of the Chief Secretary of Burma's office, who was found guilty of pretending to be the Chief Secretary in order to extract bribes from cultivators in the Irrawaddy Delta. While supporting the conviction for its salutary value, the newspaper also expressed sympathy with the convicted and his family:

> Nobody reading the charges on which Mr E. W. Vanspall and another were tried and convicted at the Criminal Sessions of the Chief Court of Lower Burma will say that the sentences are any too heavy, in view of the corrupt state of the subordinate services in Burma; and as a warning to any other evil doers ... the effect must be very good. For Mr Vanspall it is unfortunate that he should have been the first to be caught and made an example of, as there might be worse offenders than him. Mr Vanspall has many, very many, years service. He is the senior non-commissioned officer of the Volunteer Rifles and is entitled to the medal for long and good service; and his father, who is well advanced in years lives in Calcutta receiving an annuity from government.[97]

No such sentiments were extended to Burmese or Indian subordinate officials found guilty of misconduct. It was this additional empathy with the accused that characterised the manner with which deputy commissioners dealt with European subordinate officials in misconduct cases.

The somewhat farcical events of 23 February 1900 in a wharf in the Myaungmya District vividly highlight the more lenient attitude that high-ranking British officials took towards their European subordinates. A steamer called *Syriam* of the Irrawaddy Flotilla Company was unloading its cargo when some crewmembers reported to the vessel's Captain, Captain Jull, that two Burmans were 'pilfering oranges' from the cargo. One of the men was dressed as a police sergeant, and it subsequently emerged that he was indeed a local police sergeant who was enjoying leave for three months. The culprits were then brought to Captain Jull who made a complaint to the local police inspector, a young British officer called Parker. Parker apparently showed little interest in the orange theft and he simply sent the sergeant on his way, much to the ire of Jull.

The problems for the *Syriam* and her crew did not end there though. Following this initial confrontation, unseen assailants began to pelt stones at the vessel hitting one crewmember. This was also reported to Parker who, by his own admission, did nothing. When another complaint was brought to him following a crewmember being attacked on the wharf causing a head wound, Parker's actions switched from being apathetic to being arbitrary. On arriving at the scene of the attack, he arrested an unconnected Chinese man called Happa and held him at the police station without charge and without recording the arrest, but did nothing to find the actual assailants. All in all, Parker had failed to properly deal with the three criminal complaints made to him by the *Syriam*'s crew in the course of the day. In the first two complaints, he demonstrated a profound disinterest, and in the last complaint he acted only to indiscriminately arrest a passer-by at random.[98]

Unsurprisingly, Captain Jull, unimpressed by the actions of the young inspector, made a complaint of misconduct against him. At issue was less Parker's actions and more his manner. Indeed, it appeared that during the day the two men had become engaged in a heated altercation. Parker was alleged to have 'indulged in ribald language' and reportedly told Captain Jull that his crew were 'laying eggs' (embarrassing themselves).[99] Not that Jull was blameless. He apparently 'retaliated in somewhat unparliamentary language'.[100] A public quarrel of this kind would have caused a considerable scandal and no doubt would have been dealt with swiftly and firmly had it occurred between Captain Jull and a Burmese or Indian subordinate police officer, but since Parker was European, the case elicited an entirely different response.

The Deputy Superintendent of the police for Myaungmya's report on the day's events found Parker to have been entirely in the wrong, concluding that 'taking all the facts of his behaviour into consideration and the way in which he arrested the Chinaman without rhyme or reason it would appear that he was not in his right senses at the time'.[101] However, the Deputy Commissioner of Myaungmya, when remarking on the Deputy Superintendent's report and deciding Parker's fate, found himself sympathising with the young inspector's situation. He dismissed Captain Jull's actions as 'making a mountain out of a mole hill' and concluded by writing, 'my own opinion is that the whole complaint [made by Captain Jull] was a most unreasonable and unnecessary one.' Although he criticised Parker's conduct, he was able to relate to it: 'I can quite understand Mr. Parker's action. He is an office hand, and a man of but little experience and to have a complaint made to him by a *lascar* [Indian sailor] that his own surgeant[sic] was

stealing oranges must have been somewhat embarassing[*sic*] and probably on the face of it absurd.'[102] The eventual outcome of the complaint
against Parker reflected this view and he was only issued a warning for
his demonstrably dismissive and erratic behaviour.[103]

Parker was dealt with leniently in a situation in which an Indian
or a Burmese police inspector would not have been. The application
of the economy of discipline evidently took into account the race of
the accused. In a quite different case in 1907, the racial solidarity, or
at least sympathy, of high-ranking British officials when dealing with
European subordinates was openly stated. Mr Molloy, an excise inspector for Wakema, was found to have solicited for and accepted a bribe in
an excise case. The Commissioner of the Irrawaddy Division, Captain
Maxwell, was unequivocal in his condemnation of Molloy. 'The evidence against Mr Molloy is clear and distinct—he searched the house
of Ya Se and found illicit liquor—he then allowed an unknown man to
be substituted for Ya Se and there can be little room for doubt what was
the motive'. He concluded baldly that 'Mr Molloy has a bad record—he
should be dismissed from Government Service'.[104]

Maxwell's stance prompted a staunch defence of Molloy from two
of his colleagues, the Subdivisional Officer, Lawes, and the Excise
Commissioner, Thompson. Thompson argued that the evidence in the
case demonstrated that Molloy had behaved 'unsatisfactorily' but was
not conclusive enough to warrant his dismissal. Instead, he argued
that Molloy should be simply warned and transferred.[105] Thompson's
letter in defence of Molloy was met with an angry letter in reply from
Maxwell, which concluded: 'Had Mr. Molloy been an ignorant young
man just out of England with no knowledge of the people or the language I could accept your view and that of Mr. Lawes with pleasure—but
as he is a cunning intriguing and untruthful, see confidential roll, half
Burman, I am unable to accept it.'[106]

As the Molloy example suggests, although what Chatterjee described
as the 'alienness of the ruling group' may not have been pristinely pre-
served in the subordinate ranks of the administration, that 'alienness'
could be used to excuse Europeans from punishment for misconduct. An
article that appeared in the *Times of Burma* in 1900 succinctly captured
the distinction made by Maxwell between European corruption and
'native' corruption. The latter took office in order to be corrupt, whereas
the former would succumb to corruption in office through a 'very
painful' acquaintance with 'rough places'.[107] Evidently for Maxwell,
the race of Molloy was a contributing factor in his decision, and his
comment implies further that he believed that Lawes and Thompson's

defence of Molloy emanated from a misplaced sense of racial solidarity towards him: misplaced not only because Maxwell believed Molloy to be guilty but also because Molloy was mixed race.

The allowances made for subordinate European officials did not always shield them from discipline. Failing to maintain a façade of racial superiority within the subordinate ranks of the colonial administration, on occasion, resulted in formal misconduct proceedings. For example, the capabilities of Hardinge, an excise superintendent in Pyapon, were called into question in early 1905. The Deputy Commissioner of Pyapon complained that the excise department in the district was rapidly deteriorating and that as a result the illegal trade in opium and alcohol was flourishing. He located the cause of this inefficiency as Hardinge. According to the Deputy Commissioner, Hardinge was unfamiliar with the district, had failed to exert himself in his work, and was reluctant to visit hard to reach areas. More worryingly for the Deputy Commissioner was his perception that Hardinge lacked the requisite authority for the post: 'In any enquiry connected with the conduct of his subordinates Mr. Hardinge is worse than useless, for he does not appear to have the slightest knowledge of the Burman character and is altogether in the hands of the men who shout the loudest.'[108]

Although it is not explicit in the doubts expressed by the Deputy Commissioner about Hardinge, the Deputy Commissioner judged Hardinge's weaknesses according to broader expectations placed upon Europeans. Hardinge did not meet these expectations; he was weak-willed, lazy, and unable to project his authority over his Burmese subordinates. Using his poor eyesight as justification, higher-ranking British officials called for his transfer to an easier post, but in May he took extensive leave on medical grounds.[109] A similar case was that of Police Inspector White whose removal from service was sought by his Deputy Commissioner after he managed to misplace his revolver twice in three days, due apparently to a drinking problem.[110] Such examples of potentially embarrassing incompetence among British subordinate officials were intolerable.

Deputy commissioners' notions of inherent racial characteristics were implicit factors in misconduct proceedings. Sympathy and leniency were shown towards European subordinate officials in situations in which no sympathy or leniency would have been shown for Burmese or Indian officials.[111] Chatterjee's 'rule of colonial difference' certainly captures part of this, but it masks a somewhat messier reality in the subordinate ranks of the colonial bureaucracy. European subordinates were still subjected to colonial discipline if it was for gross acts of corruption, as in cases of Hadden and Vanspall, or neglectful incompetence, as in cases of Hardinge and White. As Ann Laura Stoler has argued, the tensions between the aim of maintaining strict racial divisions and the everyday compromised reality of that colonial vision were a central aspect of colonial rule.[112] While she was referring principally to sexual liaisons and miscegenation, I think similar tensions were apparent in the perhaps more banal sphere of bureaucratic discipline. Race was a perennial, if implicit, factor in how the disciplinary economy of misconduct was applied.

Misconduct in delta

The economy of discipline outlined in this chapter was in operation all over British Burma, but the scale of misconduct varied across what was a geographically large and diverse territory. At the turn of the twentieth century, corruption was a more acute problem in the tidal delta of the Irrawaddy River than it was in other parts of colonial Burma. While it was still low on imperial priorities and tacitly tolerated, misconduct was simply more pervasive there. The delta offered more opportunities for corrupt acts and greater potential rewards for malfeasance. These were provided by the development of the region into the largest and most prosperous rice-producing part of world, and the consequential prospects of rapid economic advancement. The understaffed and over-worked colonial bureaucracy further enabled subordinate level graft. As the colonial state spread into this deltaic fringe, deputy commissioners encountered corrupt subordinates with increasing frequency. Although historians have often seen this as a lawless frontier in which the state failed to impose its authority,[113] this is looking at the situation upside down. Instead, the expansion of the colonial state into the delta brought with it new forms of illegality and disorder.

In the early twentieth century, E. M. Powell-Brown spent a year travelling on the Irrawaddy. In her subsequent book, she evocatively captured the short but seemingly treacherous journey from Rangoon to the Irrawaddy Delta on one of the, what was by then, ubiquitous flotilla steamships:

> The Bassein Creek is so called because it is nowhere near Bassein. It is a channel connecting the Rangoon River with another of the delta streams. ... It is a cross between the Suez Canal and the Serpentine, shallow, tortuous and exceedingly narrow. The vagaries of the tide, the stupidity or recklessness of native boatmen, the dense jungle

obstructing the view around awkward corners, the frequent shoals and incredibly sharp turns all add to the difficulty of its navigation ... our task seems even more difficult than that of the camel or rich man of Biblical fame.[114]

The voyage was also one into a climatic frontier. Her descent into the southern tidal delta was marked by the incremental increase in both humidity and the numbers of mosquitoes, to the point where she believed European constitutions were in near mortal peril.[115]

However, the waterways that connected the colonial centre of Rangoon to the delta were not, like the eye of the needle, an inhibitor to the movement of wealth. These streams were the veins through which capital and labour flowed into the delta in exchange for rice. By the time that Powell-Brown was writing, the delta had already been transformed from a sparsely populated area covered by extensive mangrove forests to the world's largest rice-producing region.[116] Following and monitoring these transformations were British settlement officers. Their reports captured the dramatic speed and scope of the environmental changes. A tract of land visited in 1902 was 'typically deltaic'. The settlement officer reported that it was 'a flat level stretch of country intersected by innumerable rivers and tidal creeks; where ... every last inch is cultivated to the very river's edge'.[117] This comprehensive cultivation had not always been the scene that settlement officers encountered. Where a year before the officer had the 'unattractive and uninviting welcome' of mangroves trees, he was now met with 'waving rice crops stretching in their luxuriance from the river's bank as far as the eye could reach'.[118] And the transformation from forest to paddy field was still happening. With some imperial pride he wrote, 'In the southern and less developed circles the sound of the pioneer's axe is daily heard as the giants of the forest fall to make way for the great food crop. A year or two cleansing with fire and the land thus brought subject falls into line with its rich neighbour.'[119]

The image of cleansing fires clearing the way for luxuriant waving fields of wet-rice agriculture was no doubt overly romantic: it overlooked the intensive labour involved in removing the roots of mangroves, as well as the resultant deleterious health effects of the environmental upheaval and rapid demographic expansion, such as increases in cholera and malaria.[120] Nevertheless, the colonial descriptions of the tidal delta reveal the speed at which the region was integrated into the internal and world economies. In the last decade of the nineteenth century, foreign goods, credit, and migrants from Upper Burma, China, and India all made their way to the delta. Small towns of a few thousand people became thriving commercial hubs of five times the size.[121] Several times a day the steamers of the Irrawaddy Flotilla Company ferried rice and traders from the newly populous delta towns, such as Maubin, to Rangoon. Once there, the rice was sold on for milling and goods from across the globe were procured for the local markets. At the start of the twentieth century, the delta was a rapidly expanding rice frontier, large swathes of which had only recently been brought under cultivation. It was far from being a rural backwater.

The colonial bureaucracy too expanded down these same narrow streams into the southern delta, settling in the same semi-urban hubs. These rapidly growing market towns became the centres of the deltaic colonial administration. Deputy commissioners resided mainly in the largest towns, around each of which the districts were established: Maubin, Bassein, Myaungmya, and, following the creation of a new district in 1903, Pyapon. The high-ranking British officials' presence in the other major towns was often restricted to periodical tours. These towns, which included important trading nodes such as Kyaiklat, Wakema, Bogale, and Dedaye, and their immediate surrounding areas, were administered as townships by local *myo-oks*, whose offices were manned by numerous clerks. Alongside the administrative subordinate branches of the state in these delta towns were small local courts, police stations, lock-ups, dispensaries, and occasionally hospitals. In some of the smaller settlements of villages, scattered along the banks of the innumerable creeks and administered by *thugyis*, there were also police outposts. The colonial state spread with the agricultural frontier. However, it did not keep pace with the rapid economic and demographic growth of the region.

The exponential increases in the amount of rice being cultivated inevitably resulted in similar rises in the amount of government revenue that needed to be collected. Likewise, the demographic explosion in the delta inescapably meant a growth in the administrative work of almost every branch of bureaucracy. The scale of state employment in the delta, however, was not substantially altered to accommodate these escalating pressures until 1903 when the Irrawaddy Division was re-organised to create a fourth district in the delta. This alteration was a late one that had been deemed necessary by local officials since the 1880s.[122]

The deputy commissioners and the *myo-oks* shouldered the bulk of this growing burden of administrative work. As a result, *myo-oks* were regularly criticised for carelessness in their duties.[123] But of a greater concern to the upper echelons of the regime was the state of civil justice, which had suffered because it was deputy commissioners and *myo-oks* who were chiefly responsible for administering it. Despite the fact that some towns had experienced over five-fold increases in population in the 10-year period leading up to 1900, the amount of civil litigation had remained roughly at a standstill.[124] The communities of the delta were evidently wary of the languishing colonial courts and justifiably sceptical of their benefits.[125] The state bureaucracy certainly expanded into the delta, but it was not equipped to cope with onerous administrative pressures inherent to governing such a dynamic region.

In this environment of an understaffed and malfunctioning bureaucratic structure, and in the context of a relatively wealthy and highly fluid society, corruption was pervasive. The settlement reports from the delta uniformly highlighted the need to curtail the illicit practices of *thugyis* and revenue surveyors who had used their powers to obtain land.[126] In a case in 1906, a *thugyi* in Myaungmya was transferred after it was discovered that he and his immediate family had suspiciously managed to obtain the ownership of some 640 acres of land over which he was administratively responsible.[127] Deputy commissioners in the delta had fed this propensity for subordinate officials to attempt to acquire land by offering *thugyis* plots of land as part of a scheme of incentives designed to induce local Burmans to take up the otherwise unpopular post.[128] There was money to be made in the delta, and corruption offered a potential route to financial betterment. These malpractices were not confined to *thugyis*.

In 1900, after only a year in charge, the Deputy Commissioner of one delta district complained of the scale and frequency of misconduct:

> A Superintendent of Land Records, a Myook, and Inspector of Police have been dismissed; numerous Myooks and a Subdivisional Officer have been turned out of the district, while as regards the smaller fry clerks, thugyis, revenue surveyors, vaccinators, hospital assistants, jailors, scarcely a day passes but some new case of dishonesty is brought to light.[129]

This was just the tip of the iceberg. His list consisted only of the cases that he had been able to uncover in just one district in the course of barely a year. As deputy commissioners were overworked officials for whom disciplining misconduct was a minor concern, much corruption went unnoticed, wilfully as well as unknowingly. The landscape added to these difficulties of bureaucratic discipline. In the southernmost parts of the delta, the shallow waters of low tide inhibited travel on the creeks. During the wet season monsoon flooding also made movement difficult, though for opposite reasons. The timings of misconduct investigations in the Irrawaddy Division thus roughly map onto these cyclical seasonal changes. But the effect of these environmental factors can easily be overstated. By and large, the delta was a well-integrated and easily accessible region because of its network of waterways. Misconduct occurred not only because it was tolerated and because deputy commissioners were unable to effectively supervise their subordinate officials, but also because it was intrinsic to the expansion of the colonial bureaucracy.

It might be tempting to follow other historians of Burma and treat misconduct as the consequence of the imperfect implementation of bureaucratic norms, or the failure to inculcate the values of public office in the colonised society, in short, as an epiphenomenal side effect of incomplete colonial rule.[130] But misconduct was not a by-product of state expansion. Instead, it was something intrinsic to it. As we have seen in the delta, *thugyis* used their minor bureaucratic authority to acquire land, *myo-oks*, like Maung Gyi, used their magisterial powers to commit an array of malpractices, and clerks used their formal duties to embezzle government revenues. As the rest of this book demonstrates, these were only a fraction of the daily acts in which legal state power made corruption possible.[131] From these pervasive legal malpractices, we can see that misconduct was not a bureaucratic side effect, but the everyday reality of the colonial state. Thus, there was a third way in which colonial rule made misconduct, not only by discursively defining it as an illegality and then acquiescing with forms of it, as we have seen in this chapter, but also by providing the legal resources for corrupt state practices to flourish.

2
The Career of Inspector Pakiri

> For by art is created that great Leviathan called a Commonwealth, or State (in Latin, Civitas), which is but an artificial man ... To describe the nature of this artificial man, I will consider – First, the matter thereof, and the artificer; both of which is man.
>
> Thomas Hobbes, *Leviathan* (1651)

State power and subordinate officials

The relationship between the colonial state and its subordinate employees was a complex one. Part of the complexity is neatly captured in Hobbes's phrase, quoted in the epigraph above, that subordinate officials were 'the matter thereof, and the artificer' of the colonial state.[1] In other words, subordinate officials were not only employed by the colonial state, but also they made the state. This was apparent in the banal sense that the vast majority of state employees were indigenous subordinate officials. British members of the Indian Civil Service made up a tiny minority of colonial state officials across British India.[2] Additionally, the army in Burma contained indigenous Burmese soldiers and was predominantly made up of Indian subordinates.[3] There would have been no colonial state but for its overwhelmingly Burmese and Indian subordinate employees. But the proposition that the colonial state was made by its subordinate officials also has a more sophisticated implication. Subordinate officials through their everyday acts performed and enacted the colonial state.[4] Hobbes's notion of the state being created through art is apt for characterising this role of subordinate officials in making the colonial state. There was a theatrical and creative aspect to subordinate officials' everyday practices through which the colonial

47

state was enacted. It is the nature of this performative enactment of the colonial state by subordinate officials that is being explored in this chapter.

The relationship between subordinate employees and the colonial state in Burma has been depicted more simplistically in the existing historiography. The prevailing metaphor has not been corporeal (like Hobbes) or theatrical (like mine) but mechanical. Robert Taylor applied such a metaphor when he depicted the position of village headmen in post-'Pacification' Burma, describing them as 'cogs in the machine'.[5] He argued that their influence was significantly diminished and what was once a position of local, personal authority, and prestige under pre-colonial rule had become the emasculated role of a bureaucratic functionary as powers were siphoned off to specialised branches of the state. Although it was perhaps not Taylor's intention, the implication of this argument is that all subordinate officials can be characterised as cogs in the machine, although cogs of differing size and importance, since clockwork machines operate through the interaction of interlocking cogs. Taylor was not the first one to make this argument or apply this metaphor. An earlier canonical text concerning the history of colonial Burma, John Cady's *A History of Modern Burma*, also described subordinate employees, paraphrasing a British official, as 'interchangeable cogs in a vast machine'.[6] Before Cady, one of the founding scholars of Burma studies, John Sydenham Furnivall, characterised the village in colonial Burma as a 'cog-wheel in the machinery'.[7] This longstanding, reductive, mechanical metaphor diminishes to the point of obliteration the notion of subordinate officials having any creative capacity. They were simply the products of a rational, bureaucratic state. While this may have been an accurate portrayal of how some high-ranking British officials envisioned subordinate employees, it is a characterisation that leaves no room to explore the motives and intentions of subordinate employees on their own terms. Subordinate officials were simply cogs turned by the machine.

Recent scholarship on subordinate officials in colonial Africa has attempted to address precisely this gap in the history of colonialism. Much of this work successfully breaks from the dominating binary of the coloniser and colonised in colonial history by refusing to categorise these African subordinate employees as simply collaborators. Rather it has been emphasised that they were 'intermediaries' with the ability to use their positions 'to pursue their own agendas even as they served their employers'.[8] A recent edited collection of work on this topic referred to this negotiated intermediary position of subordinate officials as the 'bargain of collaboration'.[9] Other authors have re-conceptualised the position of subordinate officials in a similar way, granting them an explicitly creative role. Nancy Rose Hunt's pioneering work on medicine in the Congo portrayed subordinate employees, such as midwives, as hybrid middle-figures crucial in authoring a colonial lexicon regarding childbirth.[10] Similarly, Penny Edwards's work on the subordinate colonial official and scholar in British Burma, Taw Sein Ko, depicted him as an interlocutor producing colonial knowledge.[11]

But this new scholarship also has its limitations. The works considered here, and similar ones, while endowing subordinate officials with their own will and a capacity for creativity, do not fully capture the complexity of the position of subordinate officials. They are portrayed as intermediaries, hybrid middle-figures, or interlocutors between the colonial state and colonised population. As a result, there is an implicit separation made in these approaches between the state and its subordinate officials that is difficult to sustain. Following the logic of such a separation to its limits, the state in essence becomes reduced to a 'thin white line' of high-ranking British officials.[12] However, the colonial state in Burma connoted considerably more than a small ruling British oligarchy.

This brings us back to where we began the chapter: 'the matter thereof, and the artificer'. Subordinate officials did not merely act mechanically as part of the colonial state, nor did they simply enter into a bargain with, and mediate, the colonial state. Subordinate officials were the colonial state and, crucially, they enacted it. This was implicitly recognised at the time, in a watered-down form, by high-ranking British officials such as the Lieutenant Governor of Burma, in the early twentieth century, Herbert Thirkell White. In a passage, in his published memoirs, concerning corruption in the subordinate ranks, White exonerated deputy commissioners from blame by emphasising the independence subordinate officials had in performing their duties: 'To the mass of the people, in their daily life, the Township Officer and *Thugyi*, even more than the Deputy Commissioner, represented the government.'[13] He was not the only official to make such a claim.[14] White's words implicitly suggest a performative aspect to the colonial state, portraying the 'mass of the people' as an audience.[15] However, subordinate officials did not always 'represent' the state to their popular audience in a fashion in which White would have approved. Indeed, the colonial state was not represented (or re-presented) so much as enacted, or made real, by subordinate officials. Or, to build on Hobbes's corporeal metaphor, the body of the leviathan was animated by the acts of subordinate officials.

As we delve into this chapter, we see that the state could be theatrically enacted in the form of an arbitrary and violent spectre.

This creative, constitutive aspect of subordinate officials' everyday practices is illustrated in this chapter through the misconduct charges brought against an inspector of the civil police called Fakir Pakiri. The case against Pakiri was the largest investigation into misconduct made in the Irrawaddy Division between 1897 and 1909. Pakiri served in Bogale and Dedaye between 1899 and 1900, two townships of the southern, tidal region of the Irrawaddy Delta, which were located in the Thongwa District around the town of Pyapon. Most of the charges against him alleged that he had fabricated evidence in order to have people falsely imprisoned. His case was an extreme one. The scale of his misconduct was unequalled, although the crimes he was accused of were not rare. Nonetheless, despite the exceptional gravity of his case, Pakiri was symptomatic of the broader ability of subordinate officials to performatively enact the colonial state. In this framework, Pakiri differed from other subordinate officials only because he had greater access to the performative resources of state power.

'... of all the queer police of this queer country ...'

In early 1901, a Burmese gentleman left a manuscript in the Rangoon office of the editor of the *Times of Burma* with a request that a price be calculated for 3000 copies to be published. The document was titled *Seven Years in the Burma Police* and was described as 'being an absolutely truthful account of all the doings of the police and of the officials generally with whom the author came in contact, which came directly to his notice at the time of their occurrence'.[16] The man when depositing the text did not leave either the name of the author or his address and failed to return to complete the deal and give his consent to publication. After waiting some months, the *Times of Burma* printed in its advertisement section a request that the author return so that they could begin printing. The management team at the newspaper clearly regarded the manuscript as a potentially considerable scoop. It reported that, 'The most sensational publication of the current year will be "Seven Years in the Burma Police," as soon as the author gives instructions for its publication.'[17] They then went on to tease their readers with some of its more sordid details:

> In the book is a list of transactions in buying and selling girls ... One wretched young thing was actually bashed to death with a baulk of

firewood, in a house of ill-fame ... and the Burmese policeman ... is mentioned as accepting hush-money with the kindliest leer all over his face.[18]

The author still did not come forward, and so, in a further attempt to entice his return, and no doubt to further titillate its readership, the newspaper printed the contents list of the chapters. The manuscript promised to be a shocking exposé of the civil police, and other branches of the colonial administration, containing as it did chapter synopses such as 'CHAPTER VI; - Well paid incompetence. A reign of terror', 'CHAPTER VII; - ... The hushed up murder of a family', and 'CHAPTER XII; - The rise and fall of a Burman Head Constable. The sale of minors for purposes of prostitution; the manner in which it is conducted; its extent; and the manner in which the law is evaded.'[19] The 23 chapters covered a broad range of corruption and crimes, from fabricating evidence though to murder. Certainly, the staff at the *Times of Burma* had high hopes for the manuscript, which they believed to have been a 'true and faithful sketch'. 'We predict, for this book, an enormous sale; and the result of its publication will be many sweeping changes in the Administration of Burma.'[20] The author still did not return, and eventually the newspaper ceased its attempts to induce him back, and as far as I am aware the manuscript was not published. But the credibility of the mysteriously absent author's revelations was heightened by the stories being reported from the trial of Inspector Pakiri that was running concurrently. Indeed, both *Seven Years in the Burma Police* and the trial of Inspector Pakiri appeared to confirm what had been reported in the newspaper for years, that the police in Burma were irredeemably corrupt.

A year before the trial, the *Times of Burma* correspondent for Maubin reported that 'of all the queer police of this queer country the police of the Maubin district have certainly become the most queerly original body of preservers of the peace in Burma'.[21] In terms of the newspaper's low opinion of the police in Burma, this was quite a damning indictment. One of the newspaper's writers just a week later reported, with considerable hyperbole, that, 'It may be asked whether a community in India afflicted with plague and famine is not less miserable than the people living under certain sub-divisions of civil police in the mofussil of Burma.'[22]

This concern began to reach a fever pitch in the reports from Pakiri's trial. One article promised that complacent British officials would be forced to respond 'if only one-tenth of the disclosures now being made at Maubin are proved true' because Pakiri had been accused of 'the worst, most awful, and very heartless crimes'.[23] The nature of the case against Pakiri was revealed in the newspaper in drips: on the day of his sentencing his crimes were revealed as '"bribery", "extortion", "concocting false cases against wholly innocent persons, and perjury to obtain convictions against them", "rape", etc.; and one sergeant of police was accused of procuring young girls for the Inspector to outrage.' But the journalist was clear that despite the horror of the case, Pakiri was not to be thought of as an exception. He wrote, 'We may also ask, seeing the long run of immunity from justice a police officer like Inspector Pakeeree[sic] may enjoy, whether it is not possible that there are other members of the Civil Police ... as deeply steeped in crime as he was proved to have been at the recent trial?'[24] The underlying question raised by Pakiri's case for the readers of the *Times of Burma* was, who policed the police?

In November, it was extravagantly claimed in the columns of the newspaper that in Burma 'more than half the inmates of a jail were innocent for the offences which they were convicted.' Again the same question was posed, 'How many more Inspectors, or others, are there still in the Burma police who are yet to be found out?'[25] A letter to the editor printed in the same edition presented Pakiri's case as representative of a common experience across Burma. The writer believed that his case alone should bring about sweeping reform in 'the whole machinery of the weak government.' But the writer also made explicit the racial ideology that underpinned these concerns about the police in Burma. 'Just fancy, Pakeri[sic], *a native of India, clad with authority as an Inspector of Police*, was allowed for so long a time to do so much mischief that ... it [is] said there were 40, or 50—if not eighty—charges against him. [Emphasis added]'[26] Central to the British colonial media's concern over corruption was a fear of authority slipping away from Europeans to indigenous officials.[27] Pakiri's case was thus depicted as representative, not only of the corrupt police force, but also of the dangers of allowing Indian and Burmese subordinate officials state power.

Misconduct within the police force was not a figment of the overactive imaginations of scaremongering British newspaper writers. It was an official concern reflected in departmental discipline. The police were the most commonly dismissed of all the subordinate officials, more so than even the clerical staff that made up the majority of subordinate employees. Of those dismissed across Burma between 1886 and 1909, the police consistently made up roughly a third of the total, and from the Irrawaddy Division the figure was over 40%.[28] This also constituted a considerable proportion of the police department. In 1904, of the 10,951 men in the civil police, 561 were dismissed, 2279 were chastised with lesser departmental punishments, and 369 had criminal charges brought successfully against them.[29] For a comparison, in the same year, among the 18,439 village headmen in colonial employment, only 280 were dismissed,[30] and of the 14,655 men employed in the military police, merely 63 were dismissed.[31] It does not seem, as the *Times of Burma* had alleged, that high-ranking British officials were complacent about misconduct in the subordinate ranks of the police; subordinate policemen seem to have been at the sharp end of the colonial disciplinary economy. This suspicion of the police was also informed by the perceived hereditary inadequacies of the Burmese. John Nisbet, the former conservator of forests in Burma, wrote in his book on the administration of Burma in 1901 that, 'So adverse is the Burmese character to discipline and control in petty matters that it is impossible to get really suitable men to enlist even in the civil police.'[32]

Evidently, Pakiri was in plenty of company in facing misconduct and criminal charges within the police department. This chapter does not attempt to explore to the full the complexities of the social history of the civil police in colonial Burma at play here.[33] Nonetheless, it is necessary to briefly consider the position of Pakiri within the police force and more broadly some of the salient ambiguities of colonial policing.

The rank of an inspector was one of significant authority. In 1900, when Pakiri was arrested in a house on Mogul Street in Rangoon, he was one of only 132 inspectors employed by the colonial regime across Burma, of whom 56 were classified as 'native'[34]—an imprecise categorisation as it included immigrants from India as well as Burmese: indeed, Pakiri himself was thought to have been a half Malay, half Madrassi Muslim. As an inspector, Pakiri was responsible for the policing of an entire township and was in charge of potentially up to 100 subordinate police officers from head constables and sergeants down to low-ranking constables.[35] Indeed, as part of the trial against Pakiri, two sergeants were prosecuted as accomplices for their role in his crimes. This hierarchical authority also meant he shouldered the bulk of the responsibility for policing a sizeable population. According to the police reports, the ratio of policemen to people in the Thongwa District was one policeman for every 885 people in 1900. This was less intensive than Burma's average of one for every 640. But this only demonstrates the density of population in the tidal delta, as there were twice as many policemen to every square mile in the Thongwa District compared to the mean average across Burma.

On face value, this may appear a low ratio but, by the norms of British India, this was in fact a high concentration of police officers. The number of police to people between the years 1898 and 1900 in the Madras Presidency was roughly half, with around one to every 1700. In Bengal, it was even less, at one to nearly 3000.[36] Thus, Pakiri was directly, and indirectly through his subordinates, responsible for the policing of several thousand individuals in the delta, a region that per head of population and even more so by area, was comparatively heavily policed. As far as subordinate state employees were concerned, Pakiri was in a position to wield extensive individual power, especially given that in times of tidal flooding and the monsoon downpours, supervision by higher-ranking British officials in these southern delta townships was inhibited.[37] The engagement of a mid-ranking official like Pakiri in such wide-ranging corruption goes to establish that there were systemic problems in policing in colonial Burma at the turn of the twentieth century.

Existing research on policing in colonial India suggests that the apparent scale of misconduct in Burma was not unusual. David Arnold's work on the police in Madras highlighted the subordinate officers' ability to use their authority for their own predatory desires, as well as their tendency to act against state policy and to cooperate with local indigenous elites. He located the reason for this in the 'weakness of institutional and ideological control' over the subordinate police.[38] In this suggestion, Arnold pre-empted some of the central arguments put forward in the recent work on colonial intermediaries, crucially that subordinate police officers cannot be understood simply as collaborators but that they had the ability to act on their own accord. However, the argument that corruption was the result of a weakness of discipline does not satisfactorily account for the acts of subordinate officials of the rank of Pakiri; and to do justice to Arnold, his work did focus primarily on low-paid constables.[39] Instead, in crucial ways, Pakiri's acts of corruption demonstrated the strength of the institutions and ideology of the state. Pakiri was firmly embedded as a powerful figure in the police bureaucracy and was in a position of considerable trust having accrued many years' experience. The very creation of a bureaucratically organised colonial police force enabled Pakiri's malfeasant acts.

Anupama Rao has made a parallel argument in a convincing and closely argued article on the use of torture by the colonial police, also in the nineteenth-century Madras. She argued that the judicial demands for evidence made the extraction of evidence a priority of colonial policing, resulting paradoxically in police engaging in torture to supply this demand.[40] Thus, she conceptualises the colonial police as having been in an ambiguous position. They were both the servants of the law and the masters of legal evidence.[41] Pakiri was able to embark on his career of falsifying evidence and imprisoning innocents only because of this dual position straddled by the police. He was not only the enforcer of law, but also the creator of legal evidence. As we shall see below, it was this role in producing evidence that also contributed to the difficulties in bringing Pakiri to task for his malpractices. Misconduct was commonplace among the colonial police across British India and some of its root causes were embedded in the ambiguous structural logic of policing.

Pakiri's was an exceptional case in terms of scale, but in many other respects his example was symptomatic of the endemic tensions of policing in colonial Burma. Widespread corruption and misconduct had been associated in the British media with the civil police for some time and the subordinate branches were routinely the targets for internal discipline. These were problems that did not occur only in the lowest branches of the constabulary but also existed higher in the bureaucratic hierarchy, at the level of inspectors. Two years before Pakiri was arrested, Inspector Maung Shwe Pso of the Wakema Township was disciplined for extracting a confession from a prisoner through torture, resulting in the victim losing the use of his legs.[42] A year before Pakiri's trial, a former colleague of his, Inspector Po Ni, was criminally charged with extortion and bribery, causing a comparatively minor splash in the papers.[43] And, even while the investigation into Pakiri was ongoing, a police inspector in Thongwa involved in prosecuting Pakiri was accused of extorting bribes by threatening to falsely prosecute people in connection with the case![44] Within such an institutional context, the example of Pakiri, while extreme, was not unique.

This point can be taken beyond Pakiri's immediate departmental environment of the civil police. His example was symptomatic of the broader position of subordinate officials. If we consider state power to be a latent structural resource in need of state agents to be enacted,[45] then Pakiri's actions can be understood in a broader and more abstract framework. In such a framework, Pakiri's case, rather than being an aberration, can be read as an exploration *in extremis* of subordinate officials' ability to perform and thus enact the colonial state. In this sense, Pakiri was different from other subordinate employees only because of his greater access to the performative and latent resources of state power.[46] This will become clearer as the case against Pakiri is discussed in detail. Such was the scope of Pakiri's performative powers that he was able to have many innocent people convicted and high-ranking British officials faced what turned out to be almost insurmountable difficulties in gathering evidence to secure a conviction against him.

Inspector Pakiri

Pakiri was arrested in late November 1900 at a house on Mogul Street in Rangoon and preliminarily charged with house breaking and theft.[47] Many more accusations were subsequently added to these, 13 of which were preferred as criminal charges against him. After a lengthy trial and appeal, he was eventually found guilty in 1903 on only one count of fabricating evidence, receiving a sentence of 14 years of rigorous imprisonment.[48] Although it might be prudent as a historian to remain ambivalent in judging Pakiri's guilt, it is highly probable that there were many more malpractices that went undiscovered or were not pursued, due in part to the priorities of the officials investigating him. The surviving evidence from the investigation into his misconduct was produced with a view to securing a criminal conviction and there was never any doubt expressed concerning Pakiri's guilt. Yet, despite this unified focus, it still proved very difficult for high-level British officials to produce credible evidence on which to base a criminal prosecution.

The first official to raise concerns about the conduct of Pakiri was the Deputy Commissioner of the Thongwa District, Fraser. What first alerted his attention to Pakiri is unclear but in the last months of 1900 Fraser made enquiries into several criminal cases for which Pakiri had successfully secured convictions. Fraser then convinced the Commissioner of the Irrawaddy Division that these convictions had been successful because the evidence had been entirely fabricated by Pakiri.[49] However, this was not the first time that Pakiri had attracted attention. He already had considerable notoriety at the time of his arrest for having been implicated in fabricating evidence in a dacoity case in the early 1890s.[50] Before any investigation had begun, the *Times of Burma* local correspondent, reporting on Pakiri's transfer from Dedaye to the Bogale Township in September 1900, added the suffix 'of fame' to Pakiri's name.[51] Pakiri was not an anonymous subordinate official. The Commissioner of the Irrawaddy Division, having been convinced of the sincerity of Fraser's suspicions about Pakiri, then convinced the Lieutenant Governor of Burma of the seriousness of the situation, praising Fraser 'for bringing these cases to light and for the industry and zeal devoted to investigating them'.[52]

It remains a tantalising mystery as to why Fraser expended so much energy in investigating convictions that had already been dealt with successfully in the colonial courts without attracting any previous comment, let alone concern. Perhaps, it was his personal sense of duty. During 1900, in the Irrawaddy Division as a whole, noticeably more officials were dismissed from government service than in any other year between 1886 and 1909, and therefore Fraser's zeal may have been part of a division-wide crackdown.[53] An alternative, or additional, explanation is that there was a personal grievance between Fraser and Pakiri. In court, through his lawyer, Mr Broadbent, Pakiri made precisely this argument. They petitioned to have the case moved from Thongwa to another district because he feared 'there was a strong bias against him in the District and that the views of his character and conduct entertained by the various officials in that District were such as to create in his mind a reasonable apprehension that he would be prejudiced in his trial.'[54] In one case, in which Fraser was originally to preside, the government prosecutor consented to have the case moved because, 'he [Pakiri] alleged that amongst other officials the Deputy Commissioner before whom he was being tried had expressed very strong opinions about the man's character.'[55] As we shall see, Pakiri may have had less pure motives for wanting to have the cases moved outside of Thongwa, but it is intriguing to speculate on the possibility of a feud between Pakiri and Fraser as the trigger for the investigation. Without it, Pakiri may have never attracted any attention at all from the higher echelons of the administration.

Owing ostensibly to the growing quantity of administrative work that Fraser was responsible for in the Thongwa District, he was relieved of the duty of investigating Pakiri. In his place, a former district commissioner of the Thongwa District, Captain F. D. Maxwell, was placed on special duty to investigate. In order to achieve this, he was provided for the three-month investigation with a substantial staff, considering how overstretched officials were at this time, of two clerks, one at Rs. 100 and one at Rs. 50, and four peons.[56] The establishment of this temporary investigating body demonstrates the perceived insufficiency of standard bureaucratic supervision for dealing with Pakiri. The normal chain of command and hierarchy was not thought adequate to successfully investigate the errant Inspector and an exceptional investigatory body was deemed necessary.

The appointment of Maxwell to head this investigation team was also significant. He was chosen because of his outstanding reputation among the highest echelons of the government of Burma. He was ubiquitously praised. The Irrawaddy Commissioner wrote to the Lieutenant Governor stating that, 'It is well known to Government that the late

Deputy Commissioner, Captain Maxwell, is an officer who is capable of an immense amount of hard work and that he never spared himself.'[57] Besides his exemplary capacity for work, Maxwell was commonly called an official 'intimately acquainted' with the Irrawaddy Delta.[58] Herbert Thirkell White, who was never at a loss to compliment his fellow officials, singled out Maxwell for especially effusive praise. He claimed that Maxwell 'knew every creek and channel, and, apparently, every man, woman, and child' in the delta,[59] and further that Maxwell 'more than most of us won the intimate confidence of Burmans'.[60] Maxwell was a British colonial officer's colonial officer. He was also chosen to head this special investigation because of his previous experience in similar misconduct cases against subordinate officials in which he was said to have shown 'special aptitude'.[61] The establishment of a special body headed by Maxwell indicates that the investigation into Pakiri was a process beyond the bounds of the normal procedures of the colonial bureaucracy.[62]

Despite its importance and exceptionality, the scope of investigation was limited to specific goals. Maxwell was charged with two primary aims. One was to establish a case against Pakiri and prosecute him, and the other was to secure the release of innocent people convicted on false evidence. This narrow brief was, in practice, further limited in scope. It was expected that cases from the previous two years only would be examined, the years in which Pakiri had worked in the Thongwa District, even though Pakiri's notoriety dated back into the early 1890s.

Within these formal bounds of the investigation, there were yet further limitations, largely occurring due to the practicalities of conducting the investigation. In the process of selecting criminal cases associated with Pakiri to review, Maxwell was advised to pay particular attention to the repeated use of the same witness in several cases, as the Lieutenant Governor of Burma suspected that Pakiri had used 'professional false witnesses'.[63] However, systematically going through past criminal cases looking for suspicious convictions with only the repeated use of witnesses as a potential guide, proved an open-ended job. As Maxwell noted, 'The truth of the matter is that the detection of fraudulent cases from the mere perusal of them is most difficult. In hardly a defended criminal case can there be said to be no suspicious circumstances. I have, therefore, reduced the number of cases to the utmost.'[64] Firstly, he examined the records from the townships of Dedaye and Bogale during the times Pakiri had been stationed there, pulling out the ones that he felt were suspicious. Of those left over, he created an index and re-examined every case where a particular witness had been used to testify in multiple cases.

We know little of what guided Maxwell in distinguishing the cases he thought suspicious from the rest. In his report, he was keen to demonstrate his balanced approach, writing, 'I am not unmindful of the famous passage in Macaulay's essay on Warren Hastings in which he describes the result of an attack by Government on one of its own officers and have rejected such evidence of which I have been doubtful in consequence.'[65] If this commitment was taken seriously, his selection process may have been quite severe. Additionally, the investigation team had a great deal of material to shift through in a relatively short period. In only three months, Maxwell and his staff had two years' worth of criminal cases to examine and had many interviews to conduct. It seems highly probable, even considering Maxwell's applauded capacity to work, that only a fraction of potential cases were investigated. Moreover, the role of policemen as the producers of evidence clearly posed substantial problems when retrospectively investigating criminal cases.[66] There was always a cause for suspicion.

In his subsequent report, Maxwell presented 26 bundles of criminal cases that he felt had suspicious connections with Pakiri. Some of the bundles contained only one case, some three or four connected cases. The next tasks were to first release any innocents still in prison and then to judge the utility of the cases for securing convictions against Pakiri. The first task was relatively easily achieved, except for the issue of compensation, and here Maxwell found the most expedient solution to be avoidance. He wrote, 'These questions are very difficult to answer. So difficult indeed that until people thinking themselves aggrieved come forward and apply for compensation they might reasonably be allowed to remain unanswered.'[67] More than 20 individuals were released from their sentences, one of which had been sentenced to transportation. Understandably, none came forward to claim compensation. The second task was considerably more problematic.

Two of the first cases brought to light by Fraser had collapsed because of difficulties regarding the credibility of key witnesses. Such difficulties plagued not only the Pakiri case, but also many other misconduct cases.[68] In one early case against Pakiri, Fraser had been advised that 'owing to the inconsistencies between the witnesses' statements and the bad character of the principal witnesses' prosecution would not be sanctioned.[69] In the other, he was told that 'the prosecution of Pakiri would not be sanctioned as all the material evidence in which the charge is based was that of men who were practically accomplices.'[70] It was calculated that the evidence of accomplices in cases like Pakiri's would be of limited use to the prosecution as they were proved to be perjures, and the defence could use this to discredit their testimonies. This contrasted to highly prioritised criminal cases in which 'approver's testimony' was used by government prosecutors to secure convictions, with accomplices offered immunity from prosecution or reduced sentences in exchange for cooperation.[71]

Finding evidence that was strong enough for court thus proved exceedingly difficult. For instance, Maxwell identified four cases in which Pakiri was alleged to have planted opium on wealthy Chinese men in Dedaye in order to extort money from them. In judging the utility of these cases for procuring a criminal conviction, Maxwell was forced to concede that 'in not one of these cases can it be said that the evidence is good, in each case there is much suspicion that the cases were fabricated by Pakiri, but further one cannot safely go.'[72] Pakiri was meticulous in covering his tracks. Even the Commissioner of the Irrawaddy Division praised Pakiri's talents, writing, 'The careful way in which he concocts evidence is amazing.'[73] Pakiri's police role as producer of evidence meant that distinguishing between genuine and fabricated evidence was almost impossible. Suspicion was all Maxwell often had to act on, and this would stand little chance of success in a courtroom. Useful evidence was at a premium.

Accessing the utility of criminal cases occasionally led Maxwell to abandon investigations into some of the most serious allegations against Pakiri. One of the clearest examples of this discriminating selection process in Maxwell's report was his analysis of a rape charge made against Pakiri. Maxwell had highlighted three 'seduction' allegations in which Pakiri had represented to women that he would in some way benefit a male relative whom he was holding in prison if the women were to have sex with him. The term 'seduce' was the one used by Fraser, Maxwell, and the other British officials in the higher echelons of the administration. It is an inappropriate term to apply to such serious allegations and such acts are better called rape: but at the time in only one case was the charge of rape actually made. The remaining cases fell under the category of receiving illegal gratifications. In Maxwell's eyes, the accuser in making a rape charge had undermined the strength of the case for its use in court. The issue turned on physical coercion, 'In as much however as the girl will have it that she was raped and the evidence goes to show that she surrendered her person to her tormentor in the hopes of doing her brothers good I do not think there would be any chance of a conviction.'[74] The implication was that consent under duress was still consent. He contrasted this to the other 'seduction' cases that he felt were stronger, because 'the woman there says that she did not call out while she [the woman making the rape charge] says that she did call out but the evidence shows that she did not do so.'[75] Maxwell did not explore the case any further or reveal the nature of the contrary evidence. Instead, he simply recommended that the case be pursued only in a departmental enquiry, if no criminal convictions were secured. Maxwell was not being exceptionally callous in making this judgement.[76] Rather it was the result of a process of enquiry in which a real event was distilled into the abstract logics of disciplinary judicial discourse on crime.[77] The demands of judicial utility severely curtailed the extent of the investigation.

It was not the only utility of the cases for disciplinary imperatives that shaped Maxwell's investigation, Pakiri and his followers proved to be a continuing thorn in his side. On hearing that Pakiri had received bail, Maxwell complained that, 'the Inspector has immense influence in the District and creates a fright by spreading all sorts of rumours about his power for instance he recently said that he has got rid of Frazer[sic] &c. and of course he has done so, sufficiently for his purpose, that is, to gull [deceive] the villagers.'[78] The immediate problem was of keeping prosecution witnesses in the face of Pakiri's intimidation. Maxwell strongly recommended a police officer 'well known and trusted by the people' to look after the witnesses, as he had reported 'while I was making enquiries two witnesses were openly assaulted and many more intimidated. Pakiri and his emissaries have been all over the Pyapon subdivision and are openly vowing vengeance against everyone concerned with the case even ... a subdivisional officer.'[79] In his report, Maxwell confessed that one of the 'seduction' cases had to be abandoned even before his investigations had finished because the witnesses had been 'squared'.[80]

It is in this light that we must also understand Pakiri's attempts to have the case moved to another court. Maxwell argued that moving the case out of the district was a tactic employed in order to give Pakiri greater opportunities to tamper with the witnesses. In supporting his point, he cited the case of the European head constable of the civil police, Hadden, who had been charged with misconduct about a year before. Hadden had done exactly what Maxwell feared Pakiri would if the case were moved.[81] The case of Hadden is worth momentarily commenting on as it illuminates the legal context of Pakiri's case.

Hadden was accused of suppressing evidence—or 'burking' evidence—in a rape case by having the documents destroyed and was taken to court on criminal charges.[82] The result, as it was depicted in the *Times of Burma*, was somewhat of a farce. The witnesses for the prosecution one after another contradicted each other's statements, culminating in the testimony of Po Kyun: 'Twice in the witness box during the two hours he was being subject to cross-examination, he fainted, was carried outside, revived, and brought back again. He begged the counsel for the accused to put no more questions to him.' On the last day of the trial, the presiding magistrate sanctioned the prosecution of the witnesses for perjury.[83] The *Times of Burma* initially reported on the trial from a position of sympathy with Hadden, due to a racial solidarity that was in awkward tension with the newspaper's campaign against corruption: but Maxwell's implication that Hadden had intimidated the witnesses casts the behaviour of the witnesses in a less comic and more tragic light. Hadden was eventually convicted in a different trial of receiving illegal gratifications in March 1900.[84]

Maxwell's investigation had to counteract the violent threats of Pakiri's machinations in order to have any success in court. He explicitly did not want Pakiri's trial to end up like Hadden's first, ridiculed and derided in the press. As a result, his investigation was shaped by the willingness of individuals to come forward and give evidence against Pakiri, as well as Maxwell's ability to shield them from the influence of Pakiri. Perhaps, it was for this reason that the Lieutenant Governor of Burma stressed to Maxwell the importance of going to the scene where alleged events were said to have taken place and 'examine the witnesses on the spot'.[85] It was not only Pakiri's skilled manufacturing of evidence that made investigating him a challenge, but also his enduring notoriety and influence in the Thongwa District. Both no doubt were mutually supporting.

Pakiri's role as an inspector meant that gathering evidence against him was an exceptionally difficult task. The high-ranking British officials investigating him were in the inherently trying position of using the evidence from successful criminal convictions to convict the producer of that evidence. Pakiri was also able to evade prosecution by using his authority to 'square' the witnesses. These were the inherent challenges of policing the police, of disciplining an agent of discipline. The difficulties faced by Maxwell were ultimately apparent in the muted success of the 13 criminal charges in court, despite being judged the most secure of the many suspicious cases that went through the rigorous selection process discussed above. At his trial, Pakiri was acquitted of most charges but where found guilt was sentenced to 19 years of rigorous imprisonment. He was then acquitted on all but one of the charges on appeal and had his sentence reduced to 14 years.[86]

Pakiri was evidently largely independent of the control of his British superior officers. He was able to evade them during his career and almost managed to escape criminal prosecution. However, it would be wrong to judge that this is demonstrative of the weakness of the colonial state in Burma or that it signifies the fragility of colonial discipline. As we have seen, it was Pakiri's position in the police that made his prosecution so difficult. This argument can be expanded; Pakiri's acts of misconduct were possible only through his manipulation of colonial discipline and his ability to enact the state.

The acts of corruption and misconduct that Pakiri was engaged in were not born out of his evasion of the colonial state, even though he did evade the supervision of deputy commissioners. Nor were they strictly the result of an intermediary position between the colonial state and colonised. Pakiri's misconduct was possible only *through* the application of the disciplinary procedures of the colonial state. It is not sufficient to argue that Pakiri as a subordinate official had an intermediary position between the state and society that he was able to exploit, because Pakiri was able to satisfy his predatory appetite only through enacting and performing the state. It is also inadequate to describe him as a malfunctioning cog in the machine of the colonial state, as the dominant metaphor in the historiography would imply. If this metaphor has any descriptive value, it is only in reverse. The cog could turn the machine. This was apparent in the various malpractices of Pakiri brought to light by Maxwell's investigation, from the banal and petty to the grievous. The colonial state was constituted in the daily life of the people of the delta through the performances of subordinate officials like Pakiri, and in the delta, the state was a threateningly arbitrary manifestation.

Among the more banal of Pakiri's acts of misconduct were his interactions with other subordinate officials. These were, as they are in many institutional relationships, often strained and hostile. In this administrative context, Pakiri appears less as an errant official and more a product of his malfunctioning bureaucratic environment. During his time serving in the Dedaye Township during 1898 and 1899, Pakiri was embroiled in a feud with a local *myo-ok* called Aung Gyi. Aung Gyi was as notorious as Pakiri. Maxwell described him as 'a gentleman with as bad a reputation as, if not worse than that of Pakiri himself'.[87] The quarrel between them became so entrenched that Aung Gyi and Pakiri used their authority to victimise each other's friends and followers. Maxwell, who was the Deputy Commissioner of Thongwa at the time, freely admitted that he allowed the dispute between them to go on, 'on the principle of honest men coming by their own when thieves fall out.'[88] At the time of its occurrence, then, Maxwell tolerated their misconduct.

This state of affairs was not left to continue indefinitely and the two warring parties were eventually separated. Aung Gyi was sent to Yandoon, and Pakiri was dispatched to Bogale. Aung Gyi's career, like Pakiri's, was thereafter also blighted with controversy. At the start of 1900, he was punished for abusing his power through misconduct proceedings. It seems he had fallen out with Maung Po Maung, a legal pleader who was implicated in helping Pakiri in his corrupt acts (he was thought to have helped procure a woman for Pakiri in one of the 'seduction' cases). Aung Gyi then used his position as *myo-ok* to punish Maung Po Maung's sister by not disclosing the amount of money she was expected to pay in a debtor case, so that bailiffs would be called in to take her possessions away and sell them. For this malicious act, he received the punishment of being moved to a 'reduced place in the list of 3rd grade *myo-oks*'.[89] It seems that Aung Gyi's feud with Pakiri continued by proxy even after they were separated. Thus, Pakiri's malpractices were not aberrations from bureaucratic norms in the district. His misconduct was even partly the result of the internal rivalries of administration.

Even aspects of township administration that were less overtly antagonistic were deeply problematic. Pakiri had informal influence over Maung Gale, a township magistrate also at Dedaye. The magistrate was described rather unflatteringly by Maxwell as, 'a young man ... a poor weak thing—entirely under the thumb of his wife and of Pakiri and whose honesty was not altogether above suspicion.'[90] Maung Gale was sufficiently above suspicion to avoid being implicated directly in the legal cases against Pakiri, but nevertheless having influence over a magistrate would have been of use to a police officer with a habit of fabricating evidence. Maxwell wrote more positively of the officials in administrative positions superior to Pakiri. The Subdivisional Magistrate, Aung Zan, and the Subdivisional Police Officer, Shwe O, were described as having been, 'honest and shrewd'.[91] Of Shwe O, however, he did hold some reservations, writing in his report that he was 'old, timid, and seeking after merit'—presumably bureaucratic and not spiritual merit.[92] Aung Zan was also a recipient of generous praise from the ever-complimentary Herbert Thirkell White.[93] But despite these officials' efforts, on the whole Maxwell did not present the situation in the township in a very positive light. He pointed out in his report that for a long time Dedaye had been the origin of many corruption charges and counter-charges, although he admitted that the recent allegations against Pakiri were unprecedented in scale. He summarised his view of the context for Pakiri's misconduct in the township administration succinctly, 'A powerful and unscrupulous Police Officer [Pakiri]. A weak Township Magistrate and Subdivisional Police Officer, a Subdivisional Magistrate independent but over worked and an unscrupulous population. If the result was what it was, what surprise.'[94] It was in this occasionally fractious but inherently personal and mostly ineffectual institutional environment that Pakiri operated. He was enabled in his actions by the quotidian performance of township administration in Dedaye.

Even where Pakiri's actions were exceptional, he was successful only because of his role in the colonial state, as was apparent in his manipulation of colonial disciplinary networks, particularly the judicial system. Indeed, his acts of misconduct relied on him performing and enacting the colonial state. Maxwell believed that the nine opium-planting cases had been motivated by Pakiri's desire to extort bribes from wealthy individuals. In four of the cases, the victims were described as well-to-do Chinese men. In one of these cases, two of Pakiri's sergeants, Maung Myo and Maung Lu Gale, allegedly planted opium in the home of a Chinese man in Bogale. They later returned to the house, 'found' the opium, and arrested the servant of the house but not the master. The logic behind the arrest of the servant was that the master, having had previously been charged, would face jail, whereas they could hold the servant more easily in order to extort a bribe of Rs. 700 from the master.[95] Their actions were calculated to maximise the potential for extorting a bribe. Extortion of this kind operated through the implicit threat of disciplinary state intervention. Pakiri and his sergeants were manufacturing situations in which police power could be brought to bear in order to induce their victims to pay bribes to escape charges for crimes that they had not committed. It was not Pakiri's personal authority that constituted the threat, but the whole machinery of the colonial disciplinary system. Because of a lack of evidence, only three of the nine cases involving the planting of opium on persons were recommended for prosecution. Two initially resulted in a conviction of five years each but were subsequently overturned at appeal.[96]

In one case against Pakiri, his actions appear to have had a less exploitative character. The inhabitants of a village in the Dedaye Township apparently solicited Pakiri to have two 'obnoxious' villagers arrested. The price being agreed, Pakiri staged the theft of some cattle and arrested the two unpopular villagers for the crime. Maxwell claimed that, 'The collection of the money and the falsity of the case—the actual robbery being committed under the auspices of the Inspector—are clearly proved.'[97] Pakiri's strategy was essentially the same as in the cases of opium planting, to produce a situation in which the action of the colonial police was justified, but the nature of the case was qualitatively different. The relationship between Pakiri and the villagers was one of collaboration, a deal of mutual benefit. Evidently, law enforcement could even be a service for hire, and importantly the villagers were aware of the potential service that Pakiri offered. This should not be read as a sign of the superficiality of colonial policing. Rather, it was a sophisticated manipulation of policing, based on the joint acknowledgement that it was not the *existence* of a crime that mattered for the operation of colonial justice but the *evidence* of a crime. This case suggests a shared acknowledgement between Pakiri and these villagers that the fiction of the crime did not diminish the reality of legal discipline. Following the investigation, Tun Tha and Myo Dun, the unpopular villagers, had their sentences suspended and were released, but the case was not brought as a criminal charge against Pakiri.[98]

As well as monetary gain, Pakiri's misconduct was motivated by lust, as was apparent in his use of police powers to gain access to women, and even to rape them. As in the case of opium planting and in the case of the 'obnoxious' villagers, Pakiri invoked the colonial state to achieve his ends. As I have shown above, in all three of the so-called 'seduction' cases, he conspired to have men arrested. He then offered either to have them released or benefited in some other fashion, if their female relatives had sex with him. In one of the cases, Pakiri was apparently abetted not only by a fellow police officer, but also by the legal pleader Maung Po Maung.[99] Pakiri and his accomplices performed their official duties, although concerning fictitious crimes, and then cast themselves as a negotiable barrier before further discipline. These cases further emphasise the point that the performative nature of state power did not mean that the state was fragile. For the women caught in this coercive sexual economy produced by Pakiri's acts, the state was enacted as a very real threat. Indeed, it was enacted as an expression of masculine power.[100] Only one 'seduction' case was preferred as a criminal charge against Pakiri but he was acquitted of this during the trial.[101]

In all these cases of fabricating evidence for bribery and extortion, Pakiri was able to achieve his ends only by performing his policing powers to invoke the threat of the broader disciplinary system of the colonial state. In most cases, this involved creating intricate scenarios in which to entangle his victims, most commonly through fabricating robberies. The lengths to which Pakiri would go to stage his misconduct was apparent in the one case for which he was ultimately convicted. In this case, Pakiri had elaborately and successfully framed Saw Ke. Having orchestrated the theft of some pearls and rubies from the house of one Po Myaing, Pakiri gave the pearls to one of his followers to deposit with a moneylender in the name of Saw Ke. Pakiri then employed someone else to hide the remaining rubies in Saw Ke's house. He then arrested Saw Ke for house breaking by night and theft, and used the rubies in Saw Ke's house and the testimony of the moneylender as evidence.[102] Having gathered evidence and located witnesses, Pakiri then handed the case to the judiciary to convict Saw Ke (the crimes he was accused of carried a sentence of over 17 years of imprisonment) and the prison officials to confine him. As in the other cases against him, Pakiri had used his police powers to appropriate the colonial systems of justice and incarceration. His misconduct was based on his role as a vital node in enacting the broader colonial disciplinary network.

Pakiri's case is revealing not only because of the nature of his acts, but also due to his success; the fact he managed to have so many people convicted for such a sustained period. It was suspected in the British newspapers in Burma that Pakiri's crimes dated back further than the two years for which he had been investigated. In fact, some articles went further to suggest that Pakiri's success in the police department was aided by his misconduct. For instance, a piece in the *Times of Burma* alleged that Pakiri had achieved promotion *through* corrupt acts. It has been mentioned earlier that Pakiri had a tarnished reputation before Fraser and Maxwell had begun to investigate him, stemming from a dacoity case in the 1890s. In his report, Maxwell did not discuss this episode, he simply commented that of Pakiri's earlier career in the civil police 'the less said the better'.[103] The correspondents of the *Times of Burma* retold the story of these past accusations against Pakiri at the time of his trial.

In 1894, Pakiri was a head constable working under the inspector, briefly mentioned above, Po Ni, and the two were assigned to solve a case of violent house breaking in Rangoon. Pakiri and Po Ni eventually charged a group of suspects with the crime but the individuals they had arrested were ultimately found not guilty in court. The judge in the trial believed that the evidence in the case had been fabricated and accordingly sanctioned the prosecution of Pakiri and Po Ni. The *Times of Burma* portrayed the reaction of the police department to this judgement as something akin to a cover-up:

> ... the government was too much ashamed of itself to do the just and proper thing, having promoted Po Ni over the heads of nearly forty better inspectors ... and having promoted Pakeeree[sic] in a similar

style to be an Inspector, simply because "their men made those arrests and put false evidence against innocent men." So the government concealed the crimes of its police in a departmental inquiry ... and they were reduced (not to their former ranks, but) to top of the next grade below the rank which they were promoted.[104]

It was further speculated that despite Pakiri's infamy, he had maintained good contacts within the police department up until his ultimate arrest: 'Yet, we believe, it is notorious that Pakeeree[sic] wields immense influence in the Burma Police Secretariat ... and there must be a reason for his being a "pet" of high-placed officers.'[105]

Even if Pakiri's notoriety did not have the longevity that the hostile British media in Burma claimed, during his two years in the townships of the Thongwa District he was highly successful in obtaining false convictions, having secured at least 20.[106] Pakiri was framing people at a rate of at least one person a month. It seems that when Pakiri produced false evidence and concocted a case against an individual, invariably in the subsequent trial the falsely accused was found guilty. The link between the police investigation and the decision at trial was a close one. Pakiri's staging of crimes and performance (in a theatrical sense) of his police duties had been readily accepted as genuine by other officials and branches of the colonial state. As the *Times of Burma* suggests, it may have been the case that the police department even looked upon Pakiri's conviction rate as a success. Moreover, on the level of the everyday state, Pakiri was highly successful.[107] He was able to regularly perform the state in such a way as to punish enemies, extort bribes, and gain access to women. For his victims, state power was theatrical, self-confirming, and despotic.[108]

In reaction to Pakiri's case, the *Times of Burma* published a petition from its 'numerous readers' addressed to the Viceroy, calling for the establishment of a special commission to police the police.[109] Their call went unheeded. Although Pakiri was ultimately brought to trial and found guilty, his case did not stimulate systemic change. Rao argues, about the use of torture by the colonial police in Madras, that the acts of the 'native' police were conceived of as simply an example of indigenous barbarity in a manner that erased the complicity of the colonial disciplinary regime as a whole.[110] The investigation into Pakiri, by focusing upon him as an individual, similarly acted to close any investigatory avenues that would have explored Pakiri as a symptom of the system of policing itself. Similarly, the major commissioned investigation into the police force across British India held in 1902 concluded narrowly that the pervasive corruption in the lower ranks was the result of insufficient wages and the inherent pathological traits of oriental society.[111]

There is the possibility that Pakiri's race was seen as an explanation for his malpractices. Thus, in a similar way as Rao suggests, the investigation may have shifted the blame for the endemic misconduct from the colonial regime by focusing on an indigenous subordinate who was thought hereditarily predisposed to corruption. In Maxwell's words, 'Inspector Pakiri's nationality is of some importance. As far as I have been able to gather he is half Malay half Madrassi speaking the usual Madras languages and with a foreign accent Burmese, which he also writes. By religion Pakiri is Mohammedan.'[112] His valuing of Pakiri's background as being of 'some importance' is as revealing as it is ultimately obscure. He grants Pakiri's heritage importance but why and how it was important seems to be implicit in the description. Maxwell may be assuming that his intended reader will recognise the importance of Pakiri's heritage without further comment. Various historians have argued that the bodies of the colonised were read by the colonial state as texts on the morality, as well as the physical and mental attributes, of the subject population.[113] In the colonial judicial system, race had a structuring influence, demonstrated by the tendency to judge the accused as part of a collective, with some racial groups being deemed to be more trustworthy than others who were viewed as inherently dishonest or immoral.[114] Given the importance of an individual's cultural background and body in judging their character in the colonial disciplinary systems of the time, it is likely that Pakiri's behaviour was understood at least partly in terms of his race. Being mixed race, he did not fit comfortably within colonial categorisation: his body and background were inherently difficult to read and so he was inherently suspicious. We cannot be certain of the influence of racial thinking on the investigation and ultimate conviction, as it was not made explicit, but either way, the Pakiri case did not lead to a broader investigation or systemic reform.

Although the high-ranking British officials were unwilling to explore it, Pakiri was able to successfully manipulate colonial systems of policing and justice for his own purposes. In this way, Pakiri was not so much a hybrid middle-figure, intermediary, or interlocutor for the colonial state but its artificer. To his victims, he performed the colonial state as a powerful, arbitrary weapon at his disposal. His ability to commit misconduct was not based on his relatively autonomous position *between* the colonial state and the colonised. Rather, it was based on his position *within* the colonial disciplinary system. His official duties as a police inspector, particularly his officially ordained role as a producer of legally admissible evidence, allowed him not only to extort bribes and engage in other more nefarious acts, but also to make life difficult for the British officials attempting to investigate him. The colonial state must have appeared even more intrusive and oppressive to Pakiri's victims than it has subsequently been depicted in the historiography.

Players in a theatre state

The example of Pakiri is undoubtedly extreme. No other official in the period under study generated as many misconduct allegations or caused such consternation among high-ranking British officials. An anomaly in terms of the scale of misconduct Pakiri certainly was, but his acts were not qualitatively different from those of other subordinate officials in similar positions.[115] Instead, his case was symptomatic of the constitutive effect of subordinate state employees' daily state acts. This is not to argue that any official could have had a career like Pakiri, such an argument would be patently ridiculous. The point is a more subtle one: in everyday life it was subordinate officials' performances that made the state real.

It is crucial to acknowledge that the performativity of the state was not only apparent in acts of misconduct. When acting within the bureaucratic rules, subordinate officials were also reifying the colonial state, but these practices were intrinsically linked to misconduct. Indeed, sanctioned practices often inadvertently allowed corrupt ones. As we have seen, Pakiri's acts of misconduct necessarily relied upon other subordinate officials, such as prison warders and magistrates, doing their jobs properly. Moreover, the investigation into Pakiri showed that clearly delineating between corrupt and honest practices proved to be an almost insurmountable task for investigating officials as they struggled to find criminal cases involving the Inspector which were *not* suspect. Corrupt acts were often cunningly disguised as legitimate ones and also relied on formal practices. Given the scale and pervasive presence of misconduct in the delta, it could be asked whether corruption tainted the perception of state practices, in general, regardless of whether they directly involved instances of malfeasance. Either way it was subordinate officials' everyday practices, both corrupt and straight, which reified the state.

It should be noted additionally that there were limits to an individual subordinate official's ability to performatively enact the colonial state. Possible forms of misconduct were contingent on an official's access to the performative resources of state power: the uniforms, buildings, equipment, bureaucratic duties, and other 'props' that were available to them.[116] For instance, the most common acts of misconduct committed by vaccinators were accepting bribes to avoid vaccination, falsifying vaccination reports, and performing variolations.[117] Just as Pakiri was enabled in his acts by his position in the police force and official role as producer of legal evidence, other subordinate officials' misconduct was related to their official state duties. All formal state roles were inscribed with the potential to be perverted in ways specific to that role.[118]

Despite these caveats, the case of Pakiri vividly reveals the paradox of subordinate officials' performative enactment of the colonial state. By breaking the rules of state practice as laid down in standing orders, gazettes, manuals, and legal codes, subordinate officials were simultaneously enacting the state.[119] Quite the contrary to being epiphenomenal, pathological aberrations from the norms of state practice, as historians of colonial Burma have conceptualised it,[120] misconduct involved embodied, iterative acts which produced the structural effect of the state.[121] Pakiri did not subvert the state, but enacted it. This should not suggest the superficiality or fragility of the colonial state, especially since the fiction of Pakiri's criminal cases did not diminish the reality of state punishment for his victims. But more fundamentally it is unhelpful to conceptualise misconduct as inherently weakening state power. Rather than writing in terms of the relative strength or weakness of the state, it is better to follow both Taylor Sherman and Steven Pierce in their respective works on colonial India and Nigeria to explore how corrupt practices constituted the state.[122] As it was performed by Pakiri, the state was an intrusive, arbitrary, and violent spectre, which at the same time was experienced as an embedded social entity that had to be negotiated in daily deltaic life.

Inspector Pakiri fabricated evidence to initiate police investigations and so doing performatively enacted the state. In his acts, he was simultaneously the 'matter' of the state and its 'artificer'. Taking a more general view, subordinate officials were not merely cogs in the machine or even intermediaries for the state: they *were* the state in its quotidian existence, both its substance and its maker. They were, in the terms of the anthropologist Clifford Geertz, the players in a theatre state.[123]

3
Whiter than White

In Burma ... the people looked up to the officials and recognized that they were better off under authority than if they attempted to govern themselves. Above all, they knew that in the last resort they could rely on the justice and firmness of British officers.

Herbert Thirkell White,
A Civil Servant in Burma (1913)

The whole affair, as far as I can see, is one network of intrigue and villainy. It seems impossible to believe anybody. It all comes from dealing with Burmans.

Cecil Champion Lowis,
The Machinations of the Myo-Ok (1903)

Anti-corruption and British authority

Almost all scholarly attempts to define colonial states rely, to varying degrees, on the existence of a division between the rulers and the ruled. For most post-colonial historians, this division in colonial Asia was marked primarily by conceptions of racial difference.[1] This was apparent in many formal bureaucratic structures and employment practices in which certain powers and positions were reserved for white Europeans. But while this was usually an institutionalised bifurcation evident in the formal organisation of colonial states' uppermost branches, it is less certain how this hierarchical racial division was experienced in everyday life.[2] With subordinate officials, like Inspector Pakiri, evidently capable of subverting the authority of British superior officers and enacting the state for their own ends, it might legitimately be asked whether the white upper echelons of the colonial administration were relevant in everyday deltaic life at all. Were the daily personal politics of local government, as George Orwell evocatively characterised them, always 'impervious to the European mind, a conspiracy behind the conspiracy, a plot within a plot'?[3]

Some historians of British India have taken the view that the autonomy of subordinate officials inherently weakened the colonial state as a hierarchical entity and that the malpractice of local officials meant a lack of authority at the centre.[4] Others, like Rajnarayan Chandaravakar, have argued instead that local officials could 'harness' the hierarchical bureaucratic structures of the state without diminishing their power.[5] Both positions have their problems. The first treats power as restrictive and zero-sum, rather than as productive and capillary as most philosophers and theorists prefer to conceptualise it now.[6] The second treats the state as a homogenous actor principally serving British Imperial interests. It does not provide a perspective onto the everyday state as it was made through the quotidian practices of subordinate officials.[7] Thus, we are left with an unresolved problem: if subordinate officials enacted state power in everyday life through their malpractices and corruption, were British officials relevant?

The answer from the Burma delta is yes. When we examine the state as it was manifested in everyday life, we can see that high-ranking British officials were still crucial actors. Indeed, as I show in this chapter, the misconduct of subordinate officials was crucial to establishing and maintaining British authority on a local level. That the colonised population were aware of the institutionalised racial differentiation of the rulers and the ruled was apparent in the petitions they sent to deputy commissioners complaining of subordinate level misconduct. This was the primary mechanism for making accusations against officials. The formal disciplinary network of the colonial state was structured so that in order to seek redress for subordinate officials' abuses of power, the colonised would have to appeal to European officials. In this way, allegations of corruption made by the local population enabled high-ranking British officers to discipline their largely Indian and Burmese subordinates. They also demonstrate a popular awareness of British authority over their subordinates in society.

But these appeals to British officials were not appeals to a beneficent paternal power, as in Herbert Thirkell White's self-congratulatory portrayal in the epigraph above. While these accusations were crucial sources of information for British officials framing misconduct charges, they were equally problematic. Between the lines of anti-corruption petitions, we can often read the local intrigues and feuds that motivated the petitioners. These could be complex: on occasions, subordinate officials made misconduct allegations against other subordinate officials in order to protect themselves from misconduct allegations. The discourse of anti-corruption could be duplicitously employed to manipulate and misinform deputy commissioners, a phenomenon that has also been found in William Gould's in-depth study of corruption in late-colonial India.[8] But the ambivalence of anti-corruption accusations did not subvert the authority of British officials. Even dishonest appeals to deputy commissioners implicitly acknowledged and reified the hierarchical racial division as an intrinsic part of the state.

This chapter examines how pervasive corruption in the lower branches of the state in the delta was used to justify and enable the formal racial division of the colonial state. This occurred through a contradiction and an irony. The contradiction was that British officials were expected to be aloof from their subordinate officials while also being required to be familiar with the intimate details of their subordinates' daily lives in order to supervise and discipline them. In resolving this contradiction, they acted as bureaucratic despots. The irony was that attempts by subordinate officials and the broader populace to misinform and mislead deputy commissioners through duplicitous accusations of corruption served to enable the authority of white officials over their subordinate officials and the broader populace. Attempts to appropriate the disciplinary powers of British officials enabled them to perform their disciplinary powers. Accusations of corruption were undoubtedly ambivalent, but they nonetheless enacted British authority.

Deputy commissioners as bureaucratic despots

Within the expanding bureaucracy of British Burma, as it fanned out into the delta, deputy commissioners had a vital role. The post was a linchpin in the formal hierarchical, racial, and spatial arrangement of the colonial state. The province of Burma was divided into divisions and then within these further sub-divided into districts. Deputy commissioners were in charge of the administration of the districts as well as responsible for justice, civil policing, public works, fisheries, and forestry within them.[9] The position was also marked by a substantial increase in pay in comparison to their immediate subordinates the *myo-oks*, the highest ranked administrative position for Burmese officials in Lower Burma at the turn of the century. Crucially, the deputy commissioners were the liminal face of British officialdom and until

1908 only Europeans had held deputy commissionerships.[10] More than any other branch of colonial officialdom, the deputy commissioners represented the 'thin white line' of British administration.[11] Their role was thus at the crux of maintaining a racial division and order in the state bureaucracy, intended to be above their Burmese and Indian employees whose authority was enclosed within their districts. Through the bureaucratic responsibilities allocated to the deputy commissioners, the spatial and racial structures of the state were mutually constructed and maintained.[12]

The deputy commissioners were thus the agents of colonial bureaucratic discipline within the districts of colonial Burma, responsible for policing misconduct among their subordinates. As with criminality, the colonial discourse on corruption was about disciplining 'natives': here local state employees, rather than 'criminal tribes' or dacoits.[13] But as we have seen in Chapter 1, the disciplinary economy constructed to punish misconduct within the subordinate branches of the administration allowed for a large amount of tolerance. Officials, particularly township officers, were often punished lightly, even in well-evidenced cases of grievous corruption. For deputy commissioners, policing misconduct constituted only one duty within a range of official responsibilities; allowances were made for breaches of conduct. However, this tacit tolerance of misconduct and corruption ran alongside the notion that British officials, particularly those in the upper echelons of the colonial state, were incorruptible.

Despite the many cases of European corruption, such as those that have been explored in Chapter 1, Europeans were perceived to be incorruptible and their supervision of indigenous employees was deemed to be vital for the maintenance of administrative order. Indeed, this discourse resulted in greater sympathy being shown towards corrupt European officials.[14] It was believed that only white officials could be effective in policing corruption. This was why it was proposed that in order to combat misconduct in the Irrawaddy Division, another district would be formed, thus increasing the number of deputy commissioners supervising administration.[15] The lack of European supervision was perennially cited by officials and the British colonial press as a major cause for the prevalence of corruption and bribery. The frequent transfers of deputy commissioners gave rise to complaints that they were never settled in one place long enough to get to know their subordinate staff properly or become familiar with the local population.[16] Like the tower in the centre of the Panopticon, the very presence of a European deputy commissioner within the bounded space of the district was expected to discourage corruption and misconduct among the subordinate staff.[17] Of course, the colonial state in Burma was far from being panoptic either in intent or in practice, but deputy commissioners did attempt some supervision of their subordinate officials.

On rare occasions deputy commissioners even became deeply embroiled in local intrigues in order to discipline their subordinates, investigating private aspects of subordinate officials' lives. This can be illustrated through the misconduct case against a head constable based in Bassein, Po Kyaw. In the closing months of 1899, Po Kyaw was investigated because he was suspected of having a compromising connection with a convicted dacoit called Saw Lin through a relationship with Saw Lin's sister Shwe Kyit. The local Deputy Commissioner's subsequent misconduct investigation saw many villagers from Shwe Kyit's village interviewed about Po Kyaw's connection with her. A pensioned former *thugyi* stated that he had heard that there was a relationship between the two, either of marriage or that she was Po Kyaw's mistress. Although he went on to qualify his statement saying, 'It was during the rains I heard about it first. Many people said so. I am too old to know anything about it.'[18] The statements of eight other male villagers who were questioned on the same day supported his evidence. Some recalled the number of times that Po Kyaw had visited and stayed overnight at Shwe Kyit's home. One villager, Maung Po, who claimed to have been a neighbour of Saw Lin and a go-between for Shwe Kyit and Po Kyaw, testified that 'Po Kyaw kissed her in my presence.'[19] The investigation into Po Kyaw demonstrates that deputy commissioners occasionally involved themselves in, and penetrated, local village gossip in order to supervise and discipline their Burmese subordinates. In the example of Po Kyaw, the investigation unearthed his domestic arrangements and intimate relationships.[20]

The investigation into Po Kyaw's relationship with Shwe Kyit shows the perceived need to investigate subordinate officials' daily lives. Similar investigations often became necessary because of frequent accusations of familial favouritism in the allocation of leases and government contracts and also because of concerns about officials becoming heavily in debt.[21] Investigations into the mundane and seemingly innocuous activities of subordinate officials were part and parcel of a deputy commissioner's duties. However, at the same time, deputy commissioners were reluctant to involve themselves too deeply in local intrigues. It was deemed important that British officials kept themselves at bay from their subordinate indigenous officials and the local population in order to maintain their integrity. Deputy commissioners were to be seen as removed from the daily affairs of 'native' subordinate officials, impersonal and aloof.

Maintaining social distance from the local populace was crucial to British officials' self-presentation as the incorruptible face of the state. Often, when reflecting on their careers, British officials used their apparent aloofness to deny direct responsibility for the problems of corruption in the colonial administration, a defence that can also be found from some early histories of colonial Burma.[22] The influential scholar-official G. E. Harvey commented in a report on bureaucratic corruption published in the late-colonial period that British officials were free from corruption but that they were also inaccessible to the bulk of the population.[23] This echoed the thoughts of the Lieutenant Governor of Burma from 1905 to 1910, Herbert Thirkell White, 30 years earlier. He claimed that British officials themselves were known to be honest, but they were inaccessible to the population at large except as a last resort.[24] British officials presented themselves as the detached and therefore incorruptible face of colonial rule.

Deputy commissioners were thus in a contradictory position regarding their supervisory duties and the self-image they cultivated. They were intended to have been both remote from the subject population and simultaneously accessible for the purposes of discipline. The tension of these paradoxical pressures was neatly encapsulated in the complaint of the Deputy Commissioner of Bassien about the disreputable *myo-ok* Maung Gyi, whose career was explored in Chapter 1:

> [He] is up to his old tricks. He is dragging the dignity of his appointment through the dust by wandering about at night after women and on one occasion his having a row in a *pwe*,[25] I am told ... *I do not care a row of brass pans what his private life is but I will not allowed[sic] him to publicly disgrace his position* (emphasis added).[26]

In this throwaway comment, we can perhaps see how the contradictory demands upon high-ranking British officials of aloofness and engagement could be reconciled through rhetorical nonchalance. His comment is illustrative of the overarching concern about preserving British manners and prestige in official matters.

Being aloof from 'native' intrigues was an important aspect of the acceptable conduct of the British population's lives in colonial Burma. It was part of high-ranking white officials and the non-official upper class British population attempts to preserve their own separate social spaces.[27] George Orwell described this deliberate act of distancing in *Burmese*

Days. The book's protagonist Flory, a European timber merchant, was informed by his friend Dr Veraswami, an Indian doctor, that a Burmese magistrate was intriguing against him. Orwell wrote, perhaps reflecting on his own experiences as a police officer in Burma years earlier, that Flory justified his reluctance to help Veraswami by claiming that, 'to keep out of "native" quarrels is one of the Ten Precepts of the pukka sahib.'[28] The phrase attests to the wilful passivity of British officials about local intrigues in order to maintain the façade of racial superiority.

Evocatively captured in Orwell's writings, this distancing was also apparent at the turn of the century. The British official Harold Fielding-Hall presented a similar picture in *A People At School* concerning his experiences as a deputy commissioner in the 1890s and the early 1900s. He argued that the Burmese and the English could not successfully interact socially because it would inevitably end in mutual boredom. As a result, he advised British officials to be suspicious of attempts to make friends across the racial barrier. He warned, characteristically bluntly, 'There is not ever, there could not be, any other reason for a man or woman coming to visit you except they wished some gain.'[29] Deputy commissioners, in his view, were ideally to remain independent and impersonal by being socially inaccessible.[30] The historian John Cady later claimed that Fielding-Hall's characterisation of the strained inter-actions between British officials and the local population was perhaps overstated, but probably representative.[31]

Fielding-Hall's unwillingness to engage socially with the indigenous population may have shaped his impression of the scale of the corruption among subordinate officials.[32] He contended that he had investigated hundreds of cases of misconduct during his time as a deputy commissioner but had rarely found evidence to support them. He argued further that misconduct allegations usually stemmed from 'disappointment and ignorance and malice.'[33] His faith in the honesty of subordinate officials reflected his suspicion of the Burmese populace. He wrote, 'native officials are the cock-shies for all the misrepresenta-tion that ignorance and malice and foolishness can invent …. There is nothing safer than to traduce native officials.'[34] Just as in *Burmese Days* in which Flory's concern about being a 'pukka sahib' resulted in him failing to take action to protect his friend Veraswami against a corrupt Burmese magistrate, Fielding-Hall's aloofness may have led him to hold what his contemporaries believed to be an overly optimistic opinion of his subordinate staff.[35] Deputy commissioners' attempts to distance themselves from local intrigue were tantamount to tolerating subordinate officials' quotidian malpractices.

Occasionally deputy commissioners were directly discouraged from listening to accusations of corruption coming from the local population. In 1892, the Deputy Commissioner of the Thongwa District of the delta complained that the local village headmen 'seldom interest themselves in criminal matters' and 'use the power granted them to tyrannize in a petty way over the people.'[36] The Chief Commissioner responded by dismissing his claims and encouraging him to instead 'support the authority of the village officers over their rich and stiff-necked villagers.'[37] Although empowered to investigate and discipline their subordinate officials, deputy commissioners were advised to remain a step removed from misconduct accusations and counter-accusations. Cecil C. Lowis, a long-serving judge in colonial Burma, demonstrated what he believed to be the utility of this distance in his 1903 novel *The Machinations of the Myo-ok*. By the time that the deputy commissioner in his story had found time to investigate a case in which the contents of a township's treasury had been stolen (as well as a subsequent case of a faked robbery that had been staged to cover up the crime) the money had already been returned and the culprits had been caught, although through a comically farcical set of events.[38] It was a didactic parable suggesting that in Burma it was often best for British officials to stay out of local intrigues, as things would probably sort themselves out if left alone.

But as was amply demonstrated by the extraordinary case of Inspector Pakiri in Chapter 2, things did not always just sort themselves out. Despite deploying rhetoric separating inherent 'Oriental' corruption from British incorruptibility which justified official aloofness and encouraged a broad tolerance of subordinate-level misconduct, deputy commissioners had to exercise their authority to keep some semblance of discipline within the bureaucracy. After all, their authority was also based on their ability to discipline their subordinates. Deputy commissioners thus had to be open to accusations of misconduct emanating from society, and those seeking redress had to attract the attention of these aloof British officials to have any chance of having their cases heard. In the case files, I have seen there are few better examples of the benefit of soliciting the support of a deputy commissioner in a case of misconduct, nor a more unfortunate example, than that of Abdul Razak.

In November 1906, an inspector of the civil police had Razak arrested four times. He was released on three of these occasions by two police constables serving under the same inspector. These multiple arrests and releases all occurred on the same day, which turned to be a bad one for Razak. The motive behind the four arrests and three subsequent releases were in order for the police to extort the sum of Rs. 100 from him. Having still not paid the sum demanded of him after the fourth arrest, the police charged Razak with a fabricated criminal complaint. When the complaint was heard in court, the magistrate threw it out as false, but Razak was fortunate to have this verdict returned. The charges were dismissed in court only because he had contact with the local Deputy Commissioner Stevenson after being released, briefly, for the third time during his ordeal. In the words of Stevenson:

> Now this man Abdul Razak, while he was being pressed on the 11th November to pay Rs 100/- managed to run up to my house to tell me what was happening. ... I admit that I gave little attention to what the man was telling me at the time and did not grasp the meaning of his tale. I realised the full significance of the incident only when I heard that he had been arrested and put into the lock-up. I then immediately called for all the Police papers in the matter, which were handed over to me dilatorily and reluctantly ....[39]

Stevenson's examination of the police papers formed the central evidence that secured Razak his liberty and resulted in a charge of perjury against the policemen who acted as witnesses.[40] There was still an element of aloofness apparent in Stevenson's response to Razak, evidenced by how he was initially dismissive of Razak's pleas. However, despite this, Stevenson was eventually compelled to intervene and have the perpetrators punished.

The disciplinary power invested in deputy commissioners was mitigated by their wilfully aloof manner. They could involve themselves in detailed investigations, but whether they did so was ultimately dependent upon their capricious interest. Thus, the role of deputy commissioners was a mix of bureaucratic authority and personal power, both of which rested on the racial division of the colonial state. Through this combination of autocratic highhandedness and administrative responsibility, deputy commissioners were effectively bureaucratic despots who looked down on the activities of their Burmese and Indian subordinates, usually with disinterest and occasionally with disdain. However, to maintain this position, they had to be able to mount effective investigations into misconduct. And they could not rely upon chance encounters in the street, as in the case of Abdul Razak. Deputy commissioners had to simultaneously appear removed from the everyday realities of the malfunctioning colonial bureaucracy, and yet remain amenable to accusations of misconduct coming from the colonised population. It was in resolving these contradictory demands that information gathering, and, in particular, receiving petitions, was important: they enabled deputy commissioners to discipline subordinate officials without compromising the social distance deemed necessary to preserve their racial prestige.

Producing and gathering information was crucial to colonial governmentality across British India.[41] The deputy commissioners' techniques of collecting information on their subordinates were considerably more mundane and piecemeal than the large-scale operations of cadastral mapping and census taking,[42] but shared broad commonalities with colonial policing.[43] A list was compiled, regularly updated, and circulated by deputy commissioners detailing all those who had been dismissed from government service and thereafter banned from future state employment.[44] Alongside this ever-expanding list a range of individuated documentation was amassed. From 1890, subordinate officials from clerks to township officers were required to provide lists of family members by marriage and by blood to the deputy commissioner of their district.[45] Additionally, in 1904, deputy commissioners were instructed to maintain confidential rolls on their subordinate township officers on which praise and rewards, as well as chastisements, were to be chronologically recorded.[46] This reinforced an order from 1889, which stated that confidential registers were also supposed to have been kept on *myo-oks*, village headmen, and even clerks.[47] Subordinate officials undoubtedly felt the weight of this surreptitious documenting of their actions. Even the well-respected colonial official and scholar Taw Sein Ko felt compelled to comment in 1909 that, 'The liability to be reported on confidentially, at least once a year, and the absence of any right to refute charges made behind ones back, have hitherto weighed as a heavy incubus on all members of the official hierarchy.'[48]

Alongside the dismissal list, the family lists, and confidential reports, from 1891 were official diaries. These were supposed to have been maintained by middle-ranking subordinate officials, such as *myo-oks*, and periodically passed on to their deputy commissioner, who in turn passed on their own diaries to their commissioners. However, one assumes because of the quantity of material produced, the reception of diaries was made discretionary in 1908.[49] As well as this information gathered specifically for monitoring subordinate officials, the paper work which subordinate officials produced in the normal course of their working days was available to deputy commissioners during their misconduct investigations. Like much colonial data, this information could be misleading.[50] These written records were occasionally forged, fabricated, and falsified by officials. For instance, in 1904, a police head constable had been found to have deliberately fabricated his diaries and notebooks in an attempt to frame a township officer for corruption.[51]

This concentration of what, following Pierre Bourdieu, might be called 'informational capital' in the hands of deputy commissioners was of more disciplinary use once misconduct investigations had been initiated.[52] As in the investigation of Pakiri, the extant documentation could be retrospectively studied for evidence of malpractices. However, this archive of mundane information was less useful for bringing suspicious cases worthy of investigation to the attentions of deputy commissioners. There was perhaps too much information to constantly monitor. As a result, misconduct investigations often emerged from the personal whims and suspicions of deputy commissioners. Petitions making accusations of corruption often stimulated these suspicions. Not that they were unambiguous sources of information, as deputy commissioners were themselves aware.

Misconduct accusations were often treated with scepticism. For example, in 1898, two petitions were received complaining that an inspector of the police, Maung Tun Win, took bribes and associated himself with people of bad character. Both were written in the same handwriting but purported to be from different authors. The first petition was ostensively from a local *thugyi* who, when questioned, denied writing it.[53] Even when petitions were from their purported authors, they were ambiguous because they contained potentially useful information on misconduct but carried with them the risk that they were deliberate attempts to misinform and deceive deputy commissioners. In 1903, a petition was received against Maung Po Kyu, a *myo-ok* from Lemyethna Township in the Henzada district, alleging that he had been avoiding income tax and ignoring crimes in the township. But the petition was immediately looked upon with suspicion since the author was, according to the Deputy Commissioner, 'a man of indifferent character' who was 'acting out of ill-feeling'.[54]

Nevertheless, the allegations made in petitions usually provided the doubt that inspired misconduct investigations. In this way, petitions were not only reflections of hierarchies of authority, but they were also constitutive of them.[55] They enabled the disciplinary role of the deputy commissioner without compromising their social distance. Of course, at the same time, petitions were also useful for the petitioners themselves, providing the opportunity to inform on subordinate officials. But while some petitions may have been the earnest appeals for redress against malfeasant local officials, others were motivated by a more complex intersection of interests. When the quotidian micro-politics behind these petitions is studied in detail, the ambivalent utility of anti-corruption accusations becomes apparent.

The plot within the plot

During the month of April 1900, in the Myaungmya District, the local Deputy Commissioner received three petitions concerning individuals in Wakema Township, a township less than 100 miles north of Bogale where Pakiri had been stationed. The author of one of the petitions was Maung Ka Gyi, a labourer from the Kyetsha village. His petition alleged that a forest ranger called Maung Mo, a forest guard called Maung Pyo, and an influential timber trader called Maung Pe had conspired to allow individuals to cut cane without licences.[56] The three accused were brothers and had previously had similar complaints made against them.

The other two petitions concerned the *myo-ok* of Wakema Township, Maung Tun. One petitioner was Maung Tu Nyein, a timber trader also from the village of Kyetsha. His petition listed many incidents of corruption and abuses of power committed by Maung Tun. Shwe Bo, a small-time timber trader, sent the third and final petition. His petition alleged that Maung Tun had attempted to force him to give false evidence in a criminal case.[57] Ostensibly, all three petitions were attempting to achieve similar ends. They were all informing the Deputy Commissioner of misconduct among the subordinate officials under his supervision, with the intention of having the subordinate official responsible punished. Beneath the surface, however, these three petitions were part of a local intrigue.

The petitioners and the accused were all entangled in colonial policies attempting to manage forestry, policies that favoured commercial British timber concerns against indigenous Burmese uses of the forests. These regulations fostered a black market in illegally cut timber and cane.[58] Two of the petitioners, Maung Tu Nyein and Shwe Bo, were timber traders. The petition of Maung Ka Gyi, himself a labourer employed in the timber trade, made allegations against Maung Pe, an influential timber trader in the township. Maung Pe's brothers, Maung Mo and Maung Pyo, were both employed in the forestry department. And, as part of his duties as a *myo-ok*, Maung Tun was responsible for administering justice in forestry cases. The rapid deforestation of the delta[59] as well as the bureaucratic limits on cutting cane and the resulting shadow economy provide the context for the allegations made in the petitions, as well as the intrigues that lay behind them. This was another example of how colonial legal regulations shaped illegality in Burma.[60]

These petitions were appeals to abstract legalistic authority and were not appeals to an indigenous, pre-colonial, or 'traditional' moral economy of fairness and reciprocity.[61] As such, the petitioners referred to specific breaches of bureaucratic conduct with colonial discipline in mind. This was clear in the petition concerning the *myo-ok* Maung Tun written by Maung Tu Nyein, the timber trader from Kyetsha village. His petition was written in the format that was thought best to solicit the support of the Deputy Commissioner. In its most banal manifestation, his attempt to solicit the Deputy Commissioner involved writing in a submissive, pleading tone, opening the petition with, 'The humble petition of Maung Tu Nyein ... respectfully sheweth' and closing with, 'Wherefore Petitioner prays that an enquiry may be held into the various complaints set out. And your Petitioner will ever pray.'[62] This tone was a common feature of petitions concerning misconduct. It indicates the existence of a particular literary style in petition writing that simultaneously recognised the recipient as both bureaucratic and despotic, just as Laura Bear has discovered in petitions written by workers on the Indian railway written during the 1920s and 1930s.[63]

However, the petitioner Maung Tu Nyein did more than fawn. In his petition, he detailed three specific incidences of misconduct, supplemented by a list of witnesses to support each case. All three cases were intended to substantiate his central claim that *myo-ok* Maung Tun was abusing his power. In the first of the three incidences that he listed, he claimed that Maung Tun helped a friend by bringing a charge of using an unlicensed fishing net against his enemy, Po Maung. According to Maung Tu Nyein, the result was that, 'Po Maung called witnesses in his defence but they were frightened by the *Myook* who threatened them and the *Myook* sentenced Po Maung to 2 months' R.I. [Rigorous Imprisonment].'[64] Maung Tu Nyein then followed this description with a list of six witnesses who could support his account of the events.

To further support his case against Maung Tun, Maung Tu Nyein also narrated the almost identical legal case of Maung Po Thaung Gale, who was similarly charged with the illegal use of a fishing-net. Here, it was alleged that Maung Tun set bail at the huge amount of Rs. 200 (roughly the equivalent of 50 kilograms of rice and Rs. 25 higher than the monthly wage of an inspector in the civil police),[65] even though ultimately Maung Po Thaung Gale was fined only Rs. 10. Maung Tu Nyein filled in the blanks for the Deputy Commissioner, writing, 'Po Maung's and Maung Po Thaung's [Gale] case were identical yet one gets fined

Rs 10/- presumeably [sic] owing to the bribe and the other gets 2 months R.I.'[66] On top of the accusation of abusing his office to aid a friend in his quarrel, Maung Tun was now additionally accused by Maung Tu Nyein of soliciting and accepting bribes. This case Maung Tu Nyein supported with a list of 10 further witnesses. In both these accusations, Maung Tu Nyein was appealing to the Deputy Commissioner's duties as a supervisor of subordinate officials and the ultimate enforcer of colonial policies in the district. The petition recognised the position of deputy commissioner as a despotic and bureaucratic arbiter of justice.

Maung Tu Nyein's third accusation called attention to a case where Maung Tun had set bail for the non-bailable crime of grievous hurt with a weapon. According to the petitioner, the effect was that the complainant was scared off pursuing the case any further. Through detailing these three specific incidences of misconduct, Maung Tu Nyein was depicting Maung Tun as thoroughly corrupt while simultaneously signposting avenues for the Deputy Commissioner to investigate. To this end, his petition was successful. The Deputy Commissioner investigated the cases highlighted in Maung Tu Nyein's petition and found them to have been dealt with by Maung Tun in a suspicious manner. He endeavoured to visit Kyetsha as soon possible 'and examine the witnesses named by Mg Tu Nyein in connexion with the three cases above mentioned.'[67]

It seems as though the trader Maung Tu Nyein's petition was successful. An investigation was initiated into Maung Tun that contributed to his eventual removal from the position of *myo-ok*. Superficially then it would seem that the abused and relatively powerless villagers of Kyetsha, purportedly represented in Maung Tu Nyein's petition, were able to triumph over a corrupt and tyrannical state employee by appealing to a European official for redress. The use and value attached to petitions in informing officials about misconduct under this superficial interpretation seems similar to other colonial situations, such as the use of petitions by the weaving community in early nineteenth-century colonial Andhra. In that case, one scholar has argued that 'both the weaving community and the state accorded importance to the petition as a mechanism for redressing grievances, and, in fact, it progressively became the dominant mode of expressing grievances.'[68] However, when Maung Tu Nyein's petition is examined alongside the other two petitions, as well as the Deputy Commissioner's subsequent report and *myo-ok* Maung Tun's explanation, it becomes apparent that rather than the petition simply being an implement for the articulation and redress of legitimate grievances, it is better understood as a weapon in the armory of feuding local powerbrokers.

In introducing his report into the misconduct allegations made against the influential timber trader Maung Pe (along with his brothers in the forestry department) and *myo-ok* Maung Tun, the Deputy Commissioner wrote that, 'in order that the matter may be properly understood it is necessary that mention should be made of certain matters, of which there is no proof, but of which there can be little doubt.'[69] This comment captures the world of informal information consisting of hearsay, rumour, and common knowledge, most of which was unsubstantiated, that the petitions concerning misconduct contributed to. The three petitions considered here were intended to help the Deputy Commissioner to bridge this gap between suspicion and hard evidence.

Regarding the timber trader Maung Pe, who along with his brothers in the forestry department was accused of allowing people to illegally cut cane in the petition of the labourer Maung Ka Gyi, the Deputy Commissioner already possessed a litany of illicit acts in which he was implicated. He vented in his report that, 'He [Maung Pe] is mired up in very nearly every intrigue in Wakema.'[70] Just over a year before Maung Ka Gyi's petition was received, Maung Pe and his brothers, Maung Mo and Maung Pyo, had been criminally charged with extorting a bribe of Rs. 150 on behalf of the *myo-ok* who preceded Maung Tun in Wakema. This charge had received the full support of the Deputy Commissioner. However, Maung Pe argued for a change of court and succeeded in delaying the case for a year. When the trial was eventually held, the prosecution's case collapsed, the charges against Maung Pe and his brothers were dismissed, and they were acquitted. But the suspicion around Maung Pe did not end with this failed prosecution.

Just months before the arrival of Maung Ka Gyi's petition, another criminal case had been brought against Maung Pe. The complainant in this case alleged that Maung Pe had taken a bribe from him in order to obtain a grant of land. After taking the bribe, Maung Pe produced a forged order granting the complainant land. This forged order was unsuccessful. For the second time in roughly a year, the Deputy Commissioner sanctioned the prosecution of Maung Pe. For the second time, it again ended in a suspicious acquittal. This time the court session was a farce. The complainant did not turn up and the prosecution's witnesses proved unable even to identify Maung Pe in the courtroom, despite him being, according to the Deputy Commissioner, 'the best known man in Wakema'.[71] It later transpired that the complainant had failed to make it to court through no fault of his own. He had been attacked by three assailants and forced onto a steamship and sent down the Irrawaddy

River. This assault may explain why the witnesses were unable to identify Maung Pe, the very absence of the complainant in the courtroom may have been in itself a vivid and threatening message. The Deputy Commissioner subsequently sent this case of assault on for further investigation, resulting in a third trial against Maung Pe. Unfortunately, I have been unable to find the outcome of this criminal case.

The three petitions were inextricably linked to both this ongoing legal case, as well as an underlying personal feud between Maung Pe and Maung Tun. Maung Pe's defence advocate made many applications to the court, suggesting that the series of criminal cases against him were entirely the concoction of *myo-ok* Maung Tun. Although the Deputy Commissioner dismissed this suggestion, he did acknowledge the importance of Maung Pe and Maung Tun's quarrel. He wrote that, 'They were bitter enemies for some time, it is said because Mg Tun suspected Mg Pe of being unduly familiar with his lesser wife.'[72] Although this explanation conformed to colonial gender stereotypes about over-powerful, meddling women, as we shall see in Chapter 4, it does suggest that the dispute between them was perhaps more about social status than simply monetary gain.

Although the Deputy Commissioner did not believe that the criminal charges against Maung Pe were purely the invention of Maung Tun, he did believe that the labourer Maung Ka Gyi's petition was sent with his collusion. He commented that, 'There can be no doubt that Mg Ka Gyi is one of Mg Tun's creatures.'[73] The Deputy Commissioner analysed the petition looking for Maung Ka Gyi's possible motivations. The petition did not suggest that either Maung Pe or his brothers had caused any harm to Maung Ka Gyi, and the Deputy Commissioner doubted he had made the allegations 'in order to save the Government from loss of revenue.'[74] On the basis of this logic, the Deputy Commissioner suspected that the real purpose of the petition was for *myo-ok* Maung Tun to further damage the reputation of his enemy Maung Pe, during the on-going assault trial. Already a more complex picture of how petitions were used has emerged from this case, one in which state employees solicited non-state actors to write petitions making allegations against their powerful enemies.

The petitions that the Deputy Commissioner received against Maung Tun, although given more credence than labourer Maung Ka Gyi's petition, were also intertwined with this local feud. The petition of timber trader Maung Tu Nyein, discussed at the start of this section, was successful in encouraging the Deputy Commissioner to visit Maung Tu Nyein's village of Kyetsha and question the witnesses that he had suggested. However, Maung Tu Nyein also produced a longer supplementary list of witnesses who could testify to Maung Tun frightening villagers with threats to bring false cases against them. This list was dismissed by the Deputy Commissioner with the argument that, 'the examination of his supplementary witnesses would in all probability lead to nothing. This list is headed by Maung Pe and the evidence in any case in which he is mired up is tainted.'[75] Maung Tu Nyein's largely successful petition was thus also compromised in the eyes of the Deputy Commissioner by the involvement of Maung Pe. Both petitioners had their own hidden motives and allegiances, but portrayed themselves as selflessly acting in the government's interest. Conversely, for the Deputy Commissioner, the petitioners' very claims to be looking out for the government's interest were a sure sign of suspicious motives.

The Deputy Commissioner already possessed evidence enough to support a criminal case against Maung Pe for assault, but against Maung Tun he had only unsubstantiated suspicions. It was here that the petitions against Maung Tun were useful to him. They directed him to specific acts and sources of evidence that could be used to aid any investigation into Maung Tun's conduct. In this regard, the second petition against Maung Tun sent by a small-time timber trader Shwe Bo was particularly useful. Shwe Bo alleged that his troubles with *myo-ok* Maung Tun began when one of Maung Tun's followers attempted to persuade him to give evidence in court against the notorious trader Maung Pe. Shwe Bo's petition was explicitly connected to the criminal charges against Maung Pe. His allegation was itself difficult to substantiate, but the subsequent events that were highlighted in Shwe Bo's petition left a trail of paperwork that the Deputy Commissioner was able to retrace. In his own words, 'As regards the attempt to suborn Mg Shwe Bo there is no evidence. That the other matters stated in his petition are true there can be no doubt.'[76] Shwe Bo's petition highlighted specific acts of misconduct committed by Maung Tun and provided an explanatory narrative for them.

Shwe Bo claimed to have refused the advances of Maung Tun to give, presumably false, evidence against Maung Pe. Following this, Maung Tun issued an order to Shwe Bo's village headman informing him that he had the authority to detain individuals charged with forest offences for up to a month if it was believed that they were likely to abscond. He concurrently charged Shwe Bo with cutting excess cane. The headman then seized Shwe Bo's excess cane, under the supervision of the labourer and petitioner Maung Ka Gyi, Maung Tun's aforementioned 'creature'. However, since the headman Maung Aung Gyi did not believe that Shwe Bo was likely to abscond, he did not arrest him.

Since Shwe Bo had not been arrested, Maung Ka Gyi made a written complaint about Shwe Bo to *myo-ok* Maung Tun. On this basis, a warrant was issued for Shwe Bo's arrest, with bail set at Rs. 200 and similar amounts required from two additional sureties. Shwe Bo was then arrested but managed to find bail and individuals who would stand surety for him, and was released. However, when he arrived at the court for his hearing, Maung Tun refused to hear the case demanding instead that Shwe Bo produce fresh sureties specifically from Wakema Town. When Shwe Bo again managed to find sureties, Maung Tun allegedly had him arrested and confined in the lock-up for three hours. After Shwe Bo had been released from his confinement and had returned home, Maung Tun heard the case. Shwe Bo, now being absent, was therefore forced to forfeit his bail and his sureties' bonds. In total, Shwe Bo and his sureties paid the huge sum of Rs. 600 before the case had even reached the court, the equivalent of the annual wage of a first class sergeant in the civil police.[77] When the case finally reached the local Subdivisional Magistrate, Shwe Bo was found guilty of cutting excess cane and was sentenced to a fine of just Rs five! All because, Shwe Bo alleged, he refused to testify against the powerful but suspect fellow timber trader Maung Pe.

The Deputy Commissioner largely accepted Shwe Bo's narration of the events. The credibility of his petition was enhanced because the petition of Maung Tu Nyein, the timber trader from Kyetsha, corroborated some of the allegations against the *myo-ok*. Both petitioners had detailed examples of Maung Tun demanding exceptionally high sums in bail for relatively minor infringements of the law after the accused had appeared in court, a practice that the Deputy Commissioner found in his investigation to have been common to cases overseen by Maung Tun. The Deputy Commissioner believed that Maung Tun used this strategy of setting high bail as a tool to intimidate.[78] In the examples given by Maung Tu Nyein, the predominant interpretation of events was that bail had been set in order to extort a bribe from the accused. In Shwe Bo's petition, the purpose behind setting bail was less clearly defined. Maung Tun may have been attempting to coerce Shwe Bo into giving evidence against Maung Pe, or alternatively been punishing him for refusing to give evidence; neither possible interpretation painted *myo-ok* Maung Tun in a particularly good light.

Momentarily setting aside the explanations suggested in the petitions, the amounts that Maung Tun was setting for bail were unquestionably high. Out of all the 40,539 cases in which individuals were punished by fines throughout the year 1900, 99.5% were to the amount of

Rs. 100 or less. Within that percentage, 75.9% were for fines of Rs. ten or less. Bearing in mind that Shwe Bo and his sureties lost Rs. 600, only 18 criminal cases across colonial Burma during 1900 were settled with fines of more than Rs. 500.[79] The sums demanded in bail by Maung Tun were thus considerable and were almost certain to have been much higher if forfeited than the ultimate fine. However, demanding high bail in and of itself was not sufficient evidence to punish Maung Tun, and it was here that the petitions were additionally useful to the Deputy Commissioner as they succeeded in ascribing motives to Maung Tun's actions and placed them into an explanatory framework.

In the procedure for official misconduct charges, the accused subordinate officials had the opportunity to produce a written explanation of the acts of which they were accused.[80] Maung Tun's written explanation was his opportunity to place on record his own narrative on the events that had taken place and also to cast aspersions and suspicion onto those who had petitioned against him. In doing so, he represented both the timber trading petitioners Shwe Bo and Maung Tu Nyein as collaborators with his enemy Maung Pe and his brothers in the forestry department. They were depicted as part of an illegal forestry ring. Maung Tun simultaneously recast his apparent 'creature' Maung Ka Gyi as an informer and whistle-blower.[81] His explanatory narrative was as compelling and plausible as those produced by Shwe Bo, Maung Tu Nyein, and the Deputy Commissioner. To support this description of events, Maung Tun produced a list of three witnesses for the deputy commissioner's perusal.

This broader context of Maung Pe's plotting and of widespread illegal forestry underpinned Maung Tun's explanations of his behaviour and gave them coherence. According to Maung Tun, the surrounding evidence of large-scale illegal cutting and trading of cane made the case against Shwe Bo acutely important and serious.[82] Thus, Shwe Bo's connection with the notorious Maung Pe accounted for why he set the bail so high. He claimed that Shwe Bo repeatedly failed to turn up for his hearing and that this was why fresh sureties had to be called. He claimed, in complete contradiction to Shwe Bo's petition, that he did not lock up Shwe Bo and that Shwe Bo did not subsequently fail to arrive at the court under a misapprehension but did so knowingly. Maung Tun's explanations effectively demonstrated that the paper trail of evidence against him could be interpreted completely differently under a new narrative.

Whether Maung Tun's explanation was successful in allaying the suspicions of the deputy commissioner is unclear but unlikely. Regardless of its success, the *myo-ok*'s narrative of events directly targeted the petitions and attempted to establish the 'real' motives of their writers. Specifically, he hoped to weaken the petitions against him from the traders Maung Tu Nyein and Shwe Bo and strengthen the petition against Maung Pe from the labourer Maung Ka Gyi. He undermined Maung Tu Nyein's petition by depicting him as a powerful agent in an illegal forestry racket, making the claim that in cahoots with Maung Pe and his brothers, he had illegally cut 50,000 canes. Shwe Bo was similarly depicted as being in league with Maung Pe and the others who were against Maung Tun because of his strenuous efforts in protecting government forestry revenue. Simultaneously, he imbued Maung Ka Gyi with motives for writing his petition. He did this by representing him as a disgruntled former employee of Maung Tu Nyein turned whistle-blower and informant.

The petitions formed the central battleground for the misconduct procedures. They directed the Deputy Commissioner to evidence and, furthermore, they provided narratives for interpreting it. But the deeper motives behind the writing of the petitions were obscure. The information that the petitions contained emerged out of the local feud between Maung Tun and Maung Pe that was itself never fully brought out of the shadows. Both sides of the feud made accusations of misconduct to discredit the other, but preserving bureaucratic conduct was not the primary motive behind the petitions.

Over 100 years on, it is impossible to unpick this intrigue and unveil the reality of events in the Wakema District. Unfortunately, the outcomes of the legal case against Maung Pe and the misconduct charges against Maung Tun have not survived, or at least I have been unable to locate them. However, Maung Tun does reappear many times in the misconduct files although no longer employed as a *myo-ok*. Following this scandal, he was removed from his position (but not dismissed). His subsequent behaviour reveals even more about the instrumental use of petitions in misconduct cases in the Irrawaddy Delta.

In 1901 and 1902, many petitions were received regarding the conduct of a police inspector serving in Dedaye, Maung Pyaw, who at this time was employed on the investigation into Pakiri. One petition was received from the nearby village of Kumpaline claiming that Inspector Maung Pyaw had extorted payments from individuals with false cases and would not investigate cases unless he had received a bribe. The petitioner also alleged that Maung Pyaw had attempted to extort money from him by claiming that he was responsible for a rape in the village, and when he refused to pay, Maung Pyaw expressed his intention to prosecute the petitioner 'in connection with Pakiri'.[83] However, all was not as it appeared with the petition. The purported author was one Maung Ku, but he later claimed not to have written it: 'my age is over sixty and therefore it is not likely that I would send a libellous letter to the commissioner. I have never heard about any bribes being taken by the Inspector or anyone else. I have not heard of anything detrmiental[sic] to the Inspector.'[84] Instead of Maung Ku, it was suspected that the petition was actually sent by the now former *myo-ok* Maung Tun, who bore a grudge against both Maung Ku, who had testified against the character of Maung Tun's witnesses during a case against him, and Maung Pyaw, who had been involved as an inspector in a case against him.

Less than a year later, yet more petitions were received against Maung Pyaw alleging again that he accepted bribes and made false charges, and even that he had covered up a murder.[85] These petitions were sent anonymously but the Commissioner of the Irrawaddy Division again suspected the hand of Maung Tun.[86] Even though Maung Tun had been removed from his position of authority, he still attempted to influence high-ranking British officials in matters of discipline and his chosen tool for this was the petition. At the same time, it seems that Maung Tun did not accept his removal from office. In 1903, he was still petitioning to have his case reconsidered.[87]

It was not only Maung Tun who continued to be associated with petitions regarding misconduct; although Maung Pe does not reappear in the misconduct files, both of his brothers Maung Pyo and Maung Mo do. Interestingly, their careers following their clash with Maung Tun met with starkly contrasting fortunes. Maung Pyo was dismissed from his position in October 1902 for fraudulently acquiring land by abusing his powers as a forest ranger.[88] Maung Mo similarly became the focus of allegations of misconduct but, unlike his brother, he was able to weather the storm. Three anonymous petitions were received about his conduct, along with one that purported to be from a Karen timber trader. The response from his superior officer, the Deputy Conservator of Forests, consisted of a staunch defence of Maung Mo. It is worth quoting at length:

> Ranger Maung Mo no doubt has great influence ... but has done work, and detected and brought to justice many illegal offences, consequently he had enemies, as is clearly proved by the attached petition.
>
> I would ask you to be good enough to oblige me by giving me your opinion as to what is the best thing to be done with anonymous

petitions? I can't help thinking that in the past they must have been rather encouraged as they appear to be freely distributed, they are a source of unnecessary worry and work.[89]

The suggestion of the Deputy Conservator of Forests was that the anonymous petitions should be given to Maung Mo to deal with, as he may be able to work out the identities of the authors.

As this episode shows, petitions sent to British officers did not always succeed in stimulating suspicion against an accused subordinate official. They would often turn a blind eye towards misconduct accusations and support the authority of the subordinate official. Although the Deputy Commissioner of Myaungmya actively engaged with the petitions he received, finding them useful in investigating and forming official misconduct charges against Maung Tun, the Deputy Conservator of Forests found petitions to be frustrating and time-consuming. Both British officials, however, believed that the petitions they received were written according to malicious motives.

As the examples concerning Maung Tun and Maung Pe amply demonstrate, petitions concerning misconduct were complex and deeply ambivalent sources of information for high-ranking British officials. They directed the Deputy Commissioner of Myaungmya to specific instances of Maung Tun's suspected misconduct and gave meaning to his traceable, suspicious acts. The Deputy Commissioner opened his confidential report on Maung Tun by referring to 'matters, of which there is no proof, but of which there can be little doubt.' The petitions received by him bridged this gap between suspicion and proof, between hearsay and evidence. In this way, petitions concerning misconduct formed an important part of the colonial information order, if we expand Christopher Bayly's original meaning to include more banal exchanges of information.[90] Petitions provided a link between high-ranking British officials and the subject population. However, as with Maung Ka Gyi's petition and the later petitions against Maung Mo, it is apparent that British officials could just as easily dismiss petitions without too much consideration.

But petitions were also troublesome texts for high-ranking British officials. As the Deputy Commissioner of Myaungmya discovered, the petitioners' motivations in making misconduct accusations could be duplicitous and were mired in the intrigues and quarrels of powerful local figures. In the example above, the petitioners Maung Tu Nyein, Shwe Bo, and Maung Ka Gyi were not writing their petitions for their own benefit but on behalf of the influential local agents Maung Tun and

Maung Pe. Occasionally, as in the petitions that were received against Inspector Maung Pyaw, the actual petitioners were not who they purported to be. This was a common problem for deputy commissioners.

Through this ambiguous but mutual utility of petitions, the racial division of the colonial state was enacted in everyday life. Petitions appealed to the bureaucratic disciplinary authority invested in white officials, and in so doing enabled them to exercise their authority. Without the feud between the timber trader Maung Pe and the *myo-ok* Maung Tun producing the petitions from their followers, the Deputy Commissioner would not have been able to punish Maung Tun. His role as an agent of bureaucratic discipline would not have been realisable. Petitions made European authority over their largely Indian and Burmese subordinates possible, even when they may have been inadvertently punishing innocent officials because of misleading information.

'Native' quarrels and white rule

On 27 April 1901, the *Times of Burma* published an article titled 'Shameless Depravity'. The author was attempting to send a warning to high-ranking officialdom across British Burma:

> These rumours would wake up all the [British] officials in Burma if they knew their full nature and the extent to which the people believe them. In all cases the rumours are not necessarily alike ... but on two things they apparently possess in common, the first being that they emanate from touts, or agents, or creatures of the bribe-takers and black-mailers, and secondly they suggest that the ill-gotten gain plunder goes into some other person's pocket, or to support somebodyelse's harem, or to pander to another one's vices ....[91]

In spite of deputy commissioners' attempts to distance themselves from the corruption of their subordinate officials, the author warned, they were still tainted by it. Revealingly, the author did not appeal to notions of good government in order to 'wake up' the British officials, but to their vanity. Behind their backs they were being mocked. Bribes were being extorted in their names. The author was attempting to embarrass officials into combating misconduct more vigorously by attacking their racial prestige, implying that they were widely believed to be engaging in sexual acts across the racial divide. The article spoke to the palpable tensions of maintaining distance between the rulers and the ruled.[92]

The article played upon colonial concerns about the activities of the non-official actors attached to subordinate officials: the 'touts', 'agents', 'creatures', those whom British officials most commonly called 'followers'.[93] The image of the everyday state evoked by the author was a messy one. Corruption tainted the higher echelons while hangers-on, with no official duties, acted as unscrupulous middle figures for subordinate officials. It was a picture that fits uncomfortably in the enduring sharp, homogenising binary of colonial historiography between the colonial state and the colonised society.[94] Recent works re-conceptualising indigenous officials as intermediaries, although an improvement, do not fit any better with this depiction of pervasive bureaucratic disorder.[95] There were not only intermediaries but there were also intermediaries for the intermediaries. For the author of the article, hierarchical racial authority and the separation of state from society, key features of the colonial bureaucratic order, were both under threat. Through the circulation of malicious rumours associated with this bureaucratic disorder, it was feared that the image of British rule, in general, was in danger of being tainted.

This article was not alone in arguing that corruption was damaging the prestige of British rule.[96] Yet, in spite of constant pressure on government from the British colonial press about the extent of corruption and bribery, no steps were taken to rigorously police subordinate officials. No comprehensive investigations were held into corruption until after Burma was separated from British India and given substantial scope for self-government in 1937.[97] It was not a topic broached in correspondence between Lieutenant Governors and the government of India.[98] No special anti-corruption legislation was passed. As I noted in Chapter 1, deputy commissioners relied instead on local standing orders, devised incrementally during the late nineteenth century, and the Indian penal code to punish misconduct. Combating corruption was narrowly interpreted as a matter of European supervision. As a result, in order to seek redress for misconduct, colonised subjects had to appeal directly to deputy commissioners and, by extension, to the white hierarchical oligarchy at the top of the administration.

There was much ambivalence in these appeals. The petitions were often disingenuous and duplicitous, and accusations and counter-accusations were made in order for petitioners to discredit their enemies. But even though deputy commissioners were often being manipulated through petitions, their authority was still recognised. They were appealed to as disciplinary agents above their Indian and Burmese subordinate officials. Moreover, in practice, the petitions provided deputy commissioners with information, and misinformation, that enabled them to discipline their subordinate officials. In this sense, accusations of misconduct enabled the bureaucratic racial division of the colonial state to be performatively enacted in everyday life, embodied in the figure of the deputy commissioner.

Foucault has argued that disciplinary power discursively produces delinquent groups who seem immune to reform. The stubborn presence of these delinquents then serves to justify the societal need for carceral institutions.[99] The same self-perpetuating logic was at play in colonial rhetoric. The ubiquitous British claims to be engaged in a civilising mission in Burma were not in tension with the equally common references to the innate, inherited flaws of Burmese societies. Rather, they were two sides to the same justificatory rhetorical device. Fielding-Hall depicted British rule as a 'school' for the 'young race' of Burmans, but in truth they could never hope to graduate.[100] Colonialism was always an unfinished project.[101] When it came to combating corruption, the problem was characterised as one of ill-disciplined indigenous state employees, and the solution was greater supervision by supposedly incorruptible Europeans. The disciplinary power of British officials was at once justified by and dependent upon the presence of corrupt subordinate officials. This may explain why, in this period before the rise of Burmese nationalism and an anti-colonial popular press,[102] British anti-corruption strategies remained so casual and piecemeal: by acquiescing with low-level malfeasance deputy commissioners could stand apart from '"native" quarrels' and maintain the façade of racial superiority.

4
The Male State

'Er petticoat was yaller an' 'er little cap was green,
An' 'er name was Supi-yaw-lat—jes' the same as
Theebaw's Queen,
An' I seed her first a-smokin' of a whackin' white
cheroot,
An' a-wastin' Christian kisses on an 'earthen idol's foot
Rudyard Kipling, Mandalay (1890)

Gendered subjects, gendered state

It does not take a deep psychoanalytic reading of Kipling's *Mandalay* to reveal the slippage in his words between the desires of the British soldier and the broader drives of imperialism. There is a mutual gendering at work in the poem through which British imperial power is represented as masculine and colonised Burmese society as feminine.[1] 'Supi-yaw-lat' was not only the soldier's former Burmese lover, but she represented all of the exotic attractions of the East, inviting his kisses, and drawing him back to Mandalay with its 'sunshine', 'palm trees', and 'spicy garlic smells'.[2] Like Kipling, British officials also depicted Burmese society as feminine. For them, Burman men had been emasculated by the domestic dominance of Burman women.[3] According to their writings, Burma needed male conquest in the form of British rule. This colonial literary device also had a material manifestation.[4] The colonial state was performatively enacted as male through the everyday practices of subordinate officials as well as through formal bureaucratic rules. This gendering of the state was most apparent in the corruption and misconduct of subordinate officials. In everyday life, the state was manifested as masculine, and women were marginalised from both the formal and informal uses of state power.

However, marginalisation and exclusion were not the only effects of colonialism on women's life in Burma. As Chie Ikeya's recent ground-breaking study of gender and colonial modernity in Burma shows, many Burmese women were able to find a public voice as a result of the advent of colonial rule through education and the press.[5] As her work demonstrates, the emergence of this modern woman, the *khit kala*, was deeply contested and she was an important character for negotiating and discussing modernity in Burma. This chapter does not contradict Ikeya's well-researched and persuasively argued book. Rather, my argument reveals the contrary nature of colonial modernity. The rise of the *khit kala* as a public figure in education, the press, nationalist thought, consumer advertising, and many other spheres occurred at the same time as many Burmese women in the delta were marginalised from the state in their daily life. This everyday perspective reveals the colonial state to have been a menacing entity, a quotidian reality highlighted in misconduct in cases of gendered violence.

There are some vital caveats and warnings that arise from situating this chapter alongside Chie Ikeya's book. She explores the refiguring of gender within Burmese society through a huge range of Burmese language sources. In contrast, the misconduct records that I have worked with provide only a comparatively partial view of women's interactions with the state. More importantly, they are not sources in which women's voices found unmediated expression. This colonial archive was itself gendered; it was the product of masculine state practices.[6] In using this archive, there is a risk that my argument may be misinterpreted. The primary danger is that readers may interpret the chapter as representing women one-dimensionally as passive victims of male aggression. Such a representation would serve to re-inscribe the dichotomy of active-male and passive-female, making women 'spectacles of victimisation' and unwittingly perpetuating the myths that feed gendered violence.[7] On the other hand, attempting to balance this by recovering women's agency through these sources would be an act of historical ventriloquism that risked naturalising colonial gender ideologies inscribed in the archive.[8] In order to avoid such an interpretation, I want to be clear from the outset: I do not mean to suggest that women were always passive victims of male abuses of state power, and I am not attempting to recover women's agency. My aims are more modest and my focus more precise. This chapter explores only how the colonial state was itself gendered as male in everyday life.

Although the full complexity of Burmese women's life in the delta is beyond the scope of this chapter, we can construct how the colonial state may have appeared in women's daily encounters with it. In British officials' writings, in misconduct proceedings, and in subordinate-level corruption, the state was imagined and performed as a male. In fact, masculinity was intrinsic to how the colonial state was enacted in everyday life. As a result, it does not require a stretch of historical credulity to suggest that the state was also experienced as a male.

Women in Burma (and their henpecked husbands)

The last two decades or so has witnessed the growth of gender history in the formerly very distinct fields of imperial and colonial history, as a number of edited collections demonstrate.[9] The proliferation of writing influenced by gender history has drawn attention to many aspects of colonial history that had previously been overlooked. This section builds on just two. Firstly, that colonial rule was conceived of as a masculine enterprise and that colonial subjects were gendered about a ruling masculinity, thus justifying colonial rule. And secondly, that the production of colonial categories of rule such as race and class were mutually constituted along with gender. These insights draw out the centrality of gender to the colonial project: indeed Antoinette Burton in her introduction to an edited collection described ideologies of gender and sexuality as 'foundational' to colonial modernity.[10] However, although recent work emphasises the centrality of gender ideologies to colonial rule, it does not present them simply as another facet of colonial power. Rather, as Anne McClintock has argued, masculine colonial state policies 'while deeply implicated in colonialism, are not reducible to colonialism and cannot be understood without distinct theories of gender power.'[11]

Following in this vein, this section shows the significance of gender ideologies to colonial rule, while acknowledging their broader independence. It examines the textual construction of Burman femininity, which in stark contrast to the depiction of Indian women was interpreted as one of unparalleled independence. This depiction of Burman women was a widespread and prominent feature of writings on Burma in the colonial period and beyond among groups as diverse as imperialists, first-wave feminists, missionaries, and anti-colonial nationalists.[12] In order to emphasise the specificities of colonial uses of this trope, this section focuses narrowly on the published writings of the colonial scholar-officials James George Scott, Herbert Thirkell White, Harold Fielding-Hall, and John Nisbet, all of who wrote in the period between pacification and the Great War.[13] Their writings not only reveal how high-ranking British colonial officials constructed the Burmans as racialised and gendered subjects, but also how they viewed themselves as colonial rulers.

Of course the gendering of colonial subjects was not a process that was specific to British Burma, although it took a unique form there. Historians have explored how under the Raj a variety of Indian subjects were defined according to gendered characteristics. For example, Bengalis were characterised as effeminate, supporting a self-image among the colonial European community of the manly Englishman.[14] In contrast, Pathans in the Northwest Frontier Province, and others such as Sikhs and Gurkhas, were depicted as masculine and warlike in colonial policies of military recruitment, which were based upon a theory of 'martial races' following the Great Rebellion in 1857.[15] In the Princely States, British officials showed great concern about the masculinity and sexual habits of the princes, based upon their perceptions of what constituted palatable and gentlemanly royal conduct.[16] In these examples, as in British Burma, the gendered perceptions of the subject populations informed colonial policy and official state practices. However, unlike the examples above, writings on Burma were not primarily concerned with masculinity and men but with femininity and the position of women.[17]

Chie Ikeya has recently examined the emergence of the notion of the free and independent Burmese woman from the colonial period onwards, arguing that it was based on comparisons with Indian women and upon western notions of freedom rooted in property rights.[18] This is certainly true for the writings of colonial scholar-officials who drew their points of comparison largely from India and Europe, and who dwelt upon the Burman women's business acumen. I would like to add to Ikeya's argument that colonial scholar-officials were also informed by ideas concerning their own masculinity and the masculinity perceived imperative to rule. As we shall see, officials' depictions of women often served to establish their own European masculine virility and fitness to rule in contrast to the 'henpecked husbands' of Burma. It is perhaps significant to note in passing that these gendered characterisations were produced at a time when masculinity was being called into question in the metropole and in the colony. Feminist movements in Britain were becoming increasingly vocal and active in calling for legislation to control male sexuality,[19] and in Burma, high-ranking British officials' illicit relationships with Burmese women, which were common, were being attacked in the highest echelons of the Raj.[20]

Burman women were presented as free through their independence in three main spheres: their right to own property, their prominent position in petty trade, and their agency in courting. In all these areas, the colonial officials compared them with Indian women, and even with Western women, always with Burman women being judged to have the superlative degree of freedom. In regards to marriage, Scott wrote that 'they enjoy a much freer and happier position than in any other Eastern country, and in some respects are better off than women in England.'[21] To support this, he informed his readers that the Burman woman maintained all the property that she had entering into a marriage throughout its duration and that if she was to divorce she could take her original property plus anything more that she had earned or inherited since, adding: 'Thus a married Burmese woman is much more independent than any European even in the most advanced states.'[22] John Nisbet, the onetime conservator of forests in Burma, produced an almost identical description of a Burmese marriage.[23]

The independent position of women in the domestic sphere was depicted as being more extensive than just their continued ownership of separate property. The institution of marriage in Burma was described as one of partnerships, where the wife was involved in all decision-making, domestic and public. More often than not, women were described as the dominant partner in a marriage. Scott, Nisbet, and White all provided little anecdotes in which an official's wife discharged his duties on his behalf.

> Often a wife takes great interest in her husband's official or private work. If one has business with a police-sergeant or *Thugyi*, and finds him absent, one does not seek a subordinate, but discusses and settles the matter with the *Sazin-Gadaw* [wife of the police-sergeant] or the *Thugyi-Gadaw* [wife of the village headman]. It is on record that, prisoners being brought to a police-station in the absence of any of the force, the sergeant's wife put them in the cage, and, herself shouldering a da [knife], did sentry go till relieved. After these instances it need hardly be said that in her own household the Burmese woman is supreme.[24]

This passage from White is paradigmatic. Wives were depicted as either being the equals of men in relationships or, more commonly, the dominant figure in the marriage. Nisbet commented that, 'Under the laws of Manu, power is given to the husband to correct the wife by chastisement, a procedure seldom adopted. Indeed, it is very often the other way, the hen-pecked husband being, as Burmese ... term the status, "under the slipper" of the exacting wife.'[25] In a similar fashion,

Scott pointed out that, 'The wife sits by, no matter what public business is being transacted, and very often puts in her own opinion as a matter of course; in fact, she is virtual master of the house, and henpecked husbands are not by any means uncommon.'[26]

The prevalence of these female-dominated homes, according to the officials, was often accounted for by women's superior business acumen. This reasoning was perhaps most prominent in Nisbet's writings. He wrote that although girls were not educated at monasteries like their brothers, they were able to keep a stall at markets from the age of around 17 and that 'the experience acquired sharpens her naturally keen mercantile instincts and business capacity, and makes her mentally a much readier reckoner than her brothers'. According to Nisbet, the result was women's domestic dominance, 'A Burmese girl of nineteen or twenty is consequently much smarter at business than a lad of the same age; and she undoubtedly maintains all through life the advantage thus won. Hence she naturally rules the roost'.[27]

The image of the 'henpecked husband' was prominent in the officials' writings; the lazy and cowed man mirrored the prominent position of the enterprising, even ferocious, women of Burma. In the words of Nisbet, 'No race of men throughout the whole world would take more kindly to absolute idolness and lotus-eating than the Burmese, whose womenfolk are the great workers and taskmasters.'[28] In a later passage, he repeated this assertion. 'While the men are easy-going and fond of idleness the women are energetic and rather inclined to be greedy and grasping in monetary matters.'[29] The strength of Burman women reflected the weakness of the men, and according to the officials, Burman women could be quite forceful. Nisbet wrote that, 'the women are frequently violent in temper; and then they display remarkable command of a copious and forcible language of abuse.'[30] Likewise Scott wrote, 'A more regrettable trait is the forcible character of their language when they are annoyed ... Certain it is that the *dames de la halle* and the Billingsgate fishwives would require all their powers of voice and vituperation to silence a bazaar maiden when she sets her mind to it.'[31] These descriptions contrasted sharply with characterisation of Burman men as docile, unless provoked, or drunk. Indeed, while Scott and Nisbet imply that the strength of Burman women resulted in the weakness of the men, Harold Fielding-Hall made this argument explicitly and vividly.

> At present to everyone who comes to Burma she seems the predominant partner. She attracts by her freedom, her industry, her

independence. After India, she is a very notable appearance. So all men praise her. They take her for the strength of the nation. Yet she is the symptom and a cause of its weakness. The nations who succeed are not the feminine nations, but the masculine. Women's influence is good provided it does not go too far. Yet it has done so here.[32]

For Fielding-Hall, the high position of women in Burma was a sign of its backwardness and an explanation for its colonisation. In this way, it was quite the opposite of writings on India where the degradation of women described by colonisers placed it on a low-rung in the hierarchy of civilisations. As Catherine Hall has argued, the ideal of the companionate marriage of labouring men with dependent and subservient female companions set the standard for judging other societies in the eyes of British colonisers.[33] In Fielding-Hall's writing, and to a lesser degree in Nisbet's and Scott's writing also, the dominant marital position of women in Burma constituted a societal failure,[34] a failure that Fielding-Hall believed should be corrected through colonialism.[35]

Therefore the particular charm that all travellers see in the women of Burma is bound to fade. They have had their day. They have contributed to make the nation what it is, gay, insouciant, feminine .... But it is a man's world, and now that Burma has come out of the nursery it must learn to be a man.[36]

In colonial writings, Burman women's rights of property and their superior business skills made them the dominant partners in marriages and the most industrious gender. However, this did not make them manly women to colonial officials—although their dominance was a sign of the emasculation of Burman men, and the race in general. Indeed, Burman women, despite their relative freedom, retained their 'female charms'. The role of women as petty traders in bazaars across Burma served to highlight to officials not only their domestic influence over their husbands, but also their feminine presence in the public sphere. In the words of Fielding-Hall, 'You met them everywhere. The streets were full of them.'[37] This prominence of women in public was contrasted to India and the practice of Purdah.

The freedom to work in the bazaar and the resulting public presence of women was related by colonial scholar-officials to women's freedom to choose their own partner in courtship. Women's public presence was both feminised and sexualised. Nisbet remarked, 'It is in the bazaar that the European will have by far the best opportunity of forming his opinion of the Burmese girl; and a high opinion it is bound to be.'[38] He went on to give his own favourable opinion. 'She has a grace and freedom of manner entirely devoid of anything like forwardness or "bad form", which cannot fail to charm', although he went on to qualify this high praise, writing 'though her face be not fair or, judged by western standards, possessed of even the slightest claims of beauty.'[39] A note about their vanity immediately followed these comments, followed in turn by four entire pages dedicated to documenting how the women at bazaars applied make-up, and then by a description of courtship rituals. In courtship, he wrote, women had the right to choose their partners, and the bazaar was portrayed as the ideal venue for flirting.[40] Scott too followed his discussion of the business acumen of Burmese women with a lengthy description of courtship.[41] The image of a Burman young woman smoking a cheroot and working at a bazaar stall while simultaneously flirting was ubiquitous. Colonial officials may have seen women as dominant, even overbearing partners, but they were still seen as feminine, vain, and flirtatious.

Of the authors discussed here, only Nisbet addressed the controversial issue of British officials' intimate liaisons with Burmese women. Kenneth Ballhatchet's study of imperial policies towards male sexuality under the Raj details the frequent controversies over British officials in Burma taking Burmese mistresses, a practice that the government of India proved incapable of bringing to a halt.[42] Nisbet aligned himself against government attempts to stop such relationships. I would suggest, tentatively, that his depictions of Burman women's freedom to choose a partner also served to support his belief that the virility of European male officials was supported through sexual relationships with Burmese women. He claimed that the first circular issued by government attempting to curb the practice resulted in two horses at a Rangoon race meeting in 1872 being named the 'Chief Commissioner's Confidential Circular' and 'Physiological Necessity'. 'The latter won, and the threats of the circular were thus smothered in ridicule.'[43] It is worth quoting at length his agreement with the symbolic outcome of the Rangoon race.

> This is not a very savoury topic for discussion. But the great majority of those who may perhaps feel themselves called upon to preach on this subject cannot know what they are talking about unless they have personally experienced the depressing effects of the climate and the dismal, soul deadening solitude of residence in a small out-station, where for weeks and weeks, often months, the young

European ... enjoys no companionship at all with his own fellow countrymen .... Taking into due consideration the several influences of climate, environment, human nature, and the facts of medical science, one can quite understand the position taken with regard to this matter by those—and there *are* many such—who think the lapse from virtue in respect of such connubial relation with a daughter of the land is perhaps the least pernicious of all the vices in its immediate and its ultimate effects on that noblest of temples, the human body which enshrines the soul, the image of God.[44]

This passage demonstrates Nisbet's belief that the 'temporary marriages', as he described them, between British officials and Burmese women were crucial for maintaining British officials' health and sanity, as well as warding off other vices. In novels written by officials who served in Burma, the lack of European female companionship, and subsequent jealousy and competition among officials when a young and available European woman arrived on the scene, often formed the backbone of the plot.[45] The presence of the independent Burman woman was a relief from this solitude, at least in the writings of Nisbet. In a similar vein, Rudyard Kipling's famous poem 'Mandalay' depicts the desire of a young European soldier serving in Burma for the exotic Burman woman.[46] These relationships brought solace to the British official and, Nisbet argued, did not adversely affect the woman. He opened his discussion writing, 'So far as the Burmese girl is concerned, the union is not degrading to her.'[47] And he closed it again reassuring his readers that, 'The relationship thus created is not a degrading one for her; and after its dissolution she frequently marries well, without a taint of immorality besmirching her reputation on account of such previous union.'[48]

Nisbet's plea for the, apparently medical, needs of male officials for female companionship suggests that the depiction of Burman women may have, in part, been a male fantasy supporting their own sense of masculinity. For British colonial officials, Burman women's independence as well as being based on their fiscal competence and their sometimes-fierce tongues, was also highly sexualised. Women's agency was often reduced to making themselves pretty, seducing, and being seduced. According to Scott, after the ear-boring ceremony, which marked a Burman woman's attainment of puberty, 'she will look upon every male as a possible lover.'[49] He also claimed that in Rangoon, a tattoo on a woman indicated that she wanted a European husband.[50] Both Scott's and Nisbet's descriptions of the petting that accompanied courting attempted to titillate the reader, with remarks on the thin bamboo walls of the room and the four watchful hidden eyes of the girl's parents who 'prevent too ardent love-making'.[51] Thus, Burman women were not thought of as masculine by colonial officials but as familiarly feminine and as a result they did not pose a threat to European masculinity. If anything the officials' feminine portrayal of them enhanced European masculinity through the authors' voyeuristic gaze.

It is perhaps for this reason that despite the repeated assertions of Burman women's talents and the common anecdotes regarding their ability to fulfil the role of male subordinate officials, there was no suggestion of employing them in such roles. Indeed, in 1900 the prospect of a female village headman prompted concern from high-ranking British officials who pointed out the exceptionality of a scenario in which it could be acceptable: when there were no other direct male heirs; where she was unmarried and so there was no husband to exercise her rights; and when there was no suitable guardian to take up the position on her behalf.[52] They may have been independent and skilled, but they were still female and feminine according to broader gender ideologies, and therefore deemed inherently unfit for office. This was entirely consistent with the predominantly male state practices and institutions of late Victorian Britain.[53] That the state was a male sphere was axiomatic to the British official mind and, although they may have been henpecked, only men in Burma were granted privileged access to its resources.

The depiction of Burman women in the writings of colonial officials served to feminise the whole race and naturalise the rule of the masculine British. Despite this, the position ascribed to women caused difficulties and concerns for the colonial regime. Women potentially blurred the boundary between the public and private realms idealised by the British administrators.[54] Although they were barred from holding office, the higher echelons of the administration feared that women could exert their influence through their apparently superior business intellect, seduction, and domestic dominance. This fear usually coalesced around misconduct. It was believed that the Burmese wives of both European and Burmese officials used their connections to collect bribes, unfairly influence official acts, and commit other forms of misconduct. A central part of disciplining colonial state practices and subordinate employees therefore involved ensuring women were kept out of official matters. For the subordinate ranks of the colonial state, this meant in essence separating public duties from private interests by empowering men and excluding women.

Compromising situations

The exclusion of women through the bureaucratisation of state practices during the long nineteenth century was in no way unique to British Burma. Contemporaneous parallels can be drawn from studies on British India as well as with contexts as diverse as England, Jamaica, and across Latin America.[55] Nevertheless, this process took on specific forms in Burma because of how women were understood by high-ranking British officials. This section examines this interconnection between the established colonial perceptions of women and the formulation of colonial state practices. In other words, it traces the relationship between colonial discourse and bureaucratic practice. The two met in official concerns about misconduct. Specifically, British officials were worried that Burmese women were using their influence over male family members, particularly their husbands, employed by the colonial state. It was thought that women used their domestic dominance to persuade subordinate officials to illicitly further their trade, influence official decisions, or even to collect bribes. This suspicion around Burmese women applied to those connected with Burmese subordinate employees as well as to those indigenous women who had 'alliances' with Europeans of varying ranks. These fears resulted in attempts to monitor and control the influence of women on subordinate officials.

James George Scott captured the fearful attitude of the colonial regime toward women succinctly in a 1913 article.

> ... the Government clings to old theories. It quite recognises the position that Burmese women are far ahead of their men-folk in resource and intelligence, but it cannot rid itself of the memory of the fact that Manu classed women as one of four things that cannot be trusted. The others are the bough of a tree, a ruler, and a thief. Accordingly, while it looks upon the Burmese man with a mixture of exasperation and despair as a good, easy-going, lazy person who gives no trouble, but at the same time does not make half as much of his country as he might, the Government regards the doings of the women with a vague feeling of uneasy apprehension ....[56]

In brief, women were not to be trusted, and their influence over men was a cause for particular concern. It might be recalled from Chapter 3 that the magistrate responsible for one of Inspector Pakiri's townships was denounced as being 'a poor weak thing—entirely under the thumb of his wife', according to the deputy commissioner, Maxwell.[57] Weak men with powerful wives were viewed with official suspicion. The normative subordinate official was assertively masculine and therefore not subservient to his wife.

In response to such concern, the highest ranks of the colonial regime attempted to develop procedures and penalties in order to try and curb the undue influence of spouses, and other female relatives, on subordinate officials. This meant penetrating and monitoring their private life. A local government circular of 1890 outlined that all officials subordinate to a deputy commissioner, excepting peons and menials, 'must provide a list of people related to him either through blood or by marriage—which the Commissioner should maintain and check.'[58] How far this circular was actually followed into practice is unclear, and probably doubtful, but regardless of its utility, it demonstrated the intent of the colonial regime that in order to keep private interests from affecting public duties, private life must be brought into the gaze of high-ranking British officials.[59]

In 1891, the Chief Commissioner of Burma launched an enquiry into framing an order to restrict government servants from entering into trade, asking the opinion of British officials of the rank deputy commissioner and above. The enquiry was part of the processes of defining what constituted misconduct. As I discussed in Chapter 1, central to this process was an attempt to stop private interests affecting subordinate officials' public duties. The major debate that emerged in the correspondence of the deputy commissioners, and the ranks above them, concerned how best to deal with the trading undertaken by officials' wives. So much was this a dominant theme of the subsequent discussion among the higher echelons of the colonial regime that Nisbet, eight years on, and Scott, some 21 years on, recalled the enquiries to have been specifically about whether the wives of Burmese officials abused their positions for purposes of trade.[60] The enquiries were, however, originally intended to be broader.

No clear consensus was reached among the European higher officials. All agreed that something had to be done to restrict trading by subordinate officials, but there was no unanimity as to how best to deal with the apparently unique feature of Burmese society, that wily bazaar trader the independent wife. Some officials argued that all government officials and their wives should be prohibited from trading. Others wished to apply the prohibition only to the higher ranks of the subordinate officials. Others still thought that the government should refrain from any interference in the independent activities of the wives. The Chief Commissioner took a position between the two extremes of outright prohibition on all trading by wives and a *laissez-faire* attitude towards them. He passed an order stating that no salaried government official was allowed to be directly or indirectly involved in any form of trading under punishment of removal from their position. He then turned to their wives, discouraging trade in the strongest terms.

> The independent position of women in Burma and this admitted right to deal as they please with their separate estates makes it difficult to interfere with trading by wives of officials. But the Chief Commissioner wishes to be distinctly understood that such trading on the part of wives of Gazetted officers is viewed by the Government with grave disfavour, and, if scandal or trouble arises therefrom in any case, the officer whose wife's transactions have given cause for this will be held responsible and deemed to have constructively violated the order against trading.[61]

Burmese women posed problems for the colonial regime's attempt to separate the public sphere from the private, based on the conceptions of these spheres held by the official mind. Their influence had to be monitored.

Regulating subordinate officials' relationships with women was thus a part of disciplining everyday state practices, and as such, relationships were intended targets of European official scrutiny. Information produced on intimate relationships could be used to discredit and compromise subordinate officials, and was. As we saw in Chapter 3, in 1899, a head constable of police in Bassein, Po Kyaw, was under investigation because of his relationship with the sister-in-law of a convicted dacoit.[62] Similarly, in 1901, an inspector of police in Myaungmya, Maung Shwe So, was the subject of a departmental enquiry and unsuccessful criminal proceedings because of his relationship with a woman named Marion Bee that was allegedly influencing his police investigations. He was ultimately transferred to Wakema.[63] The colonial belief in the influence of Burmese women meant that affairs and casual liaisons were not thought of as frivolous, but as potentially incriminating. A case from 1902 involving an accusation of adultery against a *myo-ok* is particularly revealing of how high-ranking officials approached and understood subordinate officials' relationships with women, and their assumed consequences. It is worth exploring in some depth.

In early 1902, a complaint of adultery was brought before the court of the District Magistrate of Myaungmya, Webb. The complainant was Gaw Ya, a young law student. He had been married to a 21-year-old

Ma Pon for six years and they had a child of about three years of age. The accused was the *Myo-ok* Ba Thu. The prosecution alleged that during Gaw Ya's absence studying, Ba Thu and Ma Pon had committed adultery. The narrative of the events given by the witnesses for the defence and for the prosecution was, save one crucial difference, the same. In Gaw Ya's absence, Ma Pon went to live with her mother, Ma Gyi Thet, and her sister, Ma Shwe I. During this time, the three women met and befriended the cousin of the *Myo-ok*, Ma Yin, who worked in his house. While the *Myo-ok* went on tour, the women began to stay over in his house with Ma Yin. This arrangement continued when the *Myo-ok* returned, and the women often ate their meals and slept in Ba Thu's house. This set up continued with the sisters un-chaperoned when their mother, Ma Gyi Thet, left Myaungmya for a trip to Henzada. Both prosecution and defence witnesses agreed that one morning, sometime between five and eight o'clock, a quarrel broke out between the sisters Ma Pon and Ma Shwe I. In the ensuing fracas, Ba Thu, the *Myo-ok*, had his arm bitten twice. These points went uncontested.

The difference between the prosecution and the defence stories revolved around the cause of the quarrel. Ma Shwe I claimed that she was sharing a room with her sister, Ma Pon, and Ma Yin when at five o'clock in the morning she was awoken by sounds and 'on looking saw Maung Ba Thu and Ma Pon in the act of sexual intercourse.'[64] On seeing this, Ma Shwe I shouted to her sister, 'Did I not tell you beforehand that such would happen?'[65] She then began to 'slipper' her sister and, when Ba Thu attempted to intervene, she bit him twice on his arm. Her sister Ma Pon denied committing adultery. She claimed instead that the quarrel began because Ba Thu had stood on Ma Shwe I's foot. The defence constructed yet another different interpretation that Ba Thu was woken at eight o'clock in the morning by the noise of Ma Pon and Ma Shwe I fighting, and in the process of separating them received the bites.

In judging the evidence before him, District Magistrate Webb came down strongly on the side of the prosecution whose interpretation of events he 'unhesitatingly' believed.[66] His decision was based on a highly gendered reading of the evidence. His first reason for believing the prosecution was the testimony of Ma Shwe I. He wrote, 'I cannot believe that *a woman* would falsely and wantonly fabricate a story of her sister's shame' (emphasis added).[67] His second reason was the demeanour of Ma Pon in court. Webb thought that she was attempting to conciliate Ba Thu and her husband, Gaw Ya. Particularly, he felt that Ba Thu held such influence over her that it undermined the defence's claims that their acquaintance was slight. These factors in shaping Webb's decision suggest the influence of broader understandings of femininity. Ma Pon was caught between two lovers, and therefore under their influence, and Ma Shwe I could not possibly have made such, to Webb's mind, shaming charges falsely. Ma Pon's demeanour was read as typically feminine, and the thought of Ma Shwe I lying about such a subject was distinctly unladylike.

A third reason that Webb gave for believing the prosecution's version of events revealed the influence of gendered understandings more specific to Burma. Ba Thu, according to Webb, was taking a considerable and obvious risk in allowing such close relations with Ma Pon, Ma Shwe I, and their mother, Ma Gyi Thet. It was a risk that was exploited by Ma Gyi Thet who was documented as having received at least one bribe of Rs. 100 in his name. To Webb's mind, there was only one plausible reason that Ba Thu would run such a risk, lust. He wrote suggestively, 'Ma Pon is a woman of considerable personal attractions. Maung Bah Thu is a widower.' He went on to argue,

> I refuse to believe that the *Myook* allowed such a person [Ma Gyi Thet] to eat and sleep in his house for the sole reason given in his para 5 [that is to keep Ma Yin company]. He must have had a more intimate knowledge of Ma Pon and I conclude that he allowed the opportunities for an offence to continue.[68]

Webb believed that Ba Thu was fully aware that such relationships were suspicious, that the motives of women like Ma Gyi Thet were not to be trusted, and that the government would look poorly on such liaisons: and that despite all this, that he continued to allow the women in his house demonstrated that he must have had some personal stake in the relationship. This was the apparent beauty of Ma Pon. Ma Pon's 'attractions' also proved to Webb that Ba Thu was fully aware that Ma Pon was married. 'Ma Pon is a woman of 21, of prepossessing appearance: Such a person would naturally be married. It would be a matter for comment if such a woman were still unmarried.'[69] The portrayal of Burman women as manipulative, untrustworthy, and seductive found in the work of colonial scholar-officials was equally apparent in the reasoning that Webb brought to bear in Ba Thu's adultery case.

There were other problems that Webb found in the defence evidence. The alternative explanation of the quarrel was flimsy. Ba Thu also attempted to use the strategy of other *myo-oks* before and after using his powers to intimidate witnesses;[70] specifically, in this case he had his brother bring 'trumped up' charges against Ma Shwe I. In this instance, however, it backfired as it only served to confirm Webb's suspicions about Ba Thu's guilt. Ba Thu was found guilty and fined Rs. 450, or in default of payment three months of simple imprisonment.[71] It was decided departmentally that Ba Thu would also be transferred to a different station. No further action was taken because, in the view of the Commissioner of the Irrawaddy Division, there was 'no suggestion that he used his official position to further his designs.'[72] Nevertheless, the whole episode rendered his position in Myaungmya untenable, as private scandal and 'scheming women' had tainted his reputation. Webb's punishment would have been stronger had he not thought that Ba Thu had been met more than half way by the desires of Ma Pon and her mother. The implication of Webb's reasoning was that Ma Gyi Thet had deliberately attempted to build an association with the *myo-ok* through her daughters and used this association between them for her own benefit. In Webb's narrative, Ba Thu was the seduced and not the seducer.

It is tempting to accept some of Webb's interpretation. In a situation in which women were systematically excluded from state power through gendered employment policies and concerns around misconduct, it might be seen as empowering to suggest that women found alternative routes to influence and power, such as through seduction. But this is misleading. It certainly seems as though Ma Gyi Thet exploited the perceived connection between herself and Ba Thu to extort bribes. It is far less certain that she sent Ma Pon to seduce Ba Thu for this purpose. It is worth noting Diana Paton's warning when she was discussing the position of women in the sexual economies of Jamaica's nineteenth-century prisons: 'It is difficult to describe the dynamics of power and desire at work in sexual relations even when the participants are able to articulate for themselves, in the context of shared political and cultural assumptions about sex, what happened or happens in a sexual encounter.' Following from this, 'we should not expect to fully diagnose and describe the sexual relations of the past.'[73] This is surely true in the example of Ba Thu and Ma Pon. There were gaping emotional gaps in the story that were bridged by the colonial logic of Webb. To accept Webb's rendering of events would be to reify the colonial perceptions and concerns about Burman women. Perhaps worse still, it would assert, along with the high-ranking European officials, that women in Burma had informal access to state power, when in fact the documents in the misconduct files suggest that the contrary was far more common: women were further marginalised through the informal performance of state power.

The perennial concern about the influence of Burmese women in causing misconduct was also apparent in the debates surrounding

British officials' intimate relationships across the established racial boundary. To be sure, the debates arose out of perhaps more prominent concerns than misconduct, most notably a sense of racial superiority, an aversion to 'scandal', and concerns about miscegenation.[74] However, often these fears about racial preservation manifested themselves in the more practical, official voice of concern about misconduct. Indeed, the earliest confidential circular discouraging unions between British officials and Burmese women written by the then governor general, Colonel Fytche, in 1867 stated, 'It is a common belief amongst the natives of the country that such women intrigue to prevent suitors and others obtaining a hearing or approaching officers of Government thus situated, except through a corrupt source.'[75] In 1895, with intimate relationships between Burmese women and British officials still common, the new Chief Commissioner Frederic Fryer attempted to transfer two officials, E. A. Moore and H. E. McColl, for marrying Burmese women. In his unsuccessful attempts, he first suggested that their Burmese wives would bring local influences to bear on the officials. When the government of India refused to transfer them because actual instances of misconduct could not be proved, Fryer insisted that it was not the reality of corruption that mattered but that the Burmese would perceive that the wives had corruptly influenced official decisions.[76] Even when misconduct did arise concerning McColl and his wife's relatives, and with the support of the Viceroy Curzon for a transfer, McColl was still not transferred although he did receive a fine and suspension.[77] Ultimately, the colonial government proved unable to stop British officials from taking Burmese mistresses or worse, in the eyes of Fryer and Curzon, wives.

It might be argued that concerns about misconduct in relationships between European officials and their Burmese partners were largely a smokescreen for attempts to preserve racial purity. Certainly, there were no cases recorded in the misconduct files of Burmese mistresses or wives of European officials using their connections for their own illicit betterment. Indeed, the only misconduct case involving a Burmese mistress of a British official, Wooster, a treasury officer in Maubin, concerned his private abuse of her and not her abuse of his public office. In October of 1908, Maxwell, then Commissioner of the Irrawaddy Division wrote, 'Last night a Burmese woman came to me about half past ten in a state of tears saying that she had been the mistress of Mr. Wooster, had been turned out the house by that officer and assaulted by other people in the house.' Maxwell's response was dictated by concerns about avoiding a scandal: he instructed the Deputy Commissioner of Maubin that,

'An open scandal of this sort cannot be permitted. Will you kindly see that Mr. Wooster ... makes proper arrangements for the lady, and report when he has done so.'[78] Despite Nisbet's repeated claims that there was no degradation for a Burman woman to enter into a relationship with a British official, it may have been that the position of the mistress was somewhat tenuous; not unlike that of the unsympathetically portrayed Burmese mistress of Orwell's anti-hero Flory, who was cast aside with the arrival of a young English woman.[79]

The vigilance of high-ranking British officials concerning Burmese wives corrupting official duties, although commonplace, did not turn up many instances of misconduct. In spite of this lack of evidence of misconduct, Burmese women continued to be excluded from most areas of formal state power throughout colonial rule. A conflation of women with private interests continued to be central to British bureaucratic thinking. The normative subordinate official was assertively masculine and the state was officially imagined and practiced as an exclusively male sphere. This was paralleled in subordinate officials' corrupt acts. Contrary to colonial claims, misconduct among subordinate officials was not the result of the great influence of women but the opposite; women were further marginalised by misconduct and subordinate officials' everyday performances of state power.

Misconduct and gendered violence

Women rarely appear as the perpetrators of corruption in the misconduct files. Rather, where the misconduct files document women's relationship with the everyday informal practices of subordinate officials, they appear to have been the victims of abuses of state power. The space created through the informal tactics of state employees did not provide room for women. Nowhere is this clearer in the misconduct files than in cases of sexual violence and exploitation. Women were sometimes assaulted and raped by subordinate state employees. More commonly, subordinate employees in a variety of posts, particularly policemen, *myo-oks*, and hospital assistants, used their positions to suppress accusations of rape and sexual assault made by women. These acts were linked to the broader processes of state formation. In the previous two sections of this chapter, we have seen how the colonial state was gendered as male through British officials' ideal imaginings of the state and the related bureaucratised practices. In short, state power was invested solely in men, and preferably those who performed an assertively masculine role of being dominant over women. The result was that women seeking redress from the state for sexual crimes were often met with intransigence, or otherwise actively undermined.

In the late nineteenth century, there were two high-profile cases of gendered violence against Burmese women committed by British officers, cases that even penetrated the media in Britain. In 1889, the British police officer Malcolm James Chisholm was charged with forcibly tattooing the words 'bazaar prostitute' onto the forehead of Ma Gnee. The offence occurred in Upper Burma during British annexation and was reported in England in *The Times*.[80] Ten years later, *The Times* was again reporting on a case of gendered violence that had been committed in Burma, this time in Rangoon. Eight soldiers belonging to the West Kent Regiment were charged with gang raping a Burmese woman called Ma Goon in front of many witnesses.[81] These cases became notorious not so much because of their violent and gendered nature but because they were committed by Europeans. As Jordanna Bailkin has argued about the Chisholm case, these events revealed the potential moral pitfalls of colonial service for British officers and undermined the colonial claims to be a civilising force.[82] Despite their notoriety, in neither case were the men found guilty in court, although the West Kent Regiment were subsequently made an example of by Curzon who ensured the eight acquitted soldiers were discharged, and posted the whole regiment to Aden, thought to be the worst possible imperial posting. More than reflecting the difficulty of securing a conviction in crimes of sexual violence, which as we shall see was difficult in British Burma, the acquittals reflected the racial bias built into colonial justice in British India.[83] Nonetheless, though they were exceptional cases in the scale of their notoriety, they were similar to many other cases of gendered violence committed by subordinate colonial officials that did not attract such attention.

The most documented cases were the three seduction allegations levelled against Inspector Pakiri, discussed in Chapter 2, none of which ended in convictions against him. In each case, he was accused of manufacturing scenarios in which he could pressure a woman to sleep with him. This involved having a male family member arrested and then offering to release or in some other way benefit him if the women agreed to have sex with Pakiri. A rape charge against Pakiri was made in only one of the seduction cases, and here Maxwell, the investigating British official, thought that it weakened her allegation. Maxwell's reasoning was based on a de-contextualised notion of consent, one that was also the fundamental factor for judging rape cases in Victorian Britain.[84] Specifically, he believed that the accuser did not physically struggle against Pakiri, and thus he treated consent extorted under duress simply as consent. The other two seduction allegations fell under the category of offence 'receiving illegal gratifications'.

Pakiri was not the only subordinate official accused of using his official authority to gain access to women: there are sporadic references to similar practices to be found in misconduct proceedings. For example, in 1901, an anonymous petition accused a *thugyi* of a village in Danubyu township of 'receiving many girls of respectable parents'.[85] In 1896, a Gibralterian called Frederico was dismissed from the Burma police for employing his constables to solicit women for him.[86] In 1907, a second grade hospital assistant Abdul Shaik Aziz was convicted of rape and removed from his position in the Dedaye civil hospital.[87] And at the end of his chequered career, the *myo-ok* Maung Gyi, discussed in Chapter 1, was accused of using his position to procure women.[88] These examples are comparatively sparsely detailed, and there may have been more subordinate officials dismissed for similar acts but listed under broad and oblique headings such as illegal gratification, assault, extortion, illegal confinement, or kidnapping. There is a similar misconduct file from 1905 that records more fully a case in which subordinate officials abused their authority in order to commit rape.

The details emerge out of a diary entry of Thornton, the Deputy Commissioner of Pyapon, that recorded an 'extraordinary' rape case that he had tried on 29 May. The tone of his writing was somewhere between amusement and despair, a sort of feigned exasperation. He did not give any names to those involved but the narrative he produced was as follows. On one evening, a woman went to her headman to report a rape that had been committed against her. The headman's response was to take her to the guard at Kyaiklat with a police sergeant to examine her. They then took her to the hospital where the sergeant went to find the hospital assistant leaving the headman with the woman. When the hospital assistant arrived and examined her, he found that she had only just finished the sexual intercourse. Initially, the woman denied having had sex after she had been raped, but the next morning she made a criminal complaint, stating that the headman had also raped her in the hospital. It was this complaint that Thornton was given to try. He summarily dismissed the case saying that it was never substantial enough to have been sent to him and that the accuser was either 'half witted' or 'very stupid'.[89] Despite this, he did view the whole affair with considerable concern. He had no doubt that the headman had engaged in sexual intercourse with the woman in the hospital and responded by dismissing the headman. Popular opinion, he claimed, also had it that the sergeant had been involved in some form of impropriety during her examination but, Thornton argued, since she had consented to the examination he could not be charged with rape. As with Maxwell, his notion of consent took no account of deception or coercion. Nevertheless, he still launched enquiries into the sergeant's conduct. He concluded the diary entry writing, 'It is this sort of thing no doubt that prevents decent girls laying complaints'.[90] Of the woman's original rape accusation, he makes no comment but it seems unlikely that any criminal investigation was made.

This example starkly portrays the potentially vulnerable position women could be in when approaching state employees for help. The rape victim's attempt to report the crime against her resulted in two additional assaults located in two sites of colonial confinement, the guard and the hospital. Additionally, Thornton's attitude towards the rape victim was unsympathetic and he applied a limited legal definition of rape that revolved around the simplistic and narrow notion of consent that was prevalent in contemporaneous British legal practice.[91]

Maxwell and Thornton's sceptical approach to rape victims was also connected to the colonial perceptions of Burman women as independent. In the eyes of Nisbet and Fielding-Hall, women's independence had the troubling effect of producing false rape charges. Nisbet saw them as a nuisance but amusing. He wrote,

> ... it will be seen that sincerity is not a leading characteristic. This want of conscientious scruple not infrequently gives rise to very peculiar cases in court. It has previously been noted that notwithstanding the freedom of intercourse between young lads and lasses there is comparatively little immorality. Cases do however occur, and if found *in flagranti delicto* the girl will often sacrifice her lover by bringing a charge of rape against him. So much so is this the case that rape charges in general tax to the utmost the discriminative powers of the magistracy.[92]

'False' rape charges may have been taxing for officials, in Nisbet's experience, but they were also a source of risqué and humorous stories: 'One or two exceedingly amusing tales might be told in connexion with cases of this sort if only the subject were less unsuitable for these pages.'[93]

In a more serious register, Fielding-Hall saw 'false' rape charges as the result of a society in which women were too powerful, a logic that was consistent with his broader argument about the damaging feminising effect women had on Burmese society. He began by describing the situation, as he believed it to have been, in pre-colonial Burma.

> The dangers that await women elsewhere when alone in fields or forests were small in Burma .... And in addition, the administration of the law in these matters was very strict and very feminine. A man who even touched the hand of an unwilling girl suffered severely for it. That she tempted him was nothing .... Men learned sometimes to fear women as one fears a nettle that has a deadly sting. Such a freedom may sound ideal. It was not then. It is not so now ....[94]

He went on to argue that the situation had not been entirely rectified under colonial rule. 'A Burman magistrate will inflict unheard-of penalties for slight offences. He will believe all that women tell him. He will condemn at their word. And, alas! Their word is often false. More than half the claims are probably false'.[95]

The belief that many rape charges were false and that women had a propensity to lie about sexual encounters was not specific to British Burma at this time. It was a belief that was also widespread back in the metropole,[96] but the depiction of Burman women as independent fed this broader propensity to treat rape charges with distrust. However, quite the contrary to Fielding-Hall's belief that false cases were commonly accepted simply on the accuser's word, there were great obstacles facing an individual wishing to secure a conviction of rape in court. Not least among them was the behaviour of subordinate officials.

A complainant attempting to take a rape allegation through to a conviction had the statistics against them in Lower Burma. According to the published reports on criminal justice, between 1890 and 1899, the percentage of reported rapes that were subsequently pursued in court averaged 69, with a high in 1899 of 77.8 and a low in 1891 of 59. Comparatively, the percentage for all crimes against the human body, including rape, came to 94.1 for the same years, and the percentage for murder was even higher at 97.7.[97] A rape case was significantly less likely to be pursued in court than any other bodily crime. The percentage of rapes reported that were taken up in court dropped further between 1900 and 1907 with a trough in 1904 of 46.1.[98] Comparing the years between 1890 and 1899 with the years 1900–1907, the percentage of cases of all forms of crime against the human body taken to court out of those reported fell 7.9% to 86.2. For rape cases, the percentage for the same period dropped by a greater margin of 11.1% to 57.9.[99] This was just getting the case to court: once there the chances of achieving a prosecution were slim.

Conviction rates were low for all bodily crimes; the overall percentage of cases that resulted in a conviction during 1900, including court cases that had not reached a conclusion during that year or in which the accused had died during the trial, was 38. For rape cases, this was even lower, at 24.3%.[100] Although these figures were low, they were by no means exceptional, nor would they be today. Figures for conviction rates in Victorian Britain were also well below half.[101] It does not appear that Fielding-Hall was remotely correct to assert the ease with which Burmese women could successfully bring rape cases to trial and secure convictions.

There are some considerable problems with these figures. Firstly, the enumeration of rapes by the colonial state reflected the official definition of rape, which as we have seen was narrowly focused on consent. It is probable that cases in which individuals believed themselves to have been raped were instead viewed and charged by colonial officers as other crimes such as assault, and thus recorded them as such. A related problem is that other recorded bodily crimes may have been instances of gendered violence but the category under which they were classified obscures this aspect of the crime. This was particularly true for cases of abduction, kidnapping, wrongful restraint, wrongful confinement, and assault. The officially published statistics reveal perhaps more about the official perspective than the subject they were intended to record.

These problems of reading the official statistics account for only some of their limitations; more interesting is what they do not address. For one thing, official statistics reveal little about the actual incidence of rape. This is a problem for all researchers of sexual violence attempting statistical quantification, as most instances go unreported and are shrouded in silence. Thornton alluded to such a difficulty in the Irrawaddy Delta when he commented that circumstances such as those around the rape accusation in 1905 were a factor preventing 'decent girls laying complaints'. This silence is impenetrable. If a case was not reported, then it did not make it into the archive. However, the misconduct files document some of the everyday practices whereby this silence was created. In other words, there were several cases of subordinate officials attempting to suppress accusations of rape. A second and related problem with the statistics is that they do not reveal how and why so many rape charges were either not pursued in court, or when in court failed. The misconduct files again provide evidence that shows that subordinate officials investigating rape cases deliberately sabotaged them in the process.

More immediate than the difficulties of securing convictions in court and the unsympathetic perspective of high-ranking British officials were the problems facing individuals attempting to negotiate subordinate officials simply to have an allegation investigated. There are many examples of subordinate officials, particularly policemen, township officers, and hospital assistants, using their positions to sabotage or entirely suppress criminal accusations of rape and other forms of gendered violence. These acts were described as 'burking', meaning suppressing evidence, and there were many officials dismissed from government service for burking rape cases. In 1899, a township officer, Maung Gyi (a different *myo-ok* to the one discussed in Chapter 1), was dismissed for, among other things, 'burking a rape case against his son.' In 1900, Maung Kyaw Ho, a police sergeant, was dismissed for 'burking a rape case that ended in death.' And in 1908, Maung Po Lwin, a head constable of the police, was dismissed for 'trying to burke a case of rape.'[102]

Other township officers and policemen in the Irrawaddy Division escaped criminal punishment for burking cases of gendered violence. A European head constable of the police, Hadden, was initially brought to trial on a charge of burking a rape in 1899. He escaped prosecution in this trial by intimidating the witnesses, but he was convicted of receiving illegal gratifications in a related case a year later. In 1905, the *myo-ok* Maung Gyi (discussed in Chapter 1) used his magisterial powers to intimidate witnesses giving evidence against his follower Po San who had broken into a woman's house and sexually assaulted her.[103] He went to some lengths to protect Po San, standing surety for him despite being the presiding magistrate in his case, and even bursting into the premises of a supporter of the complainant one night armed with a gun. For his behaviour in this case, the last in a catalogue of misconduct complaints, he was removed from his position. In the same year, a head constable of police, Maung Po Sin, attempted a more subtle approach to burking a rape case: he simply and deliberately recorded a complaint of rape as an assault.[104] All these individuals were township officers or policemen invested with the powers to investigate and punish crime, powers that they attempted to use for the opposite purpose in cases of rape and sexual assault.

Hospital assistants were another group of subordinate employees embroiled in misconduct over rape allegations. The evidence that hospital assistants produced for criminal investigations was often unreliable, and not only in rape cases.[105] In 1905, a hospital assistant from Dedaye was transferred for falsely providing evidence that claimed his follower, Mohamed Syed, had suffered internal injuries after being beaten by the police.[106] In an even more dramatic case in 1908, the hospital assistant from Bogale, S. P. Chatterjee, was found to have fabricated evidence when the bodies of two men he reported to have died from alcoholism were exhumed and they were found to have died from fractured skulls.[107] The reason for Chatterjee's lie was a mystery to the high-ranking British officials investigating him.

In rape cases, hospital assistants also proved to be unreliable in providing evidence. In 1901, Po Mya was charged with the rape of Mi Bok Son. It was alleged that he had held her against her will for two nights in the jungle while he raped her five times. The judge in the case dismissed the complainant's testimony and acquitted Po Mya 'solely on the ground that there was some doubt whether Mi Bok Son was not a willing agent in the matter.'[108] Again the case turned on the lack of evidence regarding the victim's consent, resulting in Po Mya's word against Mi Bok Son's, since he did not deny having had sex with her. Mi Bok Son had to prove that she did not consent. However, although it was not disputed that intercourse had taken place, the medical evidence of the Hospital Assistant of Pantanaw in Myaungmya, Jeycila Rao, stated that there was no evidence of sexual intercourse between the two. His evidence was not only anomalous, but it was based on somewhat dubious medical grounds. He claimed to be able to tell by examining 'a woman's private parts' whether or not she had engaged in sexual intercourse in the last three days. These skills were apparently not matched with attention to detail in other medical matters, as Rao had failed to examine wounds that had been inflicted on Mi Bok Son's arms during her ordeal.[109] Rao was suspended from duty while he was investigated for misconduct, as it was suspected that his evidence was produced in an ill-conceived attempt to save Po Mya from punishment.[110] He was later acquitted of deliberately attempting to pervert the evidence in the case.[111] It appears that in cases of medical evidence being fabricated for criminal investigations, it was difficult to distinguish between the incompetent and the corrupt medical subordinates. Rao did not appear to have had any personal connection with Po Mya and it was this that saved him from punishment.[112]

In historical circumstances such as those in colonial Burma in which the victim had to shoulder the burden of proof to show that they did not consent to sex, Rao's evidence weakened the case of Mi Bok Son through his failure to examine the wounds on her arms as signs of coercion. Signs of coercion such as these would have strengthened her position that she did not consent to sex.[113] This example, along with the recent work of Elizabeth Kolsky on case law on rape in British

India, suggests that a lack of medical evidence tended to strengthen a defendant against an accuser. Following from this, it is revealing that medical subordinates in Burma regularly, even routinely, failed to find medical evidence in cases of rape and sexual assault. This was brought to light in a misconduct case in 1905. It appears that there was an endemic problem with medical evidence provided for cases of rape and sexual assault in colonial Burma. Hospital assistants and other medical subordinates consistently failed to detect semen stains on items of clothing submitted as evidence in police investigations and in court.

During the investigation of a rape case in 1905, a hospital assistant was disciplined for submitting some suspected semen stains on an item to a chemical examination before sending it to the Chemical Examiner, which was the only official position invested with the legal power to perform such a test. The Hospital Assistant had failed to detect any stains, and his evidence was used to strengthen the accused man's case. But the concern of Deputy Commissioner H. C. Moore was whether or not a hospital assistant was suitably qualified to make such a judgement on this technical evidence. It subsequently emerged that the Hospital Assistant was not at fault and was acting in accordance with a circular of 1899. This circular stated that due to the high number of articles being sent to the Chemical Examiner for examination, hospital assistants must first judge for themselves whether or not an item needed to be sent. It also pointed out that during 1897 and 1898, the Chemical Examiner had detected no semen stains. The then Inspector General of Jails and Civil Medical Administration, who had authored the circular, thought that examinations for semen stains should be carried out only once a case had reached court and was ordered by a magistrate, and not during police investigations.[114] In essence, the Inspector General was trying to limit the number of semen examinations, and thus free up the time of the Chemical Examiner.

Deputy Commissioner Moore thought that the 1899 order was unclear. He wondered why hospital assistants were to act as a buffer for chemical examiners. Was it because hospital assistants were capable of judging for themselves whether stains were semen or not? If this was so, by extension the process of detecting the absence of semen was an easy one, and, Moore reasoned, 'its value as evidence would be far higher ... and might, in many cases, be the means of saving an innocent accused from undergoing a long term of imprisonment.'[115] Reflecting the opinions of Nisbet and Fielding-Hall, the principal concern of Moore was to protect men from false rape accusations.

Moore, however, pointed out that the circular did not suggest that the process of detection was easy. To the contrary, it claimed that finding semen stains was extremely difficult, hence none had been found during the years 1897 and 1898. If this was the case, Moore argued rhetorically, and the discovery of semen stains was prohibitively hard, should the attempt to detect semen at all be abandoned? He answered his rhetorical question using his own research comparing chemical examinations of semen in Burma with other parts of British India. In his research, he found that Burma was an anomaly and that examinations were regularly successful elsewhere (see Table 4.1).

Moore did not think that attempts to find semen stains should be abandoned but instead urged an enquiry into why chemical examinations had completely failed in Burma. Semen was evidently detectible through chemical examinations but either through incompetence or a lack of will, medical subordinates in Burma routinely failed to detect any. This blanket failure to detect semen could only have weakened women's accusations in court as it denied them precious evidence. But such matters were of little concern to the higher echelons of the colonial regime. Moore's call for an enquiry appears to have fallen on deaf ears and was not even acknowledged—again, entirely consistent with the unsympathetic attitude of British officials towards indigenous rape victims.[116]

Table 4.1 Detection of seminal stains[117]

	Cases	Detection
Bengal		
1900	35	29
1901	68	47
1902	51	28
1903	81	47
North West Province and Oudh and Central Provinces		
1900	6	1
1901	5	3
1902	6	1
North West Frontier Province		
1901	20	9
1902	10	6
Burma		
1901	49	Nil
1902	63	Nil
1903	49	Nil

Subordinate officials' everyday corrupt acts were gendered. This was especially apparent in their involvement in gendered violence and sexual crimes. In some cases, this involvement was direct, and the subordinate officials were themselves the perpetrators. In others, subordinate officials were complicit in the crimes through their attempts to suppress and sabotage investigations into rape. Building on Timothy Mitchell's argument that the state emerges through myriad quotidian material acts, it would appear that the state in lower Burma was performatively enacted as masculine.[118] It is perhaps not too great a leap of historical imagination to suggest further that those women who attempted to attain redress for sexual crimes against them experienced the colonial state as masculine. While this may have been a widespread experience of states across the world at this time, it was not inevitable. Joanna Bourke's study of rape in Britain and North America since the mid-nineteenth century, focusing on the construction of the rapist—the commonsense myths, legal definitions, and social justifications that have created and perpetuated the rapist—makes it emphatically clear that rape is not the inevitable result of the natural predisposition of men.[119] Bearing this in mind, the wider construction of gender ideologies was at play in subordinate officials' actions. This may not be reducible to an effect of colonial rule; longer standing indigenous gender ideologies present in the *habitus* of subordinate officials must too have informed their actions. But the parallel between colonial discourse and bureaucratic practice, on the one hand, and corrupt practices of subordinate officials, on the other hand, should not be underplayed. Both served to make the state male.

The fashioning of the male state

When John Furnivall wrote *The Fashioning of Leviathan*, he was probably unaware of the significance of the gender with which he imbued the colonial state.[120] Leviathan was 'he', the universal male subject. In the writings of subsequent authors who applied fewer literary flourishes than Furnivall, the state, no longer vividly depicted as a person writ large, was portrayed as gender-neutral.[121] But Furnivall was right to represent the colonial state as a man, although unintentionally. Leviathan was male both in the imaginations of high-ranking officials and in the quotidian practices of subordinate state employees. In its everyday manifestation, the masculinity of the colonial state in Burma was one of its most striking features.

In the final section of this chapter, I highlighted the most overt and explicit ways in which the state was gendered, but the masculinity of the state has been implicitly present throughout this book. Almost all the actors and characters who have appeared have been men: the British officials, the subordinate officials, and the followers of subordinate officials. Even most of the victims of extortion and corruption have been men. The episodes of corruption that have been discussed in the previous chapters have mostly been cases involving interactions between men. Women have appeared only as victims of abuses of power. However, this gender exclusivity in itself is a ubiquitous and relatively banal observation. Many archives silence women's experiences. More revealing is how officials performed their everyday acts, and corruption was often performed with bravado and machismo. This was apparent when *myo-ok* Maung Gyi threatened his opponents with a gun to protect his friend against a charge of sexual assault in an act of male solidarity. It was apparent in the notorious career of Inspector Pakiri. It was implicit in the feud between *myo-ok* Maung Tun and timber trader Maung Pe (discussed in Chapter 3), which escalated as they attempted to prove who was more powerful. When duplicitously performing state power, subordinate officials were performing an exaggerated masculinity.

But it was not only unscrupulous subordinate officials who were performing a version of masculinity when performing the colonial state, but also the British officials who were performing the role of aloof, knowledgeable gentlemen when conducting misconduct investigations. The fictional British officials in Cecil C. Lowis's novels, written and set in colonial Burma, all demonstrated their bureaucratic wisdom and administrative competence in contrast to the European women they meet. The British women in his books were either too sensitive or too cruel in their relations with the Burmese.[122] The correspondence of the deputy commissioners we have encountered here, such as Captain F. D. Maxwell who investigated Inspector Pakiri, could have been written by one of Lowis's dry, world-weary characters. This masculinity was implicit (and occasionally explicit) in the writings of Scott, Nisbet, White, and Fielding-Hall: to be a good official, one had to behave like a man.

That performing the state seems to have intrinsically involved performing masculinity, regardless of whether the acts were formal bureaucratic ones or informal corrupt ones, demonstrates a profound overlap between legal and disorderly performances of state power: their implicit gender performances. Colonialism, through the discourses and practices of misconduct it engendered in Burma, fashioned a male state.

Conclusion

'There probably was corruption in colonial times, but it wasn't as bad as today.' These were the thoughts of a Yangon resident who I spoke to about my research during the frantic weeks I spent there, most of which I passed shut away in the national archives of Myanmar. These were sentiments shared by others I met in the city as well: it was perhaps bad then, but it is worse now.

Corruption has been used as a marker of the failure of the post-colonial state in Burma.[1] The country regularly foots the table of the NGO Transparency International's global corruption index.[2] It would take a considerable act of wilful ignorance to suggest that this is nothing more than a neo-imperial discourse. Although such perspectives are indeed underpinned by pernicious Eurocentric and neoliberal models of development, it is undeniable that corruption is a feature of people's daily life in contemporary Myanmar, not all of it oppressive.[3] But the commonly espoused belief I encountered that contemporary corruption was worse than colonial corruption is more about the politics of history than it is a quantitative assessment.

The military regime that has ruled Burma for almost half a century has regularly found denigrating the colonial regime to be a useful rhetorical strategy, shifting the blame for contemporary problems into the past. The writings of some prominent post-colonial historians have come close to endorsing such a position.[4] At the same time, some sectors of the international opposition to military rule in Burma have adopted imperial logic and language.[5] These flawed political uses of history lead me to ask two questions: does exposing the failure of British colonialism in Burma exonerate the current regime from responsibility for some of the contemporary problems? And does the opposite, constructing a narrative of post-colonial deterioration, serve to bolster the arguments of imperial apologists that things were better under the British Empire, or worse, justify neo-imperialism? The history of corruption gives us the opportunity to critique both standpoints.

Throughout the book, I have argued for greater sophistication in understanding the relationship between corruption and the colonial state. Rather than corruption simply being a set of epiphenomenal aberrations from the norms of state practice (as it has usually been portrayed in the passing mentions it has had in the historiography), both its pervasive presence in the Burma Delta and its intrinsic link to legal authority demonstrate that it played a greater historical role. Corruption was performative. It was often through acts of malfeasance and misconduct that the state was manifested and experienced in everyday life. But does this argument imply that colonial rule is to blame for post-colonial corruption? In order to address the thorny problem of any post-colonial residues in corrupt practices in contemporary Myanmar, in this chapter, I will locate this study in the wider debate on the legacy of colonialism and in the longer history of state formation.

Corruption and the making of the modern state

British colonialism undoubtedly wrought huge transformations in Burma, but the nature of these is far from clear. There is no consensus among historians of colonial Burma on the precise nature of the impact that imperialism had on the state, on society, or on the imagination. It seems to have either changed everything or nothing.[6]

For some, colonial rule was a 'fleeting passing phase'[7] through which an 'autonomous history' of Southeast Asia continued largely undisturbed by the presence of the imperial powers.[8] What is today the Union of Myanmar, under this interpretation, broadly corresponds to the geography of pre-colonial states dating back to Pagan.[9] The liquidation of the monarchy and the imposition of an alien system of village administration are not denied, but these changes while disruptive were ultimately superficial for scholars such as Michael Aung-Thwin. For Aung-Thwin, colonialism was not hegemonic and it did not alter deeper Burmese mentalities.[10] Modern-day Myanmar thus has entrenched roots dating back over a millennia. The contrast with other post-colonial historians could not be greater.

Perhaps most famously Thant Myint-U has argued that modern Burma was forged in the failed attempts of the Konbaung Dynasty to reform and maintain its independence in the face of nineteenth-century British imperial expansion.[11] Some have pushed this further, arguing that the idea of Burma itself was a product of British colonialism. In this argument, the imagining of the geographical territory we call Burma or Myanmar was the result of concepts imposed through colonialism.[12] Others have argued that the post-colonial state's coercive relationship with society is directly descended from its colonial predecessor.[13] Likewise, in the aftermath of Benedict Anderson's *Imagined Communities*, historians have built on the argument that nationalism was a European modular form re-configured across the colonial world[14] and applied it to the various nationalities in Burma.[15] Inherent to this argument is the notion that Burmese mentalities were fundamentally altered by the experience of colonialism.

Although the continued extent of colonialism's impact in Myanmar is heavily disputed, it should now be clear from the preceding chapters that the nature of the colonial state has been consistently misunderstood. For nearly all scholars, colonial rule has been viewed simply as a foreign imposition: an invasive, new state forcing change in society through its bureaucratic and coercive resources. I do not want to downplay the undeniable violence of colonial occupation, which was particularly apparent after 1885,[16] but the colonial state was much more complex and a lot less unified than this familiar narrative suggests. As Foucault's work on governmentality urges in its simplest formulation, it is not enough to look at how states have arranged power. We must explore how power has been arranged to make states possible.[17]

Taking our lead from the conceptual interventions made by post-Abrams state theorists, discussed in Chapter 1, it would be more useful to work from the premise that the colonial state was the metaphysical effect of everyday practices introduced through British rule.[18] To be sure, among these daily practices were members of the Indian Civil Service drawing up plans for the administration of Burma, British-appointed headmen collecting capitation taxes, and military police tracking alleged 'dacoits'. But the colonial state was also enacted through judges extorting bribes, policemen surreptitiously releasing friends from prison, and clerks pocketing stamp money. Indeed, these latter practices were more common and quotidian than the former.

Having explored these everyday practices throughout this book, it should be apparent that the colonial state was not simply a 'thin white line' of British officials and their coercive institutions,[19] nor was it a homogenous, wilful historical actor. In short, it was not simply an agent of colonialism, but was itself the product of changes engendered by colonialism. The colonial state emerged in everyday life through new practices in Burma, practices regularised in bureaucratic rules, legal codes and institutions financially backed by the resources of imperial Britain. Crucially, corruption was not a side effect of this daily making of the colonial state and should not be dismissed as a set of ephemeral, ultimately meaningless acts committed by marginal, errant petty officials. It was pervasive and integral to the making of the state. The new formal, legal resources of the colonial bureaucracy made possible subordinate officials' informal, illegal performances of state power. Policeman *used* the law to frame innocent people. Clerks *used* bureaucratic procedures to embezzle government funds. Corrupt acts were not aberrations from norms of state practice, as high-ranking British officials attempted to depict them.

That corruption was widespread was indicative of the distinctive nature of colonial modernity and governmentality. Unlike under pre-colonial rule, as far as the existing literature is able to sustain a comparison, corruption did not undermine the colonial state. Victor Lieberman, Thant Myint-U, and Michael Adas all depict corruption in pre-colonial Burma as a force that undermined the centrally located authority of the dynastic court.[20] In the pre-colonial period, local notables would use acts such as bribery and embezzlement to develop their own reputations, build their local followings, and eventually mount a challenge to the authority of the ruling powers. For Lieberman, this was one of the central tensions of Burmese pre-colonial administrative cycles. For Adas, it was an aspect of the pre-colonial 'contest state'. To put it crudely, more power held by local administrators equated to less power for the monarchy.

In contrast, corruption within the subordinate ranks of the colonial state dispersed across *mofussil* Burma did not threaten the centralised authority of high-ranking British officials. *Myo-oks* did not commit acts of misconduct in order to increase their patronage manpower, raise an army, and attempt to overthrow the state. Local colonial officials, particularly *myo-oks* and policemen, undoubtedly used their positions to establish their personal reputations and authority, as well as for self-aggrandisement: but as we have seen under colonial rule, their personalised authority did not intrinsically detract from the authority of the state. The distribution of power between the centre and the local was not zero-sum, as it was in pre-colonial Burma. Instead, subordinate officials necessarily invoked the colonial state in order to commit their acts of misconduct and establish their personal authority. Through their acts, the state was not weakened, but enacted as a powerful and intrusive entity.

Not only was the colonial state made a despotic quotidian reality through subordinate level corruption, British policies towards corruption reified the racial division of the state. The tacit toleration of corruption through a liberal economy of discipline enabled British officials to distance themselves from their Indian and Burmese subordinates. While Europeans within the subordinate branches of the administration were also among those engaging in the daily malpractices occurring in the delta, the higher echelons of the state acted as aloof bureaucratic despots. Whether to make accusations of corruption or to defend oneself from corruption accusations, subordinate officials and the broader populace had to appeal directly to the authority of European deputy commissioners for redress. As I have shown elsewhere, there were few other official channels to have these grievances heard; the lower courts offered little in the way of justice for misconduct.[21] While it was not an explicitly stated policy, the authority of high-ranking British officials was enhanced by the disorderly daily realities of the colonial bureaucracy. It was this mixture of aloofness and acquiescence in informal British anti-corruption policy in Burma that was distinctively colonial. It contrasted notably to the official attitude taken in response to anti-corruption campaigns in nineteenth- and early-twentieth-century Britain.[22]

Far from corruption being an unacceptable illegality stamped out by the British, as they claimed in their imperial rhetoric, it is better understood as having been a product of colonial rule, acquiesced with by the colonial government, and thereafter used to justify the structural racial hierarchies of the administration. Additionally, as we have seen in Chapter 4, acts of misconduct ran parallel to the official gendering of the state. There were profound overlaps in the masculine gender performances of both formal and informal state practices. This differed from how corruption seems to have functioned in pre-colonial Burma where it was a cause and symptom of the incapacity of dynastic power and could even be a strategy for eventually overthrowing central power. It is ironic that British colonial rhetoric made such grand claims to have suppressed 'corrupt' indigenous state practices while at the same time inaugurating a more embedded regime of tolerated misconduct in their new bureaucracy.[23]

But what of corruption beyond the short timeframe which I have explored? This, after all, is the crux of the issue. Does my study of colonial corruption suggest that contemporary levels of corruption can be traced back to this period? And does this argument let the military 'off the hook'? To address these issues without descending into moralistic polemics requires a greater degree of nuance than the historiography and charged political atmosphere has often allowed. Moreover, its resolution is not particularly exciting. At its heart, this is a problem of periodisation.

Anti-corruption campaigns reveal the changing and contingent cultural meanings of corruption, and as such they are useful for locating corruption historically.[24] As we have seen, during this middle period of colonial rule, corruption was tolerated and its policing was organised according to the logic of racial difference. Combating corruption also informed the activities of anti-colonial peasant organisations in Burma, which according to Robert Taylor, by 1924 had spread across the colony.[25] However, it did not enter the legally endorsed mainstream of political debate until the late 1930s in the run up to the official enquiry into corruption, which published its findings in 1940. Nationalist politicians then used the issue to attempt to discredit their opponents. U Saw, in particular, was successful in mobilising the suspicion of political corruption (which was outside the remit of the official enquiry) against Dr Ba Maw's government.[26] Since then, anti-corruption rhetoric has periodically been part of political discourse in Burma. Endemic corruption in the post-colonial bureaucracy was perceived to be one of the many challenges to the credibility of U Nu's democratic government. As a result, Ne Win's military regime used fighting corruption as a justification for its establishment.[27] Since this time, corruption has commonly featured among the charges made by opposition movements to the junta, in its various guises. No longer are anti-corruption campaigns solely a concern about the daily, low-level abuses of subordinate officials, as they were in the period up to 1940 and in the run up to 1962. Criticisms are now levelled at the open secret of the military's illicit relationships with drug lords.[28] Things are not the same as they were over a century ago: corruption does not have exactly the same meanings and resonances; the policies of the various governments in Burma concerning corruption have been different and have changed over time, and will continue to do so.

The history of corruption in Burma has not been static. Nevertheless, there are good reasons for considering the colonial period onward as a distinct one: a period in which corruption has been intrinsic to how the modern state has been seen and performed in its various colonial and post-colonial forms. At no point have low-level acts of corruption and misconduct seriously threatened the state, although its presence has been used as a rhetorical political weapon against each of the various regimes. Minor abuses of public office, such as petty officials collecting 'tea money' (taking small amounts of money as informal additional charges for government services), cannot be meaningfully described as anti-government acts. They are better understood as small acts in the politics of everyday life.[29] Nor can quotidian acts of corruption be helpfully conceived of as aberrations from norms of state practice. As Monique Skidmore has shown, the arbitrary abuses of state power by local officials in the last decade or so have mimicked the authoritarianism of the military regime.[30] Moreover, like Inspector Pakiri in the colonial period, state officials have continued to mobilise legal authority to perform their illegal acts. The history of post-colonial corruption is one of change within a deeper continuity. The state is still performatively enacted through pervasive corruption.

This deeper chronology in the history of corruption suggests that historians are not forced into an unattractive choice between blaming colonialism/exonerating the military and blaming the military/justifying imperialism. Indeed, both positions share the same assumption that corruption signifies a failure of state formation. Such a position overlooks the role corruption has played in the making of the modern state. As we have seen, through pervasive administrative disorder the colonial state was enacted, and corruption continues to be constitutive of the modern state in contemporary Myanmar. In this, Burma is probably not an exceptional case; scholars of post-colonial societies have often noted a complex combination of disciplinary, legal power, and arbitrary, despotic authority in state practices.[31] Although my focus has been on Burma, I would tentatively suggest that it might prove instructive to consider corruption as performative of the modern state in colonial contexts beyond this quarter of British India. Moreover, I believe that this more sophisticated understanding is helpful to counter the implicit and simplistic equation of corruption with contemporary state failure that has had serious effects. Since the 1990s, neoliberal reforms under the anti-corruption rhetoric of 'good governance' in post-colonial nations have undermined democratic and welfare-providing state structures.[32] It may be that in order to develop a framework to address these global issues on different and more radical terms, corruption needs to be studied as a set of deeply embedded modern state practices of long precedent rather than as recent symptoms of post-colonial weakness.

Notes

Preface

1. Lowell Dittmer, 'Burma vs. Myanmar: What's in a Name?', *Asian Survey*, vol. 48, no. 6 (2008), 885–888.
2. Michael Aung-Thwin and Maitrii Aung-Thwin, *A History of Myanmar Since Ancient Times: Traditions and Transformations* (London: Reaktion Books, 2012), 8.
3. Benedict Anderson, *Imagined Communities: Reflections on the Origins and Spread of Nationalism*, second edition (London: Verso, 1991).

Introduction

1. M. Adas (1974) *The Burma Delta: Economic Development and Social Change on an Asian Rice Frontier, 1852–1941* (Madison, WI: University of Wisconsin Press) pp. 38, 60. Wet-rice production had been present in the delta for centuries before its colonisation by the British, and similar processes were occurring contemporaneously in the Mekong delta and Chao Phraya delta, but the scale was greater in late-nineteenth-century Burma. See P. A. Coclanis (1993) 'Southeast Asia's Incorporation into the World Rice Market: A Revisionist View', *Journal of Southeast Asia Studies*, 24, 2, 251–67.
2. *Imperial Gazetteer of India: Provincial Series, Burma. Vol. 1. The Province; Mountains, Rivers, Tribes; and the Arkan, Pegu, Irrawaddy, and Tenasserim Divisions* (Calcutta: Superintendent of Government Printing, 1908) pp. 350–5.
3. I. Brown (1997) *Economic Change in South-East Asia, c. 1830–1980* (Kuala Lumpur: Oxford University Press) p. 115; M. Adas (2009) 'Continuity and Transformation: Colonial Rice Frontiers and Their Environmental Impact on the Great River Deltas of Mainland Southeast Asia', in E. Burke and K. Pomeranz (eds) *The Environment and World History* (Berkeley, CA: University of California Press) p. 198.
4. For more on criminality in colonial Burma, see I. Brown (2007) 'A Commissioner Calls: Alexander Paterson and Colonial Burma's Prisons', *Journal of Southeast Asian Studies*, 38, 2, 293–308; J. Saha (2012) 'Madness and the making of a colonial order in Burma', *Modern Asian Studies* (Advanced online publication via *firstview*), 1–30. Doi: 10.1017/S0026749X11000400; J. Saha (2012) 'A Mockery of Justice? Colonial Law, the Everyday State and Village Politics in the Burma Delta, c.1890-1910', *Past & Present*, 217, 2, 187–121; M. Aung-Thwin (2011) *The Return of the Galon King: History, Law, and Rebellion in Colonial Burma* (Athens, OH: Ohio University Press) pp. 47–75.
5. J. Nisbet (1901) *Burma Under British Rule—and Before*, Vol. 1 (Westminster: Constable) pp. 112–13.
6. J. McC. Heyman and A. Smart (1999) 'States and Illegal Practices: An Overview', in J. McC. Heyman (ed.) *States and Illegal Practices* (Oxford,

New York: Berg) pp. 1–24; M. Nuijten and G. Anders (2007) 'Corruption and the Secret of Law: An Introduction', in M. Nuijten and G. Anders (eds) *Corruption and the Secret of Law: A Legal Anthropological Perspective* (Aldershot: Ashgate) pp. 9–12.

7. National Archives of Myanmar, Yangon, hereafter NAM, 1/15 (E), 6965, 1897 File No. 7M-19, 11 January 1897.

8. Their names do not appear on the government's published list of those dismissed from public service. NAM, 1/15 (E), 7350, 1908 File No. 7M-9.

9. Foucauldian insights run through this book and structure my conceptualisations in ways which defy acknowledgement through references at every potentially relevant occurrence. M. Foucault (1979) *Discipline and Punish: The Birth of the Prison*, trans. Alan Sheridan (Harmondsworth: Penguin Books).

10. For some excellent works exploring the logics behind colonial policies against criminality and their implementation, see Radhika Singha (1993) '"Providential" Circumstances: The Thuggee Campaign of the 1830s and Legal Innovation', *Modern Asian Studies*, 27, 1, 83–146; M. Brown (2003) 'Ethnology and Colonial Administration in Nineteenth-Century British India: The Question of Native Crime and Criminality', *British Journal for the History of Science*, 36, 2, 201–19; S. B. Frietag (1991) 'Crime in the Social Order of Colonial North India', *Modern Asian Studies*, 25, 2, 227–61; V. Lal (1999) 'Everyday Crime, Native Mendacity and the Cultural Psychology of Justice in Colonial India', *Studies in History*, 15, 1, 145–66; N. Sinha (2008) 'Mobility, Control and Criminality in Early Colonial India, 1760s–1850s', *Indian Economic and Social History Review*, 45, 1, 1–33.

11. M. Aung-Thwin, *The Return of the Galon King*; M. Aung-Thwin (1985) 'The British "Pacification" of Burma: An Order Without Meaning', *Journal of Southeast Asian Studies*, 16, 2, 245–61; P. Ghosh (2000) *Brave Men of the Hills: Resistance and Rebellion in Burma, 1825–1932* (London: Hurst).

12. M. P Callahan (2002) 'State Formation in the Shadow of the Raj: Violence, Warfare and Politics in Colonial Burma', *Southeast Asian Studies*, 39, 4, 513–36.

13. See J. Saha (2011) 'Histories of Everyday Violence in British India', *History Compass*, 9, 11, 844–53; T. Sherman (2009) 'Tensions of Colonial Punishment: Perspectives on Recent Developments in the Study of Coercive Networks in Asia, Africa and the Caribbean', *History Compass*, 7, 3, 659–77. For some exceptions, see Ranajit Guha (ed.) (1987) 'Chandra's Death', in *Subaltern Studies V: Studies in India History and Society* (Delhi: Oxford University Press, 1987) pp. 135–65; T. Sherman (2010) *State Violence and Punishment in India* (London: Routledge); E. Kolsky (2010) *Colonial Justice in British India: White Violence and the Rule of Law* (Cambridge: Cambridge University Press).

14. D. Scott (1995) 'Colonial Governmentality', *Social Text*, 43, 191–220; U. Kalpagam (2000) 'Colonial Governmentality and the "Economy"', *Economy and Society*, 29, 3, 418–38; N. Dirks (2001) *Castes of Mind: Colonialism and the Making of Modern India* (Princeton, NJ: Princeton University Press).

15. P. Howell (2005) 'Race, Space and the Regulation of Prostitution in Colonial Hong Kong', *Urban History*, 31, 2, 229–48; S. Legg (2007) *Spaces of Colonialism: Delhi's Urban Governmentalities* (Malden: Blackwell); A. Tambe

(2009) *Codes of Misconduct: Regulating Prostitution in Late Colonial Bombay* (London: University of Minnesota Press).

16. J. L Comaroff (2001) 'Colonialism, Culture, and the Law: A Foreword', *Law and Social Inquiry*, 26, 2, 305–14.

17. Saha, 'Mockery of Justice?'

18. NAM, 1/15 (E), 7276, 1906 File No. 7M-6, 20 April 1906.

19. Ibid.

20. NAM, 1/15 (E), 7310, 1907 File No. 7M-1, 17 November 1906.

21. Ibid., 9 November 1906.

22. For some exceptions, see R. E. Frykenberg (1965) *Guntur District, 1788–1848: A History of Local Influence and Central Authority in South India* (Oxford: Clarendon Press); R. Chandravakar (1998) *Imperial Power and Popular Politics: Class, Resistance and the State in India, c. 1850–1950* (Cambridge: Cambridge University Press); T. Sherman, *State Violence and Punishment*; W. Gould (2010) *Bureaucracy, Community and Influence in India: Society and the State, 1930s–1960s* (Abingdon: Routledge).

23. A good example of this is Michael Adas's notion of a shift under colonialism away from a pre-colonial 'contest state'. See M. Adas (1980) '"Moral Economy" or "Contest State": Elite Demands and the Origins of Peasant Protest in Southeast Asia', *Journal of Social History*, 13, 4, 521–46; M. Adas (1986) 'From Footdragging to Flight: The Evasive History of Peasant Avoidance Protest in South and South-east Asia', *Journal of Peasant Studies*, 13, 2, 64–86.

24. J. S. Furnivall (1991) *The Fashioning of Leviathan: The Beginnings of British Rule in Burma* (Canberra: Department of Anthropology, Australian National University).

25. N. Englehart (2011) 'Liberal Leviathan or Imperial Outpost? J. S. Furnivall on Colonial Rule in Burma', *Modern Asian Studies*, 45, 4, 759–90; J. Pham (2004) 'Ghost Hunting in Colonial Burma: Nostalgia, Paternalism and the Thoughts of JS Furnivall', *South East Asia Research*, 12, 1, 237–68.

26. See, for instance, the similarities in their depictions of the changing role of the village headman: J. S. Furnivall (1948) *Colonial Policy and Practice: A Comparative Study of Burma and Netherlands India* (Cambridge: Cambridge University Press) pp. 74–6; R. H. Taylor (2008) *The State in Myanmar* (London: Hurst) pp. 82–91.

27. See M. P. Callahan (2003) *Making Enemies: War and State Building in Burma* (Ithaca, NY: Cornell University Press) pp. 21–31; M. W. Charney (2009) *A History of Modern Burma* (Cambridge: Cambridge University Press) pp. 7–10. Although there is significant debate over the extent of impact colonial state formation had: M. Aung-Thwin, 'The British "Pacification" of Burma'; V. Lieberman (1987) 'Reinterpreting Burmese History', *Comparative Studies in Society and History*, 29, 1, 162–94.

28. This assumed separation between the state and society is a prominent feature of highly acclaimed and influential, self-proclaimed 'non-statist' schools of Asian history, see, for instance: J. Smail (1961) 'On the Possibility of An Autonomous History of Modern Southeast Asia', *Journal of Southeast Asian History*, 2. 2, 72–102; R. Guha (ed.) (1983) 'The Prose of Counter-Insurgency' in *Subaltern Studies II: Studies in Indian History and Society* (Delhi: Oxford University Press) pp. 1–42; J. C. Scott (2009) *The Art of Not Being*

Governed: An Anarchist History of Upland Southeast Asia (New Haven, CT, London: Yale University Press).

29. Subordinate officials are dealt with in R. L. Bryant (1997) *The Political Ecology of Forestry in Burma, 1824–1994* (London: Hurst); A. Naono (2009) *State of Vaccination: The Fight Against Smallpox in Colonial Burma* (Hyderabad: Orient Black Swan); J. Warren (2002) 'The Rangoon jail riot of 1930 and the prison administration of British Burma', *South East Asia Research*, 10, 1, 5–29. However, these studies do not devote any space to conceptualising the place of subordinate officials as their focus is only on one particular branch of the colonial state. Two interesting exceptions to this are P. Edwards (2004) 'Relocating the Interlocutor: Taw Sein Ko (1864–1930) and the Itinerancy of Knowledge in British Burma', *South East Asia Research*, 12, 3, 277–335; A. Turner (2011) 'Narratives of Nation, Questions of Community: Examining Burmese Sources without the Lens of Nation', *Journal of Burma Studies*, 15, 2, 263–82, which look at two rather exceptional indigenous colonial officials.

30. R. H. Taylor (1987) *The State in Burma* (London: C. Hurst & Co) p. 82; J. F. Cady (1958) *A History of Modern Burma* (Ithaca, NY: Cornell University Press) p. 153; J. S. Furnivall, *Colonial Policy and Practice*, p. 75.

31. F. Cooper and A. L. Stoler (eds) (1997) 'Between Metropole and Colony: Rethinking a Research Agenda', in *Tensions of Empire: Colonial Cultures in a Bourgeois World* (Berkeley, CA: University of California Press) pp. 6–9; J. L. Comaroff (1998) 'Reflections on the Colonial State, in South Africa and Elsewhere: Factions, Fragments, Facts and Fictions', *Social Identities*, 4, 3, 321–61.

32. See, for instance, the difficulties of writing the history of African colonial intermediaries: B. N. Lawrance, E. L. Osborn, and R. L. Roberts (eds) (2006) *Intermediaries, Interpreters, and Clerks: African Employees in the Making of Colonial Africa* (Madison, WI: University of Wisconsin Press).

33. P. Abrams (1988) 'Notes on the Difficulty of Studying the State', *Journal of Historical Sociology*, 1, 1, 58–89.

34. Along with Abrams's ideas, he also builds on Michael Foucault's writings on 'governmentality', which urge scholars to focus on how societies arrange themselves to be governable, instead of simply examining how they are governed over. M. Foucault (1991) 'Governmentality', in G. Burchell, C. Gordon, and P. Miller (eds) *The Foucault Effect: Studies in Governmentality* (Chicago, IL: Chicago University Press) pp. 87–104. T. Mitchell (1991) 'The Limits of the State: Beyond Statist Approaches and Their Critics', *American Political Science Review*, 85, 1, 77–96; T. Mitchell (2006) 'Society, Economy, and the State Effect', in Aradhana Sharma and Akhil Gupta (eds) *Anthropology of the State: A Reader* (Oxford: Blackwell) pp. 169–86.

35. S. Corbridge, et al. (eds) (2005) *Seeing the State: Governance and Governmentality in India* (Cambridge: Cambridge University Press); C. J. Fuller and V. Bénéï (eds) (2001) *The Everyday State and Society in Modern India* (London: Hurst); T. B. Hansen and F. Stepputat (eds) (2001) *States of Imagination: Ethnographic Explorations of the Postcolonial State* (Durham, NC: Duke University Press); L. I. Rudolph and J. K. Jacobsen (eds) (2006) *Experiencing the State* (Delhi: Oxford University Press); and the essays in T. Sherman, W. Gould, and S. Ansari (eds) (2011) 'Special Issue: Society and the Everyday State in India and Pakistan', *Modern Asian Studies*, 45, 1, 1–224.

36. Akhil Gupta (1995) 'Blurred Boundaries: The Discourse of Corruption, the Culture of Politics, and the Imagined State', *American Ethnology*, 22, 2, 375–402; C. Jeffreys (2002) 'Caste, Class, and Clientelism: A Political Economy of Everyday Corruption in Rural North India', *Economic Geography*, 78, 1, 21–41; W. Gould, *Bureaucracy, Community, and Influence*; S. Pierce (2006) 'Looking Like a State: Colonialism and the Discourse of Corruption in Northern Nigeria', *Comparative Studies in History and Society*, 48, 4, 887–914.
37. A. L. Stoler (2009) *Along the Archival Grain: Epistemic Anxieties and Colonial Commonsense* (Princeton, NJ: Princeton University Press).
38. A similar point has been made about white violence against Indians: J. Bailkin (2006) 'The Boot and the Spleen: When was Murder Possible in British India?', *Comparative Studies in Society and History*, 48, 2, 462–93.
39. NAM, 1/15 (E), 7276, 1906 File No. 7M-6, 20 April 1906.
40. Until 1908, all deputy commissioners were always European. J. F. Cady, *A History of Modern Burma*, p. 151.
41. G. Orwell (1989) *Burmese Days* (London: Penguin) p. 44.
42. P. Chatterjee (1993) *The Nation and its Fragments: Colonial and Postcolonial Histories* (Princeton, NJ: Princeton University Press) pp. 14–34.
43. This ambivalence towards some forms of cultural practices that came to be defined as 'corrupt' has also been noted in W. Gould, *Bureaucracy, Community, and Influence*.
44. Here I am following in the work of historians of crime in colonial Asia who have attempted to go beyond deconstructing colonial discourses as inventions and explore the social meanings of the practices defined as 'criminal'. For the historiographic discussion of Thuggee, see K. Wagner (2004) 'The Deconstructed Stranglers: A Reassessment of Thuggee', *Modern Asian Studies*, 38, 4, 931–63.
45. R. H. Taylor, *The State in Burma*, p. 91; J. F. Cady, *A History of Modern Burma*, pp. 176–8; F. S. Donnison (1953) *Public Administration in Burma: A Study of Development During the British Connexion* (London: Royal Institute of International Affairs) pp. 80–6; M. Adas (1981) 'From Avoidance to Confrontation: Peasant Protest in Precolonial and Colonial Southeast Asia', *Comparative Studies in Society and History*, 23, 2, 242–3.
46. For similar approaches, see S. Pierce, 'Looking Like a State'; T. Sherman, *State Violence and Punishment*.
47. *Times of Burma*, 5 June 1901.
48. Of course, it has been famously argued that the state as a concept is but a fiction in A. R. Radcliffe-Brown (1940) 'Preface', in M. Fortes and E. E. Evans-Pritchard (eds) *African Political Systems* (London: Oxford University Press, for the International African Institute) pp. xi–xxiii.
49. J. L. Comaroff, 'Reflections on the Colonial State', p. 336.
50. L. I. Rudolph and J. K. Jacobsen (eds) (2006) 'Framing the Inquiry: Historicizing the Modern State', in *Experiencing the State* (New Delhi: Oxford University Press) pp. xii–xiii; T. B. Hansen and F. Stepputat (eds) (2001) 'Introduction: States of Imagination', in *States of Imagination: Ethnographic Explorations of the Postcolonial State* (Durham, NC: Duke University Press) p. 14.
51. J. Pham, 'Ghost Hunting in Colonial Burma'.
52. J. Butler (1988) 'Performative Acts and Gender Constitution: An Essay in Phenomenology and Feminist Theory', *Theatre Journal*, 40, 4, 519–31.

53. K. C. Dunn (2010) 'There is No Such Thing as the State: Discourse, Effect and Performativity', *Forum for Development Studies*, 37, 1, 79–92; C. Weber (1998) 'Performative States', *Millennium: Journal of International Studies*, 27, 1, 77–95.

54. C. Geertz (1980) *Negara: The Theatre State in Nineteenth Century Bali* (Princeton, NJ: Princeton University Press) p. 13.

55. A. McClintock (1992) 'The Angel of Progress: Pitfalls of the Term "Post-Colonialism"', *Social Text*, 31/32, 84–98; Ranjana Khanna (2003) *Dark Continents: Psychoanalysis and Colonialism* (Durham, London: Duke University Press).

56. M. Aung-Thwin, 'The British "Pacification" of Burma'.

57. M. Aung-Thwin and M. Aung-Thwin (2012) *A History of Myanmar Since Ancient Times: Traditions and Transformations* (London: Reaktion Books) p. 17.

58. T. Myint-U (2001) *The Making of Modern Burma* (Cambridge: Cambridge University Press); indeed, M. Aung-Thwins' *A History of Myanmar* is in many respects a commercial rival to T. Myint-U (2007) *A River of Lost Footsteps: A Personal History of Burma* (New York: Faber and Faber).

59. T. Myint-U (2011) 'In Myanmar, Seize the Moment', *New York Times*, 5 October 2011, p. A27.

60. M. Aung-Thwin (2001) 'Parochial Universalism, Democracy Jihad and the Orientalist Image of Burma: The New Evangelism', *Pacific Affairs*, 74, 4, 483–505.

61. See particularly, C. Ikeya (2011) *Refiguring Women, Colonialism and Modernity in Burma* (Honolulu: University of Hawai'i Press).ap 2.

62. M. T. Taussig (1992) *The Nervous System* (New York, London: Routledge) p. 113.

1   Making Misconduct

1. Commentators on corruption have long highlighted this, but it continues to be necessary to point this out. For recent work commenting on corruption as a depiction of non-Western 'others', see: D. Haller and C. Shore (2005), 'Introduction—Sharp Practice: Anthropology and the Study of Corruption' in D. Haller and C. Shore (eds) *Corruption: Anthropological Perspectives* (London: Pluto) pp. 1–26. For a much earlier complaint about this tendency, see J. C. Scott (1969) 'The Analysis of Corruption in Developing Nations', *Comparative Studies in Society and History*, 11, 3, 315–41.

2. P. Perry (2005) 'Corruption in Burma and the Corruption of Burma' in N. Tarling (ed.) *Corruption and Good Governance in Asia* (London: Routledge) p. 188.

3. O. P. Dwivedi (1967), 'Bureaucratic Corruption in Developing Countries', *Asian Survey*, 7, 4, 245–53.

4. H. T. White (1913) *A Civil Servant in Burma* (London: E. Arnold) p. 143.

5. C. H. T. Crosthwaite (2001) 'The Administration of Burma' in P. H. Kratoska (ed.) *Southeast Asia: Colonial History*, Vol. 2 (London: Routledge) p. 213.

6. This imperialist argument is explicitly made in F. S. Donnison (1953) *Public Administration in Burma: A Study of Development during the British Connexion* (London: Royal Institute of International Affairs).

7. D. G. E. Hall (2001) 'Anglo-Burmese Conflicts in the 19th Century: A Reassessment of their Causes' in P. H. Kratoska (ed.) *Southeast Asia: Colonial History*, Vol. 2 (London: Routledge) p. 201.

8. R. H. Taylor (1987) *The State in Burma* (London: Hurst & Co.) p. 84.

9. White, *A Civil Servant in Burma*, p. 262.

10. A similar argument has been made in Anupama Rao (2001) 'Problems of Violence, States of Terror: Torture in Colonial India', *Interventions: The International Journal of Postcolonial Studies*, 3, 2, 186–205.

11. My conceptualisation of misconduct as an illegality owes much to M. Foucault (1979) *Discipline and Punish: The Birth of the Prison*, trans. Alan Sheridan (Harmondsworth: Penguin Books).

12. For British India, see S. B. Freitag (1991) 'Crime in the Social Order of Colonial North India', *Modern Asian Studies*, 25, 2, 227–61; A. A. Yang (ed.) (1985) *Crime and Criminality in British India* (Tucson, AZ: University of Arizona Press); C. Anderson (2004) *Legible Bodies: Race, Criminality and Colonialism in South Asia* (Oxford: Berg); Meena Radhakrishna (2001), *Dishonoured by History: 'Criminal Tribes' and British Colonial Policy* (Hyderabad: Orient Longman). For Southeast Asia, see V. L. Rafael (ed.) (1999) *Figures of Criminality in Indonesia, the Philippines, and Colonial Vietnam* (Ithaca, NY: Cornell University Press). For Burma, see J. Saha (2012) 'Madness and the Making of a Colonial Order in Burma', *Modern Asian Studies* (Advanced online publication via *Firstview*), 1–30. Doi: 10.1017/S0026749X11000400; M. Aung-Thwin (2011) *The Return of the Galon King: History, Law, and Rebellion in Colonial Burma* (Athens, OH: Ohio University Press).

13. V. Lal (1999) 'Everyday Crime, Native Mendacity and the Cultural Psychology of Justice in Colonial India', *Studies in History*, 15, 1, 145–66.

14. A. A. Yang (1987) 'Disciplining "Natives": Prisons and Prisoners in Early Nineteenth Century India', *South Asia: Journal of South Asian Studies*, 10, 2, 29–45.

15. Foucault, *Discipline and Punish*, p. 272.

16. J. McC. Heyman and A. Smart (1999) 'States and Illegal Practices: An Overview' in J. McC. Heyman (ed.) *States and Illegal Practices* (Oxford, New York: Berg) pp. 1–24; A. Tambe (2009) *Codes of Misconduct: Regulating Prostitution in Late Colonial Bombay* (London: University of Minnesota Press).

17. See, for example, the diaries and official correspondence of Lieutenant Governor Fryer who served in the highest post in Burma continuously from 1895 to 1903. India Office Records, British Library, London; hereafter, IOR, MSS Eur E 355.

18. *Local Government Circulars Issued from the General Secretariat, 1888 to the 31 March 1915* (Rangoon: Office of the Superintendent, Government Printing, 1916) pp. 18–20.

19. An assistant superintendent of police called Maung Tun Min was successful in having charges of extorting a confession from a convict through torture dropped in 1900 due to his written explanation (National Archive of Myanmar, Yangon; hereafter, NAM, 1/15 (E), 7036, 1900 File No. 7M-27, 1 August 1900). Similarly, a subdivisional officer in Maubin, Maung Tha No, escaped punishment for breaking standing orders regarding the allocation of grants of land by pleading ignorance of the orders in his written explanation (NAM, 1/15 (E), 7032, 1900 File No. 7M-23, 10 August 1900).

20. *Local Government Circulars*, p. 25.
21. Ibid., p. 26.
22. This may explain why, although dismissed subordinate officials sent many petitions requesting that the decision in their case be reconsidered, decisions were rarely overturned (ibid., pp. 24–5).
23. *The Indian Penal Code, (Act XLV of 1860): As Modified Up to the 1st June, 1910, with an Index* (Calcutta: Superintendent of Government Printing, India, 1915).
24. Saw U White, a treasury officer in Bassien district, was investigated for misconduct after he was found at work in a 'state of hopeless intoxication' and his correspondence was found to be incomprehensible (NAM, 1/15 (E), 7008, 1899 File No. 7M-23, 11 November 1899).
25. Other less controversial orders involved broad issues such as how to regulate land-ownership among subordinate officials. Other orders were more specific, such as those to prohibit clerks bidding in government auctions.
26. IOR, P/4037, (GOB) Home Dept. (Appointment/Miscellaneous) 1892, February 1892.
27. IOR, P/5800, (GOB), Home Dept. (Appointments) 1900, 7 April 1900.
28. Ibid., 5 April 1900.
29. NAM, 1/15 (E), 7276, 1906 File No. 7M-6.
30. NAM, 1/15 (E), 7017, 1900 File No. 7M-1, 21 December 1899.
31. NAM, 1/15 (E), 7021, 1900 File No. 7M-9.
32. *Local Government Circulars*, pp. 25–8.
33. For example, in 1899, a police sergeant employed in Henzada district called Maung Shwe Po was dismissed from government service for fabricating the evidence in a case of robbery. The case was not strong enough for a criminal conviction against Maung Shwe Po, but it was deemed that the balance of the evidence was against him and so he was charged departmentally with misconduct and dismissed (NAM, 1/15 (E), 6991, 1899 File No. 7M-2, 20 March 1899). In contrast, a year later, also in Henzada, a *myo-ok* charged with the less serious misconduct of incompetence in court proceedings was punished more lightly with a transfer (NAM, 1/15 (E), 7041, 1900 File No. 7M-34, 30 October 1900).
34. NAM, 1/15 (E), 7030, 1900 File No. 7M-19, July 1900.
35. NAM, 1/15 (E), 7174, 1904 File No. 7M-46, 14 December 1904.
36. NAM, 1/15 (E), 7006, 1899 File No. 7M-21, 16 October 1899.
37. NAM, 1/15 (E), 7022, 1900 File No. 7M-10, 15 March 1900.
38. NAM, 1/15 (E), 6995, 1899 File No. 7M-8.
39. NAM, 1/15 (E), 7224, 1905 File No. 7M-38.
40. NAM, 1/15 (E), 7350, 1908 File No. 7M-10.
41. The corruption among *thugyis* has been noted ubiquitously in studies of colonial Burma, if only in passing. But for references to corruption in other administrative positions, albeit brief, see R. L. Bryant (1997) *The Political Ecology of Forestry in Burma, 1824–1994* (London: Hurst) pp. 124–5; A. Naono (2009) *State of Vaccination: The Fight against Smallpox in Colonial Burma* (Hyderabad: Orient Blackswan) pp. 149–60; J. Warren (2002) 'The Rangoon Jail Riot of 1930 and the Prison Administration of British Burma', *South East Asia Research*, 10, 1, 5–29.
42. NAM, 1/15 (E), 7350, 1908 File No. 7M-10.

43. A. Ireland (1907) *The Province of Burma: A Report Prepared on Behalf of the University of Chicago*, Vol. 1 (Boston, New York: Houghton, Mifflin & Co.) p. 149.
44. B. N. Lawrance, E. L. Osborn, and R. L. Roberts (eds) (2006) *Intermediaries, Interpreters, and Clerks: African Employees in the Making of Colonial Africa* (Madison, WI: University of Wisconsin Press); J. Rich (2004) 'Troubles at the Office: Clerks, State Authority, and Social Conflict in Gabon, 1920–45', *Canadian Journal of African Studies*, 38, 1, 58–87; J. Derrick (1983) 'The "Native Clerk" in Colonial West Africa', *African Affairs*, 82, 326, 61–74.
45. NAM, 1/15 (E), 7064, 1901 File No. 7M-24, 29 May 1901.
46. NAM, 1/15 (E), 7009, 1899 File No. 7M-24, 22 December 1899.
47. NAM, 1/15 (E), 7350, 1908 File No. 7M-10.
48. Ibid.
49. C. C. Lewis (1903) *The Machinations of the Myo-Ok* (London: Methuen).
50. NAM, 1/15 (E), 7056, 1901 File No. 7M-12, 13 April 1901.
51. NAM, 1/15 (E), 7350, 1908 File No. 7M-10.
52. *Times of Burma*, 4 February 1899.
53. NAM, 1/15 (E), 7381, 1909 File No. 7M-15, 19 October 1909.
54. NAM, 1/15 (E), 7350, 1908 File No. 7M-10.
55. NAM, 1/15 (E), 7281, 1906 File No. 7M-11, 5 June 1906; NAM, 1/15 (E), 7282, 1906 File No. 7M-11, 14 June 1906.
56. There was some debate among officials over which method resulted in the best candidates that was still unresolved during the first decade of the twentieth century.
57. IOR, P/6036, (GOB) Home Dept. (Appointments/Miscellaneous) 1901, 9 September 1901.
58. NAM, 1/15 (E), 7200, 1905 File No. 7M-8, 13 February 1905.
59. Ibid., 14 February 1905.
60. Ibid.
61. NAM, 1/15 (E), 7195, 1905 File No. 7M-1; NAM, 1/15 (E), 7178, 1904 File No. 7M-51.
62. NAM, 1/15 (E), 7215, 1905 File No. 7M-28, 17 August 1905.
63. Rich, 'Troubles at the Office'; Sumit Sarkar (2002) *Beyond Nationalist Frames: Postmodernism, Hindu Fundamentalism, History* (Bloomington: Indiana University Press) pp. 28–37.
64. R. H. Taylor (2008) *The State in Myanmar* (London: Hurst & Co.) pp. 164–5.
65. NAM, 1/15 (E), 7176, 1904 File No. 7M-48, 22 September 1904.
66. For example, see, H. Fielding-Hall (1899) *The Soul of a People*, 3rd edn (London: Macmillan); J. Nisbet (1901) *Burma under British Rule—and Before*, Vol. 1 (Westminster: Constable); J. G. Scott (1910) *The Burman: His Life and Notions*, 3rd edn (London: Macmillan).
67. NAM, 1/15 (E), 7216, 1905 File No. 7M-29, 14 June 1905.
68. Ibid.
69. NAM, 1/15 (E), 7055, 1901 File No. 7M-10, 11 March 1901.
70. Ibid., 15 June 1901.
71. Ibid., 12 August 1901.
72. Ibid., 31 July 1901.
73. *Times of Burma*, 29 April 1899.

74. *Times of Burma*, 5 March 1902.

75. *Times of Burma*, 3 May 1902.

76. *Times of Burma*, 6 February 1901.

77. Lowis, *The Machinations of the Myo-Ok*.

78. G. Orwell (1989) *Burmese Days* (London: Penguin). For more on the tradition Orwell was writing within, see S. L. Keck (2005) 'Text and Context: Another Look at *Burmese Days*', *SOAS Bulletin of Burma Research*, 3, 1, 27–40.

79. Due to there being many individuals named Maung Gyi in government employ the administration took to adding numbers to the ends of their names to distinguish between them in correspondence, this being Maung Gyi number eight. As there is only one Maung Gyi in our narrative, the number has been dropped from his name.

80. For more on this strategy, see Chapter 3 on the use of petitions in misconduct cases.

81. NAM, 1/15 (E), 7107, 1903 File No. 7M-11, 10 March 1903.

82. Ibid., 28 March 1903.

83. NAM, 1/15 (E), 7112, 1903 File No. 7M-17, 22 April 1903.

84. Ibid.

85. NAM, 1/15 (E), 7179, 1904 File No. 7M-52.

86. NAM, 1/15 (E), 7196, 1905 File No. 7M-2, 5 January 1905.

87. For the important gendered aspect of Maung Gyi's behaviour, see Chapter 4 in which his acts are placed in the context of the broader gendering of the colonial state.

88. NAM, 1/15 (E), 7222, 1905 File No. 7M-35, 2 November 1905.

89. Ibid., 3 November 1905.

90. NAM, 1/15 (E), 7273, 1906 File No. 7M-3, 25 May 1906.

91. NAM, 1/15 (E), 6995, 1899 File No. 7M-8, 30 March 1899.

92. Partha Chatterjee (1994) *The Nation and Its Fragments: Colonial and Postcolonial Histories* (Delhi: Oxford University Press) p. 18.

93. J. F. Cady (1958) *A History of Modern Burma* (Ithaca, NY: Cornell University Press) p. 151.

94. *Times of Burma*, 7 January 1899.

95. NAM, 1/15 (E), 6994, 1899 File No. 7M-7, 24 March 1899; the details of his trials were also reported, but became more muted during his second trial in which he was convicted of bribery.

96. *Times of Burma*, 26 August 1899.

97. *Times of Burma*, 19 June 1901.

98. NAM, 1/15 (E), 7027, 1900 File No. 7M-15, 13 March 1900.

99. Ibid.

100. Ibid.

101. Ibid.

102. Ibid.

103. Ibid., 3 October 1900.

104. NAM, 1/15 (E), 7315, 1907 File No. 7M-7, 27 May 1907.

105. Ibid., 14 June 1907.

106. Ibid., 18 August 1907.

107. *Times of Burma*, 25 August 1900.

108. NAM, 1/15 (E), 7203, 1905 File No. 7M-11, 13 March 1905.

109. Ibid., 17 February 1905 and 15 May 1905.

110. NAM, 1/15 (E), 7351, 1908 File No. 7M-11, 31 October 1908.
111. This was also apparent in criminal punishment, see H. Fischer-Tine (2009) 'Hierarchies of Punishment in Colonial India: European Convicts and the Racial Dividend, c. 1860–1890' in H. Fischer-Tine and S. Gehermann (eds) *Empires and Boundaries: Rethinking Race, Class, and Gender in Colonial Settings* (New York: Routledge) pp. 41–65.
112. A. L. Stoler (2002) *Carnal Knowledge and Imperial Power: Race and the Intimate in Colonial Rule* (Berkeley, CA: University of California Press).
113. Cady, *A History of Modern Burma.*
114. E. M. Powell-Brown (1911) *A Year on the Irrawaddy* (Rangoon: Myles Standish & Co.) pp. 13–14.
115. Ibid., pp. 94, 160.
116. M. Adas (1974) *The Burma Delta: Economic Development and Social Change on an Asian Rice Frontier, 1852–1941* (Madison, WI: University of Wisconsin Press) pp. 38, 60.
117. J. Mackenna (1903) *Report on the Settlement Operations in the Myaungmya and Thongwa Districts, Season 1902–03* (Rangoon: British Burma Press) p. 1.
118. Ibid.
119. Ibid., p. 2.
120. I. Brown (1997) *Economic Change in South-East Asia, c. 1830–1980* (Kuala Lumpur: Oxford University Press) p. 115; M. Adas (2009) 'Continuity and Transformation: Colonial Rice Frontiers and Their Environmental Impact on the Great River Deltas of Mainland Southeast Asia' in E. Burke and K. Pomeranz (eds) *The Environment and World History* (Berkeley, CA: University of California Press) p. 198.
121. *Imperial Gazetteer of India: Provincial Series, Burma. Vol. 1: the Province; Mountains, Rivers, Tribes; and the Arkan, Pegu, Irrawaddy, and Tenasserim Divisions* (Calcutta: Superintendent of Government Printing, 1908) pp. 350–5.
122. IOR, P/6275, (GOB) Home Dept. (Appointments/Miscellaneous) 1902.
123. Several *myo-oks* were disciplined through the misconduct proceedings for their incompetence, negligence, and inefficiency in dealing with the proceedings of civil courts at this time. For instance, Maung Po Thin of Zalun in Henzada was transferred for his incompetence in court procedures in 1900 (NAM, 1/15 (E), 7041, 1900 File No. 7M-34, 30 October 1900). Months later, a second *myo-ok* in Henzada was transferred for causing delays and for having careless omissions in his work (NAM, 1/15 (E), 7051, 1901 File No. 7M-6, 11 February 1901).
124. IOR, P/6275, (GOB) Home Dept. (Appointments/Miscellaneous) 1902, 24 March 1902.
125. See J. Saha (2012) 'A Mockery of Justice? Colonial Law, the Everyday State, and Village Politics in the Burma Delta', *Past & Present*, 217, 187–212.
126. J. Mackenna (1899) *Report on Revision Settlement Operations in Bassein District, Season 1897–98* (Rangoon: British Burma Press) pp. 29–30; Mackenna, *Myaungmya and Thongwa Districts, Season 1902–03*, p. 14; D. Chalmers (1908) *Report on the Revision Settlement Operations in Pyapon District, Season 1906–07* (Rangoon: British Burma Press) p. 10.
127. NAM, 1/15 (E), 7287, 1906 File No. 7M-16, 3 August 1906.

128. Chalmers, *Pyapon District, Season 1906–07*, p. 2.
129. IOR, P/6275, (GOB) Home Dept. (Appointments/Miscellaneous) 1902, 8 September 1900.
130. Taylor, *The State in Burma*, p. 91; M. Adas (1981) 'From Avoidance to Confrontation: Peasant Protest in Precolonial and Colonial Southeast Asia', *Comparative Studies in Society and History*, 23, 2, 242–3; Cady, *A History of Modern Burma*, pp. 176–8; D. G. E. Hall (1974), *Burma* (New York: AMS Press), p. 149; Donnison, *Public Administration in Burma*, pp. 80–6.
131. M. Nuijten and G. Anders (eds) (2007) 'Corruption and the Secret of Law: An Introduction' in *Corruption and the Secret of Law: A Legal Anthropological Perspective* (Ashgate: Aldershot) pp. 9–12.

2   The Career of Inspector Pakiri

1. T. Hobbes (1996) *Leviathan* (Cambridge: Cambridge University Press).
2. D. Gilmour (2006) *The Ruling Caste: Imperial Lives in the Victorian Raj* (New York: Farrar, Straus and Giroux).
3. M. P. Callahan (2003) *Making Enemies: War and State Building in Burma* (Ithaca, NY: Cornell University Press) pp 21–44.
4. Timothy Mitchell's writings on the state are central to my theoretical formulation of this chapter. T. Mitchell (1991) 'The Limits of the State: Beyond Statist Approaches and Their Critics', *The American Political Science Review*, 85, 1, 77–96.
5. R. H. Taylor (1987) *The State in Burma* (London: C. Hurst & Co) p. 82.
6. J. F. Cady (1958) *A History of Modern Burma* (Ithaca, NY: Cornell University Press) p. 153.
7. J. S. Furnivall (1948) *Colonial Policy and Practice: A Comparative Study of Burma and Netherlands India* (Cambridge: Cambridge University Press) p. 75.
8. B. N. Lawrance, E. L. Osborn, and R. L. Roberts (eds) (2006) 'Introduction: African Intermediaries and the "Bargain" of Collaboration', in *Intermediaries, Interpreters, and Clerks: African Employees in the Making of Colonial Africa* (Madison, WI: University of Wisconsin Press) p. 7.
9. Ibid.
10. N. R. Hunt (1999) *A Colonial Lexicon of Birth Ritual, Medicalization, and Mobility in the Congo* (Durham, NC: Duke University Press) pp. 1–26.
11. P. Edwards (2004) 'Relocating the Interlocutor: Taw Sein Ko (1864–1930) and the Itinerancy of Knowledge in British Burma', *South East Asia Research*, 12, 3, 277–335.
12. A. H. M. Kirk-Greene (1980) 'The Thin White Line: The Size of the British Colonial Service in Africa', *African Affairs*, 79, 314, 25–44.
13. H. T. White (1913) *A Civil Servant in Burma* (London: E. Arnold) p. 262.
14. See also H. Fielding-Hall (1906) *A People at School* (London: Macmillan); J. Nisbet (1901) *Burma Under British Rule—and Before*, Vol. 1 (Westminster: Constable).
15. My conceptualisation of the performative is derived from my reading of J. Butler (1988) 'Performative Acts and Gender Constitution: An Essay in Phenomenology and Feminist Theory', *Theatre Journal*, 40, 4, 519–31.
16. *Times of Burma*, 25 September 1901.

17. Ibid.
18. Ibid.
19. *Times of Burma*, 5 October 1901.
20. Ibid.
21. *Times of Burma*, 10 February 1900.
22. *Times of Burma*, 17 February 1900.
23. *Times of Burma*, 7 August 1901.
24. *Times of Burma*, 4 September 1901.
25. *Times of Burma*, 30 November 1901.
26. Ibid.
27. This was discussed in more detail in Chapter 1.
28. I have calculated these statistics using the list of dismissed persons from 1908, and a supplementary list for the year 1909: NAM, 1/15 (E), 7350, 1908 File No. 7M-10 and NAM, 1/15 (E), 7377, 1909 File No. 7M-10, respectively.
29. A. Ireland (1907) *The Province of Burma: A Report Prepared on Behalf of the University of Chicago*, Vol. 1 (Boston, New York: Houghton, Mifflin & Co.) p. 219.
30. A. Ireland (1907) *The Province of Burma: A Report Prepared on Behalf of the University of Chicago*, Vol. 2 (Boston, New York: Houghton, Mifflin & Co.) p. 718.
31. A. Ireland, *The Province of Burma*, Vol. 1, p. 227.
32. J. Nisbet, *Burma Under British Rule—and Before*, Vol. 1, p. 235.
33. Lalita Hingkanonta is now engaged on exactly this project.
34. A. Ireland, *The Province of Burma*, Vol. 1, p. 208.
35. Ibid., pp. 200–201, 208.
36. *Report on the Police Administration of Burma 1898* (Rangoon: Home Department, 1899) pp. 28–9; *Report on the Police Administration of Burma 1899* (Rangoon: Home Department, 1900) pp. 20–1; *Report on the Police Administration of Burma 1900* (Rangoon: Home Department, 1901) pp. 70–1.
37. J. C. Scott (2009) *The Art of Not Being Governed: An Anarchist History of Upland Southeast Asia* (New Haven, CT: Yale University Press) pp. 51–61.
38. D. Arnold (1985) 'Bureaucratic Recruitment and Subordination in Colonial India: The Madras Constabulary, 1859–1947', in Ranajit Guha (ed.) *Subaltern Studies IV: Writings on South Asian History and Society* (Delhi: Oxford University Press) p. 33.
39. Ibid., p. 53.
40. Anupama Rao (2001) 'Problems of Violence, States of Terror: Torture in Colonial India', *Interventions: The International Journal of Postcolonial Studies*, 3, 2, 199.
41. Ibid., p. 191.
42. NAM, 1/15 (E), 6982, 1898 File No. 7M-15, 29 June 1898.
43. *Times of Burma*, 1 January 1899, 28 January 1899. Escaping prosecution in this trial, he was again criminally charged in 1902 when working as an inspector in Pakiri's old township of Dedaye, NAM, 1/15 (E), 7083, 1902 File No. 7M-10, 30 April 1902.
44. NAM, 1/15 (E), 7066, 1901 File No. 7M-29.
45. This understanding is influenced by Giddens's idea of the 'duality of structure', see A. Giddens (1979) *Central Problems in Social Theory: Action, Structure and Contradiction in Social Analysis* (London: Macmillan) pp. 49–95.
46. Bourdieu's notion of the state as the concentration of various types of capital is useful in supporting this argument; Pakiri had more coercive and

informational capital than other subordinate officials. P. Bourdieu (1999) 'Rethinking the State: Genesis and Structure of the Bureaucratic Field', in G. Steinmetz (ed.) *State/Culture: State-Formation After the Cultural Turn* (Ithaca, NY: Cornell University Press) pp. 53–75.

47. *Times of Burma*, 24 November 1900.
48. NAM, 1/15 (E), 7113, 1903 File No. 7M-21.
49. IOR, P/5801 (GOB) Home Dept. (Police) 1900, November Part B, vii, December Part B, pp. xiv–xv.
50. *Times of Burma*, 7 August 1901.
51. *Times of Burma*, 29 September 1900.
52. IOR, P/5801 (GOB) Home Dept. (Police) 1900, December Part B, pp. xv–xvi.
53. This is suggested in Chapter 1. NAM, 1/15 (E), 7350, 1908 File No. 7M-10.
54. *Times of Burma*, 22 December 1900.
55. Ibid.
56. IOR, P/6037 (GOB) Home Dept. (Police) 1901, March Part B, p. xi.
57. IOR, P/6276 (GOB) Home Dept. (Appointments/Miscellaneous) 1902, 21 September 1900.
58. The phrase 'intimately acquainted' is often applied to Maxwell, but two specific examples are from IOR, P/6276 (GOB) Home Dept. (Appointments/Miscellaneous) 1902, 8 September and IOR, P/6037 (GOB) Home Dept. (Police) 1901, 20 December 1901.
59. White, *A Civil Servant in Burma*, p. 51.
60. Ibid., p. 198.
61. IOR, P/6037 (GOB) Home Dept. (Police) 1901, 20 December 1901.
62. The investigation could perhaps be described as one of those numerous exceptional, improvised, and informal aspects of colonial rule that were part what has been called a 'coercive network'. See T. Sherman (2010) *State Violence and Punishment in India* (London: Routledge) pp. 1–17.
63. IOR, P/6037 (GOB) Home Dept. (Police) 1901, 20 December 1900.
64. NAM, 1/15 (E), 7049, 1900 File No. 7M-1, 29 March 1901.
65. Ibid.
66. Some of these problems have been discussed in Anupama Rao (2005) 'Death of a Kotwal: Injury and the Politics of Recognition', in S. Mayaram, M. S. S. Pandian, and A. Skaria (eds) *Muslims, Dalits, and the Fabrications of History: Subaltern Studies 12* (New Delhi: Permanent Black and Ravi Dayal Publisher) pp. 140–87.
67. NAM, 1/15 (E), 7113, 1903 File No. 7M-21, 27 June 1903.
68. See the section on *myo-oks* in Chapter 1 for the case of Maung Gyi suspected of bribery.
69. IOR, P/5801 (GOB) Home Dept. (Police) 1900, December Part B, p. xiv.
70. IOR, P/5801 (GOB) Home Dept. (Police) 1900, December Part B, p. xv.
71. The use of approver's testimony was a legal innovation applied to forms of criminality deemed urgent by the British in India, that it was not invoked for corruption cases reflected their low priority for the higher echelons of the administration, see: S. Amin (1987) 'Approver's Testimony, Judicial Discourse: The Case of Chauri Chaura', in R. Guha (ed) *Subaltern Studies V: Writings on South Asian History and Society* (Delhi: Oxford University Press) pp. 166–202; Radika Singha (1993) '"Providential Circumstances": The Thuggee Campaign of the 1830s and Legal Innovation', *Modern Asian Studies*, 27, 1, 83–146.

72. NAM, 1/15 (E), 7049, 1901 File No. 7M-1, 29 March 1901.
73. NAM, 1/15 (E), 7040, 1900 File No. 7M-33, 27 November 1900.
74. NAM, 1/15 (E), 7049, 1901 File No. 7M-1, 29 March 1901.
75. Ibid.
76. This unsympathetic attitude among British high-ranking officials concerning rape is explored in Chapter 4.
77. R. Guha (ed.) (1987) 'Chandra's Death', in *Subaltern Studies V: Writings on South Asian History and Society* (Delhi: Oxford University Press) p. 141.
78. NAM, 1/15(E), 7049, 1901 File No. 7M-1, 7 January 1901.
79. NAM, 1/15 (E), 7049, 1900 File No. 7M-1, 29 March 1901.
80. Ibid.
81. Ibid.
82. The term 'burking' has macabre origins; it derives from the infamous nineteenth-century grave robber and murderer William Burke who suffocated his victims in order to provide bodies for dissection.
83. *Times of Burma*, 12 August 1899.
84. NAM, 1/15 (E), 7350, 1908 File No. 7M-10.
85. IOR, P/6037 (GOB) Home Dept. (Police) 1901, 20 December 1900.
86. NAM, 1/15 (E), 7113, 1903 File No. 7M-21.
87. NAM, 1/15 (E), 7049, 1901 File No. 7M-1, 29 March 1901.
88. Ibid.
89. NAM, 1/15 (E), 7026, 1900 File No. 7M-14, 1 June 1900.
90. NAM, 1/15 (E), 7049, 1901 File No. 7M-1, 29 March 1901.
91. Ibid.
92. Ibid.
93. White, *A Civil Servant in Burma*.
94. NAM, 1/15 (E), 7049, 1901 File No. 7M-1, 29 March 1901.
95. Ibid.
96. NAM, 1/15 (E), 7113, 1903 File No. 7M-21.
97. NAM, 1/15 (E), 7049, 1901 File No. 7M-1, 29 March 1901.
98. NAM, 1/15 (E), 7113, 1903 File No. 7M-21.
99. Maung Po Maung was the legal pleader who was entangled in a feud with Pakiri's enemy the *myo-ok* Aung Gyi mentioned earlier. NAM, 1/15 (E), 7049, 1901 File No. 7M-1, 29 March 1901.
100. This point is explored at length in Chapter 4.
101. NAM, 1/15 (E), 7113, 1903 File No. 7M-21.
102. NAM, 1/15 (E), 7075, 1902 File No. 7M-1, 12 April 1902.
103. NAM, 1/15 (E), 7049, 1901 File No. 7M-1, 29 March 1901.
104. *Times of Burma*, 7 August 1901.
105. *Times of Burma*, 30 November 1901.
106. The overall number is unclear as in many suspicious convictions for minor crimes the individuals had already served their sentences and been released by the time Maxwell had begun his investigation and so they were not investigated further.
107. The everyday state is an approach that focuses on the way in which the state is inserted into peoples' daily lives. For an espousal of this approach, though in a different context, see C. J. Fuller and V. Bénéï (eds) (2001) *The Everyday State and Society in Modern India* (London: Hurst & Company).

108. Anupama Rao argues that this was a spectre of colonial power raised by torture in the administration. I would argue in the case of Pakiri that this was a reality of colonial power. Rao, 'Torture in Colonial India', p. 193.
109. *Times of Burma*, 21 September 1901.
110. Rao, 'Torture in Colonial India', p. 187.
111. D. A. Champion (2003) 'Authority, Accountability and Representation: The United Provinces Police and the Dilemmas of the Colonial Policeman in British India, 1902–1939', *Historical Research*, 79, 192, 217–37.
112. NAM, 1/15 (E), 7049, 1900 File No. 7M-1, 29 March 1901.
113. C. Anderson (2004) *Legible Bodies: Race, Criminality and Colonialism in South Asia* (Oxford: Berg) pp. 57–99; N. B. Dirks (2001) *Castes of Mind: Colonialism and the Making of Modern India* (Princeton, NJ: Princeton University Press) pp. 125–228; D. Arnold (2004), 'Race, Place and Bodily Difference in Early Nineteenth-Century India', *Historical Research*, 77, 196, 254–73; S. Kapila (2007), 'Race Matters: Orientalism and Religion, India and Beyond c. 1770–1880', *Modern Asian Studies*, 41, 3, 471–513.
114. Vinay Lal (1999), 'Everyday Crime, Native Mendacity and the Cultural Psychology of Justice in Colonial India', *Studies in History*, 15, 1, 145–66; S. B. Freitag (1991), 'Crime in the Social Order of Colonial North India', *Modern Asian Studies*, 25, 2, 227–61.
115. See, for example, Maung Gyi, a *myo-ok* discussed in the previous chapter, and in respect to the gendered nature of Pakiri's acts see Chapter 4.
116. T. Mitchell, 'Limits of the State'.
117. NAM, 1/15 (E), 7350, 1908 File No. 7M-10.
118. M. Nuijten and G. Anders (2007) 'Corruption and the Secret of Law: An Introduction', in M. Nuijten and G. Anders (eds) *Corruption and the Secret of Law: A Legal Anthropological Perspective* (Aldershot: Ashgate) pp. 9–12.
119. This amounts to a reconfiguring of some aspects of Timothy Mitchell's approach to the modern state. His suggestion that discipline (in the Foucauldian meaning of the term) was central in transforming everyday practices into the state, and the state into everyday practices, requires space for the performative nature of the process. As we have seen in this chapter, misconduct and illegality can also reify the state. T. Mitchell, 'The Limits of the State'.
120. R. H. Taylor, *The State in Burma*, p. 91; J. F. Cady, *A History of Modern Burma*, pp. 176–8; F. S. Donnison (1953) *Public Administration in Burma: A Study of Development During the British Connexion* (London: Royal Institute of International Affairs) pp. 80–6; M. Adas (1981) 'From Avoidance to Confrontation: Peasant Protest in Precolonial and Colonial Southeast Asia', *Comparative Studies in Society and History*, 23, 2, pp. 242–3.
121. J. Butler, 'Performative Acts and Gender Constitution'; K. C. Dunn (2010) 'There is No Such Thing as the State: Discourse, Effect and Performativity', *Forum for Development Studies*, 37, 1, 79–92; C. Weber (1998) 'Performative States', *Millennium: Journal of International Studies*, 27, 1, 77–95.
122. S. Pierce (2006) 'Looking Like a State: Colonialism and the Discourse of Corruption in Northern Nigeria', *Comparative Studies in History and Society*, 48, 4, 887–914. T. Sherman, *State Violence and Punishment*.
123. See 'Introduction'. C. Geertz (1980) *Negara: The Theatre State in Nineteenth Century Bali* (Princeton, NJ: Princeton University Press).

3 Whiter than White

1. D. Arnold (2004) 'Race, Place and Bodily Difference in Early Nineteenth-Century India', *Historical Research*, 77, 196, 254–73; Partha Chatterjee (1994) *The Nation and Its Fragments: Colonial and Postcolonial Histories* (Delhi: Oxford University Press) pp. 14–34; F. Cooper (2005) *Colonialism in Question: Theory, Knowledge, History* (California: University of California Press) pp. 171–90; S. Kapila (2007) 'Race Matters: Orientalism and Religion, India and Beyond c. 1770–1880', *Modern Asian Studies*, 41, 3, 471–513; A. L. Stoler (2002) *Carnal Knowledge and Imperial Power: Race and the Intimate in Colonial Rule* (Berkeley, CA: University of California Press).

2. Considerable headway has been made in research on the everyday experience of racial difference in E. Kolsky (2010) *Colonial Justice in British India: White Violence and the Rule of Law* (Cambridge: Cambridge University Press).

3. G. Orwell (1989) *Burmese Days* (London: Penguin) p. 44.

4. R. E. Frykenberg (1965) *Guntur District, 1788–1848: A History of Local Influence and Central Authority in South India* (Oxford: Clarendon Press).

5. R. Chandavarkar (2009) 'State and Society in Colonial India', in *History, Culture and the Indian City* (Cambridge: Cambridge University Press) pp. 84–93.

6. S. Lukes (1974) *Power: A Radical View* (London: Macmillan); M. Foucault (1991) 'Governmentality', in G. Burchell, C. Gordon, and P. Miller (eds) *The Foucault Effect: Studies in Governmentality* (Chicago, IL: Chicago University Press) pp. 87–104.

7. C. J. Fuller and V. Bénéï (eds) (2001) *The Everyday State and Society in Modern India* (London: Hurst and Co.); T. Sherman (2010) *State Violence and Punishment in India* (London: Routledge) pp. 1–16.

8. W. Gould (2010) *Bureaucracy, Community, and Influence in India: Society and the State, 1930s–1960s* (New York: Routledge) pp. 104–36.

9. A. Ireland (1907) *The Province of Burma: A Report Prepared on Behalf of the University of Chicago*, Vol. 1 (Boston, New York: Houghton, Mifflin & Co.) p. 122; J. Nisbet (1901) *Burma Under British Rule—and Before*, Vol. 1 (Westminster: Constable) p. 227.

10. J. F. Cady (1958) *A History of Modern Burma* (Ithaca, NY: Cornell University Press) p. 151.

11. A. H. M. Kirk-Greene (1980) 'The Thin White Line: The Size of the British Colonial Service in Africa', *African Affairs*, 79, 314, 25–44.

12. The anthropologists James Ferguson and Akhil Gupta have argued that states are imagined spatially as both above and enclosing society through myriad material practices. From the position ascribed to deputy commissioners, the colonial state in Burma was imagined as hierarchical and compartmentalised both spatially and racially. J. Ferguson and A. Gupta (2002) 'Spatializing States: Toward an Ethnography of Neoliberal Governmentality', *American Ethnologist*, 29, 4, 981–1002.

13. A. A. Yang (1987) 'Disciplining "Natives": Prisons and Prisoners in Nineteenth-Century India', *South Asia: Journal of South Asian Studies*, 10, 2, 29–45; M. Aung-Thwin (2011) *The Return of the Galon King: History, Law, and Rebellion in Colonial Burma* (Athens, OH: Ohio University Press).

14. This has been called the 'racial dividend': H. Fischer-Tine (2009) 'Hierarchies of Punishment in Colonial India: European Convicts and the Racial Dividend, c.1860–1890', in H. Fischer-Tine and S. Gehermann (eds) *Empires and Boundaries: Rethinking Race, Class, and Gender in Colonial Settings* (New York: Routledge) pp. 41–65.
15. The new district was created in 1903. IOR, P/6275 (GOB) Home Dept. (Appointments/Miscellaneous) 1902.
16. This complaint is echoed in D. G. E. Hall (1956) *Burma*, 2nd edn (London: Hutchinson's University Library).
17. M. Foucault (1979) *Discipline and Punish: The Birth of the Prison*, trans. Alan Sheridan (Harmondsworth: Penguin Books).
18. NAM, 1/15(E), 7005, 1899 File No. 7M-20, 30 November 1899.
19. Ibid.
20. The gendered nature of this investigation was not unusual but part of a broader gendered access to the resources that were brought through colonial disciplinary practices, as I show in the following chapter.
21. For example, the secretary of the Lemyethna town committee had misconduct proceedings brought against him when a building contract was offered to his brother. NAM, 1/15 (E), 7060, 1901 File No. 7M-18, 11 October 1901.
22. See, for example, F. S. Donnison (1953) *Public Administration in Burma: A Study of Development During the British Connexion* (London: Royal Institute of International Affairs); Hall, *Burma*.
23. G. E. Harvey (1946) *British Rule in Burma, 1824–1942* (London: Faber and Faber) p. 38.
24. H. T. White (1913) *A Civil Servant in Burma* (London: E. Arnold) pp. 262–3.
25. A *pwe* is a word roughly equivalent to festival in this context.
26. NAM, 1/15 (E), 7196, 1905 File No. 7M-2, 5 January 1905.
27. This was most apparent in the institution of the club in British India: Mrinalini Sinha (2001) 'Britishness, Clubbability, and the Colonial Public Sphere: The Genealogy of an Imperial Institution in Colonial India', *Journal of British Studies*, 40, 4, 489–521. For more on how this was negotiated in colonial Burma, see P. Edwards (2002) 'Half-Cast: Staging Race in British Burma', *Postcolonial Studies*, 5, 3, 279–85; P. Edwards (2003) 'On Home Ground: Settling Land and Domesticating Difference in the "Non-Settler" Colonies of Burma and Cambodia', *Journal of Colonialism and Colonial History*, 4, 3.
28. Orwell, *Burmese Days*, p. 44.
29. H. Fielding-Hall (1906) *A People at School* (London: Macmillan) pp. 165–6.
30. Ibid., p. 172.
31. J. F. Cady, *A History of Modern Burma*, p. 154.
32. H. Fielding-Hall, *A People at School*, p. 221.
33. Ibid., p. 222.
34. Ibid., p. 224.
35. Certainly some of his contemporaries retrospectively viewed it as an overly optimistic portrayal. See the introduction to the *Report of the Bribery and Corruption Enquiry Committee 1940* (Rangoon: Superintendent of Government Printing, 1941) p. 9.
36. IOR, P/4037 (GOB) Home Dept. (Appointments and Miscellaneous) 1892, 5 July 1892.

37. Ibid.
38. C. C. Lowis (1903) *The Machinations of the Myo-Ok* (London: Methuen).
39. NAM, 1/15 (E), 7318, 1907 File No. 7M-11, 9 April 1907.
40. Ibid.
41. For two contrasting approaches to colonial information gathering, see A. Appadurai (1993) 'Number in the Colonial Imagination', in C. A. Breckenridge and P. Van Der Veer (eds) *Orientalism and the Postcolonial Predicament: Perspectives from South Asia* (Philadelphia, PA: University of Pennsylvania Press) pp. 114–135; C. A. Bayly (1996) *Empire and Information: Intelligence Gathering and Social Communication in India, 1780–1870* (Cambridge: Cambridge University Press).
42. The full extent of this recorded material has only recently been explored in its more minutial detail. A. Mizuno (2011) 'Identifying the "Agriculturists" in the Burma Delta in the Colonial Period: A New Perspective on Agriculturists Based on a Village Tract's Registers of Holdings from the 1890s to the 1920s', *Journal of Southeast Asian Studies*, 42, 3, 405–34. For more on the census in Burma, see J. Richell (2005) *Disease and Demography in Colonial Burma* (Copenhagen: NIAS).
43. For the use of descriptive rolls to monitor criminals, see C. Anderson (2004) *Legible Bodies: Race, Criminality and Colonialism in South Asia* (Oxford: Berg). Or having to provide information on their families, see A. J. Major (1999) 'State and Criminal Tribes in Colonial Punjab: Surveillance, Control and Reclamation of the "Dangerous Classes"', *Modern Asian Studies*, 33, 3, 657–88.
44. By 1908, this document ran into 83 pages. NAM, 1/15 (E), 7350, 1908 File No. 7M-10.
45. *Local Government Circulars Issued from the General Secretariat, 1888 to the 31st March 1915* (Rangoon: Office of the Superindendent, Government Printing, 1916) pp. 39–40.
46. Ibid., p. 34.
47. Ibid., pp. 81–83.
48. Taw Sein Ko (1913) *Burmese Sketches* (Rangoon: British Burma Press) p. 310; P. Edwards (2004) 'Relocating the Interlocutor: Taw Sein Ko (1864–1930) and the Itinerancy of Knowledge in British Burma,' *South East Asia Research*, 12, 3, 277–335.
49. *Local Government Circulars*, p. 88.
50. For instance, see I. Brown (2005) '"Blindness Which we Mistake for Sight": British Officials and the Economic World of the Cultivator in Colonial Burma', *Journal of Imperial and Commonwealth History*, 33, 2, 181–93.
51. NAM, 1/15 (E), 7174, 1904 File No. 7M-46.
52. P. Bourdieu (1999) 'Rethinking the State: Genesis and Structure of the Bureaucratic Field', in G. Steinmetz (ed.) *State/Culture: State-Formation After the Cultural Turn* (Ithaca, NY: Cornell University Press) pp. 53–75.
53. NAM, 1/15 (E), 6980, 1898, File No. 7M-5, 2 April 1898.
54. NAM, 1/15 (E), 7119, 1903, File No. 7M-31, 3 October 1903.
55. A notion also raised in M. Foucault (2000) 'The Lives of Infamous Men', in J. D. Faubion (ed.) *Power: Essential works of Foucault, 1954–1984*, Vol. 3, trans. Robert Hurley (New York: New Press) pp. 157–75.
56. NAM, 1/15 (E), 7029, 1900, File No. 7M-18, 10 April 1900.

57. NAM, 1/15 (E), 7035, 1900, File No. 7M-26.
58. For more on the politics of colonial forestry in Burma, see R. L. Bryant (1997) *The Political Ecology of Forestry in Burma, 1824–1994* (London: Hurst).
59. M. Adas (1983) 'Colonization, Commercial Agriculture, and the Destruction of the Deltaic Rainforests of British Burma in the late Nineteenth Century', in P. P. Tucker and J. F. Richards (eds) *Global Deforestation and the Nineteenth-Century World Economy* (Durham: Duke University Press) pp. 95–110.
60. J. McC. Heyman and A. Smart (1999) 'States and Illegal Practices: An Overview', in J. McC. Heyman (ed.) *States and Illegal Practices* (Oxford, New York: Berg) pp. 1–24.
61. For a study making use of a moral economy framework, see J. C. Scott (1976) *The Moral Economy of the Peasant: Rebellion and Subsistence in Southeast Asia* (New Haven, CT: Yale University Press).
62. NAM, 1/15 (E), 7035, 1900, File No. 7M-26, 21 April 1900.
63. L. Bear (2006) 'An Economy of Suffering: Addressing the Violence of Discipline in Railway Workers' Petitions to the Agent of the East Indian Railway, 1930–47', in S. Pierce and Anupama Rao (eds) *Discipline and the Other Body: Correction, Corporeality, Colonialism* (Durham, NC: Duke University Press) pp. 243–72.
64. NAM, 1/15 (E), 7035, 1900, File No. 7M-26.
65. These comparative amounts come from MacKenna, *Report on the Settlement Operations in the Myaungmya and Thongwa Districts*, p. 24; Ireland, *The Province of Burma*, Vol. 1, p. 219.
66. NAM, 1/15 (E), 7035, 1900, File No. 7M-26, 21 April 1900.
67. Ibid.
68. P. Swarnalatha (2001) 'Revolt, Testimony, Petition: Artisanal Protests in Colonial Andhra', *International Review of Social History*, 46, S9, 128.
69. NAM, 1/15 (E), 7035, 1900, File No. 7M-26, 20 August 1900.
70. Ibid.
71. Ibid.
72. Ibid.
73. Ibid.
74. Ibid.
75. Ibid.
76. Ibid.
77. Ireland, *The Province of Burma*, Vol. 1, p. 219.
78. NAM, 1/15 (E), 7035, 1900, File No. 7M-26, 20 August 1900.
79. Ireland, *The Province of Burma*, Vol. 1, p. 493.
80. This order was circulated among the District Commissioners on the 14 November 1898. *Local Government Circulars*, pp. 23–4.
81. NAM, 1/15 (E), 7035, File No. 7M-6, 25 September 1900.
82. Ibid.
83. NAM, 1/15 (E), 7066, 1901, File No. 7M-29, 12 August 1901.
84. Ibid.
85. NAM, 1/15 (E), 7083, 1902, File No. 7M-10, 12 May 1902, 5 March 1902.
86. Ibid., 28 September 1902.
87. NAM, 1/15 (E), 7103, 1903, File No. 7M-5, 17 March 1903.
88. NAM, 1/15 (E), 7077, 1902, File No. 7M-3, 28 October 1902.
89. Ibid.

90. Bayly, *Empire and Information*, pp. 1–9.
91. *Times of Burma*, 27 April 1901.
92. Chatterjee, *The Nation and Its Fragments*; A. L. Stoler (1995) *Race and the Education of Desire: Foucault's History of Sexuality, and the Colonial Order of Things* (Durham, NC: Duke University Press).
93. This is not the first time that followers of subordinate officials have appeared in this book. In Chapter 2, Deputy Commissioner Maxwell made repeated references to Pakiri's followers as well as the followers of his enemy, *Myo-ok* Maung Aung Gyi. He also complained of Pakiri's followers going about the Pyapon area to frighten potential witnesses. Similarly, in Chapter 1, I have shown that throughout his chequered career, the *myo-ok* Maung Gyi employed intermediaries. He used his follower Maung Ba Cho to solicit for and collect his bribes. In the last misconduct case against him, it also emerged that he used his magisterial powers in an ill-fated attempt to protect his follower Po San from prosecution.
94. For two important critiques of such structuring binaries, see S. Sarkar (2002) *Beyond Nationalist Frames: Postmodernism, Hindu Fundamentalism, History* (Bloomington: Indiana University Press); F. Cooper and A. L. Stoler (eds) (1997) 'Between Metropole and Colony: Rethinking a Research Agenda', in *Tensions of Empire: Colonial Cultures in a Bourgeois World* (Berkeley, CA: University of California Press) pp. 1–56.
95. B. N. Lawrance, E. L. Osborn, and R. L. Roberts (eds) (2006) *Intermediaries, Interpreters, and Clerks: African Employees in the Making of Colonial Africa* (Madison, WI: University of Wisconsin Press).
96. See my discussion of press depictions of the lower courts in J. Saha (2012) 'A Mockery of Justice? Colonial Law, the Everyday State and Village Politics in the Burma Delta, c. 1890–1910', *Past & Present*, 217, pp. 187–212.
97. Report of the Bribery and Corruption Enquiry Committee.
98. See, for example, the diaries and official correspondence of Lieutenant Governor Fryer who served in the highest position in Burma continuously from 1895 to 1903. MSS Eur E 355.
99. M. Foucault, *Discipline and Punish*.
100. H. Fielding-Hall, *A People at School*.
101. A. M. Burton (ed.) (1999) 'Introduction: The Unfinished Business of Colonial Modernities', in *Gender, Sexuality, and Colonial Modernities* (London: Routledge) pp. 1–16.
102. For an excellent analysis of the changing meanings and responses to corruption in a late-colonial context, see Gould, *Bureaucracy, Community, and Influence*.

4   The Male State

1. Following Joan W. Scott, I use gender in its radical sense—that sexes are socially and culturally constructed and not biological or natural essences—and not as a euphemism for women or simply to describe the differences between men and women. J. W. Scott (1999) *Gender and the Politics of History*, revised edn (New York: Columbia University Press).
2. R. Kipling (1994) 'Mandalay' in *The Collected Poems of Rudyard Kipling* (Ware: Wordsworth Editions) pp. 431–2.

3. This first section looks specifically at writings on Burman women, because colonial gender ideologies were crucial for defining and differentiating between different ethnic groups in Burma. Even though the authors themselves would often use the terms Burman and Burmese interchangeably, today this is more problematic, as Burmese can be used to describe all nationals of Myanmar. See T. Lwyn (1994) 'Stories of Gender and Ethnicity: Discourses of Colonialism and Resistance in Burma', *Australian Journal of Anthropology*, 5, 1, 60–85.

4. For more on the relationship between 'rhetoric and reality', see A. A. Powell and S. Lambert-Hurley (eds) (2006) 'Introduction: Problematizing Discourse and Practice', in *Rhetoric and Reality: Gender and the Colonial Experience in South Asia* (New Delhi: Oxford University Press) pp. 1–15.

5. C. Ikeya (2011), *Refiguring Women, Colonialism, and Modernity in Burma* (Honolulu: University of Hawaii Press) pp. 46–74.

6. A. L. Stoler (2009) *Along the Archival Grain: Epistemic Anxieties and Colonial Commonsense* (Princeton, NJ: Princeton University Press) pp. 28–31. Working in the archive is also experienced differently according to gender, as has been discussed by Antoinette Burton; see A. M. Burton (2004) 'Archive Stories: Gender in the Making of Imperial and Colonial Histories', in P. Levine (ed.) *Gender and Empire* (Oxford: Oxford University Press) pp. 281–93.

7. J. Bourke (2007) *Rape: A History from 1860 to the Present Day* (London: Virago) pp. 6–7.

8. Some historians' attempts to deal with these issues are explored fruitfully in Anupama Rao (2008) 'Affect, Memory, and Materiality: A Review Essay on Archival Mediation', *Comparative Studies in Society and History*, 50, 2, 559–67. And for a longer and fuller discussion of some of the philosophical difficulties raised here, see G. C. Spivak (1988) 'Can the Subaltern Speak?' in C. Nelson and L. Grossberg (eds) *Marxism and the Interpretation of Culture* (Basingstoke: Macmillan Education) pp. 271–316.

9. A. M. Burton (ed.) (1999) *Gender, Sexuality, and Colonial Modernities* (London: Routledge); P. Levine (ed.) (2004) *Gender and Empire* (Oxford: Oxford University Press); A. McClintock (ed.) (1995) *Imperial Leather: Race, Gender and Sexuality in the Colonial Contest* (New York: Routledge); C. Midgley (ed.) (1995) *Gender and Imperialism* (Manchester: Manchester University Press); A. A. Powell and S. Lambert-Hurley (eds) (2006) *Rhetoric and Reality: Gender and the Colonial Experience in South Asia* (New Delhi: Oxford University Press).

10. A. M. Burton (ed.) (1999) 'Introduction: The Unfinished Business of Colonial Modernities', in *Gender, Sexuality, and Colonial Modernities* (London: Routledge) p. 2.

11. A. McClintock (ed.) (1995) 'Introduction: Postcolonialism and the Angel of Progress', in *Imperial Leather: Race, Gender and Sexuality in the Colonial Contest* (New York: Routledge) p. 14.

12. C. Ikeya (2005) 'The "Traditional" High Status of Women in Burma', *Journal of Burma Studies*, 10, 51–81; Lwyn, 'Stories of Gender and Ethnicity'.

13. The James George Scott book *The Burman: His Life and Notions* was originally published in 1882 before the annexation of Upper Burma, but I have used the revised third edition published in 1910.

14. Mrinalini Sinha (1995) *Colonial Masculinity: The 'Manly Englishman' and the 'Effeminate Bengali' in the Late Nineteenth Century* (Manchester: Manchester University Press) pp. 1–32.

15. G. Rand (2006) '"Martial Races" and "Imperial Subjects": Violence and Governance in Colonial India, 1857–1914', *European Review of History*, 13, 1, 1–20; N. B. Dirks (2001) *Castes of Mind: Colonialism and the Making of Modern India* (Princeton, NJ: Princeton University Press) pp. 77–81.

16. S. Kapila (2005) 'Masculinity and Madness: Princely Personhood and Colonial Sciences of the Mind in Western India 1871–1940', *Past & Present*, 187, 121–56.

17. This is not a clean-cut difference. The title of Scott's book *The Burman: His Life and Notions* clearly demonstrates the gendered nature of his subject, the Burmans, as male. And, of course, the discussions of masculinity given as examples above often dealt with the position of women too, for example, the effeminacy of the Bengali man was understood about the degradation of Bengali women: see C. Hall (2004) 'Of Gender and Empire: Reflections on the Nineteenth Century', in P. Levine (ed.) *Gender and Empire* (Oxford: Oxford University Press) pp. 52–3. However, when authors approached the national traits and characteristics of the Burmese, it was often the women that were discussed, and the position of women was paramount in gendering the Burmans as a race.

18. Ikeya, 'The "Traditional" High Status of Women in Burma', p. 85.

19. F. Mort (2000) *Dangerous Sexualities: Medico-Moral Politics in England Since 1830*, 2nd edn (London: Routledge & Kegan Paul) pp. 81–110.

20. K. A. Ballhatchet (1980) *Race, Sex and Class Under the Raj: Imperial Attitudes and Policies and Their Critics, 1793–1905* (London: Weidenfeld and Nicholson) pp. 144–55.

21. J. G. Scott (1910) *The Burman: His Life and Notions*, 3rd edn (London: Macmillan) p. 52.

22. Ibid.

23. J. Nisbet (1901) *Burma Under British Rule—and Before*, Vol. 2 (Westminster: Constable) p. 214.

24. H. T. White (1913) *A Civil Servant in Burma* (London: E. Arnold) pp. 68–9.

25. Nisbet, *Burma Under British Rule—and Before*, Vol. 2, p. 182.

26. Scott, *The Burman*, p. 53.

27. Nisbet, *Burma Under British Rule—and Before*, Vol. 2, p. 204.

28. Ibid., pp. 216–17.

29. Ibid., p. 224.

30. Ibid., p. 225.

31. Scott, *The Burman*, p. 69.

32. H. Fielding-Hall (1906) *A People at School* (London: Macmillan) p. 266.

33. Hall, 'Of Gender and Empire', pp. 50–1.

34. Certainly Scott does not write explicitly that the role of women was harmful, damaging to Burmese society, but he does write in a fashion that marks out Burmese society as inherently different to European civilisation, and one that was less developed. The role of women was one important marker of difference that Scott employed to achieve this 'othering' effect: in this sense, his writings serve similar purposes as Fielding-Hall's. For the now ubiquitously footnoted, famous discussion of this literary strategy, see E. Said (1979) *Orientalism* (New York: Vintage Books).

35. It was in this that the male colonial gaze differed from that of European female travellers who found in Burmese women modernity and a cause to celebrate, not a need for correction. E. Cooper (1983) *The Harim and the*

Purdah: Studies of Oriental Women (Delhi: Bimla Pub. House) pp. 179–210; G. Trench-Gascoigne (1896) *Among Pagodas and Fair Ladies: An Account of a Tour Through Burma* (London: A. D. Innes & Co.) pp. 43–61.

36. Fielding-Hall, *A People at School*, p. 266.
37. Ibid., pp. 25–6.
38. Nisbet, *Burma Under British Rule—and Before*, Vol. 2, p. 204.
39. Ibid.
40. Ibid., pp. 205–13.
41. Scott, *The Burman*, pp. 53–7.
42. Ballhatchet, *Race, Sex and Class Under the Raj*, pp. 144–55.
43. Nisbet, *Burma Under British Rule—and Before*, Vol. 2, p. 251.
44. Ibid., pp. 251–2.
45. G. Orwell (1989) *Burmese Days* (London: Penguin); C. C. Lowis (1899) *The Treasury-Officer's Wooing* (London: Macmillan). Indeed, this conspicuous presence of white women was a central feature of Anglo-Indian novels across British India: see Indrani Sen (2002) *Woman and Empire: Representations in the Writings of British India, 1858–1900* (London: Sangam Books) pp. 80–3.
46. R. Kipling (1994) *The Collected Poems of Rudyard Kipling* (Ware: Wordsworth Editions) pp. 431–3.
47. Nisbet, *Burma Under British Rule—and Before*, Vol. 2, p. 250.
48. Ibid., p. 253.
49. Scott, *The Burman*, p. 48.
50. Ibid., p. 43.
51. Scott, *The Burman*, p. 56; Nisbet, *Burma Under British Rule—and Before*, Vol. 2, p. 211.
52. IOR, P/5800 (GOB) Home Dept. (Appointment/Miscellaneous) 1900, 29 August 1900.
53. P. Corrigan and D. Sayer (1985) *The Great Arch: English State Formation as Cultural Revolution* (Oxford: Blackwell) p. 12.
54. The importance of this distinction in misconduct procedures has been discussed in Chapter 1.
55. P. Corrigan and D. Sayer, *The Great Arch*; L. Davidoff and C. Hall (2002) *Family Fortunes: Men and Women of the English Middle Class, 1780–1850*, 2nd edn (London: Routledge); E. Dore (2000) 'One Step Forward, Two Steps Back: Gender and the State in Latin America', in E. Dore and M. Molyneux (eds) *Hidden Histories of Gender and the State in Latin America* (Durham, NC: Duke University Press) pp. 3–32; D. Paton (2004) *No Bond but the Law: Punishment, Race, and Gender in Jamaican State Formation, 1780–1870* (Durham, NC: Duke University Press) p. 61; K. Sangari and S. Vaid (eds) (1990) 'Recasting Women: An Introduction', in *Recasting Women: Essays in Indian Colonial History* (New Jersey: Rutgers University Press) pp. 1–26.
56. J. G. Scott (1913) 'The Position of Women in Burma', *The Sociological Review: Journal of the Sociological Society*, 6, 2, 145.
57. NAM, 1/15 (E), 7049, 1901 File No. 7M-1, 29 March 1901.
58. *Local Government Circulars Issued from the General Secretariat, 1888 to the 31st March 1915* (Rangoon: Office of the Superintendant, Government Printing, 1916) p. 40.
59. In Chapter 3, we have seen in the case of Po Kyaw how high-ranking British officials would sometimes explore the personal lives of their subordinates.

60. Nisbet, *Burma Under British Rule—and Before*, Vol. 2, p. 182; Scott, *The Position of Women in Burma*, p. 145.
61. IOR, P/4037 (GOB) Home Dept. (Appointment/Miscellaneous) 1892, February 1892.
62. NAM, 1/15(E), 7005, 1899 File No. 7M-20, 30 November 1899.
63. NAM, 1/15(E), 7050, 1901 File No. 7M-5, 28 February 1901.
64. NAM, 1/15(E), 7078, 1903 File No. 7M-5, 28 February 1902.
65. Ibid.
66. Ibid.
67. Ibid.
68. Ibid.
69. Ibid.
70. See the section on *myo-oks* in Chapter 2 for more details.
71. Ibid.
72. Ibid., 15 March 1902.
73. Paton, *No Bond but the Law*, p. 103.
74. For the official concerns about, perceptions of, and policies towards, the children of mixed-race unions in colonial Burma, see P. Edwards (2002) 'Half-Cast: Staging Race in British Burma', *Postcolonial Studies*, 5, 3, 279–95.
75. Quoted in Ballhatchet, *Race, Sex and Class Under the Raj*, p. 146.
76. Ibid., 148–9.
77. Ibid., p. 151.
78. NAM, 1/15(E), 7357, 1908 File No. 7M-18, 19 October 1908.
79. Orwell, *Burmese Days*.
80. This case has been thoroughly explored in J. Bailkin (2005) 'Making Faces: Tattooed Women and Colonial Regimes', *History Workshop Journal*, 59, 1, 33–56.
81. This case has been highlighted in both Ballhatchet, *Race, Sex and Class Under the Raj*, p. 142; D. M. Peers (1998) 'Privates off Parade: Regimenting Sexuality in the Nineteenth-Century Indian Empire', *The International History Review*, 20, 4, 823–4; and at length in J. Neill (2011) '"A Most Disgusting Case": Imperial Policy, Class, and Gender in the "Rangoon Outrage" of 1899', *Journal of Colonialism and Colonial History*, 12, 1.
82. J. Bailkin, 'Making Faces'.
83. For more on how European violence against 'natives' was dealt with under colonial rule, see J. Bailkin (2006) 'The Boot and the Spleen: When Was Murder Possible in British India?', *Comparative Studies in Society and History*, 48, 2, 128–92; M. J. Wiener (2009) *An Empire on Trial: Race, Murder, and Justice Under British Rule, 1870–1935* (Cambridge: Cambridge University Press) pp. 128–92; E. Kolsky (2010) *Colonial Justice in British India: White Violence and the Rule of Law* (Cambridge: Cambridge University Press).
84. Bourke, *Rape*.
85. NAM, 1/15(E), 7062, 1901 File No. 7M-21.
86. IOR, L/PJ/6/420, Public and Judicial Proceedings file 830, 2 May 1896.
87. NAM, 1/15(E), 7350, 1908 File No. 7M-10.
88. NAM, 1/15 (E), 7222, 1905 File No. 7M-35, 2 November 1905.
89. NAM, 1/15(E), 7211, 1905 File No. 7M-22, 31 May 1905.
90. Ibid.

91. Following the approach of Joanna Bourke's groundbreaking study of rape for the purposes of my analysis, any claim of rape made by a victim, perpetrator, or a third party is accepted: I do not attempt any abstract definition of rape. This way it is hoped that I avoid universalising narrow definitions of sexuality or the body. Bourke, *Rape*, pp. 9–11.

92. Nisbet, *Burma Under British Rule—and Before*, Vol. 2, pp. 222–3.

93. Ibid., p. 223.

94. Fielding-Hall, *A People at School*, p. 260.

95. Ibid., pp. 260–1.

96. Indeed, as Joanna Bourke has shown, this belief has been persistent and continues to be a commonsense myth about rape charges, obscuring the larger problem of the silence of victims. Bourke, *Rape*.

97. I have calculated these percentages using the statistical returns for Lower Burma published in the appendices of the following: *Report on Criminal Justice in Burma, for the Year 1890* (Rangoon: Judicial Department, 1891) and every subsequent year until, *Report on Criminal Justice in Burma, for the Year 1899* (Rangoon: Judicial Department, 1900).

98. *Report on Criminal Justice in Burma, for the Year 1904* (Rangoon: Judicial Department, 1905).

99. *Report on Criminal Justice in Burma, for the Year 1900* (Rangoon: Judicial Department, 1901) and every subsequent year until, *Report on Criminal Justice in Burma, for the Year 1907* (Rangoon: Judicial Department, 1908).

100. *Report on Criminal Justice in Burma, for the Year 1900*.

101. C. A. Conley (1986) 'Rape and Justice in Victorian England', *Victorian Studies*, 29, 4, 519–36.

102. The first two cases can be found in NAM, 1/15(E), 7350, 1908 File No. 7M-10 and the last case is from NAM, 1/15 (E), 7377, 1909 File No. 7M-10.

103. For more on this case, see the section on *myo-oks* in Chapter 2. NAM, 1/15 (E), 7222, 1905 File No. 7M-35, 2 November 1905.

104. NAM, 1/15 (E), 7219, 1905 File No. 7M-33.

105. See J. Saha (2012) '"Uncivilized Practitioners": Medical Subordinates, Medico-Legal Evidence, and Misconduct in Colonial Burma', *South East Asia Research*, 20, 4, 423–43.

106. NAM, 1/15(E), 7199, 1905 File No. 7M-6, 28 May 1905.

107. NAM, 1/15(E), 7350, 1908 File No. 7M-8, 21 September 1908.

108. NAM, 1/15(E), 7057, 1901 File No. 7M-13, 25 April 1901.

109. Ibid., 24 April 1901.

110. Ibid., 25 July 1901.

111. NAM, 1/15(E), 7080, 1902 File No. 7M-7, 27 May 1902.

112. NAM, 1/15(E), 7199, 1905 File No. 7M-6, 28 May 1905.

113. E. Kolsky (2010) 'The Body Evidencing the Crime: Rape on Trial in Colonial India, 1860–1947', *Gender and History*, 22, 1, 109–30.

114. NAM, 1/15(E), 7198, 1905 File No. 7M-5, 9 October 1899.

115. Ibid., 18 January 1905.

116. The lack of response from high-ranking British officials may also have been a reflection of Deputy Commissioner H. C. Moore's marginalisation in the administration as he, like his brother E. A. Moore mentioned above, had married a Burmese woman. Whether this closer association with Burmese women engendered in the Deputy Commissioner a more

sympathetic attitude to indigenous rape victims than his more callous colleagues, it is impossible to say. Ballhatchet, *Race, Sex and Class Under the Raj*, p. 151.

117. This table is taken from Deputy Commissioner Moore's correspondence, NAM, 1/15(E), 7198, 1905 File No. 7M-5, 18 January 1905.

118. T. Mitchell (1991) 'The Limits of the State: Beyond Statist Approaches and Their Critics', *The American Political Science Review*, 85, 1, 77–96.

119. Bourke, *Rape*.

120. J. S. Furnivall (1991) *The Fashioning of Leviathan: The Beginnings of British Rule in Burma* (Canberra: Department of Anthropology, Australian National University).

121. Any number of studies could be cited as examples of where gender is not considered, but it suffices to highlight its absence even in the most rigorously researched and influential study of the state in Burma; see R. H. Taylor (1987) *The State in Burma* (London: C. Hurst & Co.).

122. Lowis, *The Treasury-Officer's Wooing*; C. C. Lowis (1903) *The Machinations of the Myo-Ok* (London: Methuen).

Conclusion

1. P. Perry (2005) 'Corruption in Burma and the Corruption of Burma', in N. Tarling (ed.) *Corruption and Good Governance in Asia* (London: Routledge) pp. 186–97.

2. www.transparency.org/policy_research/surveys_indices/cpi/2009/cpi_2009_ table, last accessed 9 June 2010.

3. See the discussion of 'tea money' and officials' uses of the black market in A. M. Thawnghmung (2011) 'The Politics of Everyday Life in Twenty-First Century Myanmar', *Journal of Asian Studies*, 70, 3, 641–56. For a discussion of the more negative aspects of low-level corruption, see Monique Skidmore's mentions of 'line-money' in M. Skidmore (2004) *Karaoke Fascism: Burma and Politics of Fear* (Philadelphia, PA: University of Pennsylvania Press).

4. This is most apparent in M. Aung-Thwin (2001) 'Parochial Universalism, Democracy Jihad and the Orientalist Image of Burma: The New Evangelism', *Pacific Affairs*, 74, 4, 483–505.

5. This is pointed out in the conclusion of M. Aung-Thwin (2011) *The Return of the Galon King: History, Law, and Rebellion in Colonial Burma* (Athens: Ohio University Press), albeit in a somewhat a-historical fashion.

6. For a more nuanced discussion of the impact of colonialism, see C. Ikeya (2011) *Reconfiguring Women, Colonialism, and Modernity in Burma* (Honolulu: Hawai'i University Press) pp. 14–45.

7. I am borrowing this phrase from N. Tarling (2001) *Imperialism in Southeast Asia: A Fleeting Passing Phase* (Abingdon: Routledge).

8. J. Smail (1961) 'On the Possibility of an Autonomous History of Modern Southeast Asia', *Journal of Southeast Asian History*, 2, 2, 72–102.

9. M. Aung-Thwin (2011) 'A Tale of Two Kingdoms: Ava and Pegu in the Fifteenth Century', *Journal of Southeast Asian Studies*, 42, 1, 1–16.

10. M. Aung-Thwin (1985) 'The British "Pacification" of Burma: Order without Meaning', *Journal of Southeast Asian Studies*, 16, 2, 245–61.

11. T. Myint-U (2001) *The Making of Modern Burma* (Cambridge: Cambridge University Press).
12. M.-L. Heikkilä-Horn (2009) 'Imagining "Burma": A Historical Overview', *Asian Ethnicity*, 10, 2, 145–54.
13. M. P. Callahan (2003) *Making Enemies: War and State Building in Burma* (Ithaca, NY: Cornell University Press).
14. Partha Chatterjee (1986) *Nationalist Thought and the Colonial World: A Derivative Discourse* (London: Zed Books).
15. See, for example, Ananda Rajah (2002) 'A "Nation of Intent" in Burma: Karen Ethno-Nationalism, Nationalism and Narrations of Nation', *The Pacific Review*, 15, 4, 517–37.
16. M. P. Callahan (2002) 'State Formation in the Shadow of the Raj: Violence, Warfare and Politics in Colonial Burma', *Southeast Asian Studies*, 39, 4, 513–36; Parimal Ghosh (2000) *Brave Men of the Hills: Resistance and Rebellion in Burma, 1825–1932* (London: Hurst and Company); M. Aung-Thwin, *The Return of the Galon King*. The pre-1885 period of colonial rule has recently been re-evaluated in N. A. Englehart (2011) 'Liberal Leviathan or Imperial Outpost? J. S. Furnivall on Colonial Rule in Burma', *Modern Asian Studies*, 45, 4, 759–50.
17. M. Foucault (1991) 'Governmentality', in G. Burchell, C. Gordon, and P. Miller (eds) *The Foucault Effect: Studies in Governmentality* (Chicago, IL: University of Chicago Press, 1991).
18. P. Abrams (1988) 'Notes on the Difficulty of Studying the State', *Journal of Historical Sociology*, 1, 1, 58–89; T. Mitchell (1991) 'The Limits of the State: Beyond Statist Approaches and Their Critics', *The American Political Science Review*, 85, 1, 77–96; J. L. Comaroff (1998) 'Reflections on the Colonial State, in South Africa and Elsewhere: Factions, Fragments, Facts and Fictions', *Social Identities*, 4, 3, 321–61.
19. I am borrowing this phrase from A. H. M. Kirk-Greene (1980) 'The Thin White Line: The Size of the British Colonial Service in Africa', *African Affairs*, 79, 314, 25–44.
20. M. Adas (1981) 'From Avoidance to Confrontation: Peasant Protest in Precolonial and Colonial Southeast Asia', *Comparative Studies in Society and History*, 23, 2, 217–47; V. Lieberman (1984) *Burmese Administrative Cycles: Anarchy and Conquest, C. 1580–1760* (Princeton, NJ: Princeton University Press); T. Myint-U, *The Making of Modern Burma*; M. J. Braddick (2000) *State Formation in Early Modern England, c. 1550–1700* (Cambridge: Cambridge University Press).
21. J. Saha (2012) 'A Mockery of Justice? Colonial Law, the Everyday State and Village Politics in the Burma Delta c.1900', *Past & Present*, 217, pp. 187–212.
22. For how some practices deemed corrupt were sanitised and made routine in Britain between the eighteenth and twentieth centuries, see P. Harling (1995), 'Rethinking "Old Corruption"', *Past & Present*, 147, 127–58; N. Dirks (2006) *The Scandal of Empire: India and the Creation of Imperial Britain* (Cambridge, MA: Harvard University Press); M. Pugh (1993) *The Making of Modern British Politics, 1867–1939* (Oxford: Blackwell) pp. 10–15.
23. Although in the abstract it is a process, which in a bigger frame has been discussed in N. Dirks, *Scandal of Empire*.
24. M. Nuitjen and G. Anders (eds) (2007) 'Corruption and the Secret of Law: An Introduction', in *Corruption and the Secret of Law: A Legal Anthropological Perspective* (Aldershot: Ashgate) pp. 9–12.

25. R. H. Taylor (1987) *The State in Burma* (London: C. Hurst & Co).
26. R. H. Taylor (1976) 'Politics in Late Colonial Burma: The Case of U Saw', *Modern Asian Studies*, 10, 2, 161–93.
27. M. W. Charney (2009) *A History of Modern Burma* (Cambridge: Cambridge University Press).
28. For the complexity of this relationship, see P. Meehan (2011) 'Drugs, Insurgency and State-Building in Burma: Why the Drugs Trade Is Central to Burma's Changing Political Order', *Journal of Southeast Asian Studies*, 42, 3, 376–404.
29. A. M. Thawnghmung, 'The Politics of Everyday Life'.
30. M. Skidmore, *Karaoke Fascism*.
31. J. Comaroff and J. L. Comaroff (eds.) (2006) *Law and Disorder in the Postcolony* (Chicago, IL: Chicago University Press); A. Mbembe (2001) *On the Postcolony* (Berkeley and Los Angeles: University of California Press).
32. J. Cloke and Ed Brown (2004) 'Neoliberal Reform, Governance and Corruption in the South: Assessing the International Anti-Corruption Crusade', *Antipode*, 36, 2, 272–94; W. Brown (2003) 'Neo-liberalism and the End of Liberal Democracy', *Theory & Event*, 7, 1.

Index